Writing and European thought, 1600–1830 argues for the central importance of writing to conceptions of language, technological progress and Western civilisation during the Early Modern era. Attitudes to the written language changed radically between the late Renaissance and Romanticism, and Nicholas Hudson traces the development of thought about language during this period, challenging some central assumptions of modern historical scholarship. He asserts that European thinkers have not been uniformly prejudiced against writing, and he questions the assumption that the rise of print and literacy produced a more visually oriented culture. Through detailed readings of major writers, Hudson shows how writing became the emblem of the superiority of European culture, and how, with the expansion of print culture, European intellectuals became more aware of the virtues of 'orality' and the deficiencies of literate society.

WRITING AND EUROPEAN THOUGHT, 1600–1830

WRITING AND EUROPEAN THOUGHT 1600–1830

NICHOLAS HUDSON

University of British Columbia

CAMBRIDGE
UNIVERSITY PRESS

Published by the Press Syndicate of the University of Cambridge
The Pitt Building, Trumpington Street, Cambridge, CB2 1RP
40 West 20th Street, New York, NY 10011-4211, USA
10 Stamford Road, Oakleigh, Melbourne 3166, Australia

First published 1994

Printed in Great Britain at the University Press, Cambridge

A catalogue record for this book is available from the British Library

Library of Congress cataloguing in publication data
Hudson, Nicholas
Writing and European thought, 1600–1830 / Nicholas Hudson.
p.   cm.
Includes bibliographical references (p.) and index.
ISBN 0 521 45540 5 (hardback)
1. Written communication – History.   2. Europe – Intellectual life.   3. Language and
languages – Philosophy.   I. Title.
P211.H83   1994
302.2′244–dc20   94-7062   CIP

ISBN 0 521 45540 5 hardback

For Julia

Contents

ix

Plates

Preface and acknowledgements

This book germinated with a simple observation: the development of attitudes towards written language has been little studied, despite a wealth of material related to this subject, and the importance of this medium in Western intellectual history. Such a project seemed particularly needed at a time when the books of Jacques Derrida had brought so much attention to the issue of writing in European philosophy. Histories of literacy and print culture had also cultivated an interest in visual media. These studies nonetheless generally focused on print rather than writing. Moreover, they concerned the social and political impact of printed materials, rather than the evolution of theories about writing as a form of language. Relatively neglected were the views of scholars in the seventeenth and eighteenth centuries about the origin and nature of written language, and about how writing had influenced language and society, though these were popular themes in Early Modern scholarship. As I started my investigation, my reading had already suggested to me that the history of ideas concerning writing differed from what was widely assumed. European thinkers displayed no consistent prejudice against the letter or written mark, as indicated by Derrida. And I was unconvinced by the argument that the post-Gutenberg era became progressively dominated by a visual understanding of language and the world, as often claimed by historians of print and the media.

But the idea of 'writing', my research soon revealed, is huge and multifaceted. Numerous branches of modern scholarship study written language from varying perspectives. Writing is a theme not only in deconstructive philosophy or in histories of literacy and media. In fact, it also concerns students of linguistics, rhetoric, education, anthropology and the archaeology of ancient scripts. Researchers in all these fields seldom give much attention to the work of colleagues in other departments, though their interests often intersect. One challenge of this book, therefore, was to discover some common ground between the different preoccupations and approaches of our modern scholarly disciplines. Another task was to keep the topic of 'writing' from overwhelming me with its hydra-like propensity to grow new heads of discussion with every encounter. My solution, in large part, has been to stay close to what scholars from the Renaissance to the Romantic era were themselves saying about writing. Their predominant interests lay with the origin and history of writing, its importance to 'civilisation', and its relationship with speech. And in focusing on these problems, I could detect a complex but definite pattern of change. I could see the gradual emergence of our modern indecision and controversy concerning the benefits of writing for language and culture.

The subject of this book is thus the study of writing or 'grammatology' during the Early Modern era. I nonetheless hesitate to mention the term 'grammatology', which, in present academic discourse, has become charged with associations with sceptical philosophy and the critical techniques of deconstruction. In fact, the term 'grammatology' was first coined long ago in English by the grammarian George Dalgarno in *Didascalocophus: or the deaf and dumb man's tutor* (1680). It was revived in our century not by Derrida, but by the archaeologist I. C. Gelb, to describe merely the scholarly discipline devoted to the history and nature of written language. In the few places where I have used the term 'grammatology' (prudently deleted from a former title of this book), it should be interpreted only in this restricted sense. It is a minor hope of mine, however, that we might once again deploy 'grammatology' as a useful technical term without implying the whole philosophical apparatus of deconstruction, and without stirring either anti-institutional fervour or defensive indignation.

The research for this book was funded by a grant from the Social Sciences and Humanities Research Council of Canada, and by grants from the University of British Columbia and the Voltaire Foundation, Oxford. My sincere thanks to Ed Hundert for his thoughtful and enlightening comments on a late draft. A late version of the book was read for the Press by Hans Aarsleff and by Vivian Salmon, both of whom had already taught me a great deal in their scholarship, and whose commentary helped to make my scholarship better. Thanks to Carey McIntosh for his thorough and insightful response to a prospectus. Over the years I have accumulated a vast range of intellectual debts from colleagues in Vancouver and elsewhere, including Nigel Smith, Fraser Easton, Don Nichol, Kevin Cope, Kay Stockholder, Roger Seamon, Philippa Spoel, Ron Hatch, Mark Vessey and Hermann Real. I am grateful to Richard Cavell for his help with translation. To Alex Hudson I owe some exemplary drawings of Hermes, god of writing, along with much spiritual uplifting. Finally, the book is dedicated to Julia, whose help and support made everything else possible.

Note on translations

Wherever possible, I have used the most reliable translation available of non-English texts. In cases where no such translation was available, my own translation follows the original passage in parentheses. The reader will notice unusual spellings in passages from the works of some eighteenth-century French authors. As I discuss, the eighteenth century was a time of much idiosyncratic experimentation with French orthography.

Introduction

> View *writing's art*, that like a sovereign queen,
> Amongst her subject *sciences* are seen;
> As she in *dignity* the rest transcends,
> So far her pow'r of *good* and *harm* extends;
> And strange effects in both from her we find,
> The *Pallas* and *Pandora* of mankind.[1]

These lines by the English poet laureate Nahum Tate (1652–1715) express the mixed adulation and suspicion that has long characterised European attitudes towards written language. Few have questioned the title of writing as 'sovereign queen' of the sciences, for this invention has made all the learned arts possible. Writing has been considered the very emblem of 'civilisation', a sign of the intellectual superiority of the West, and a justification for Europe's colonial ascendance over pre-literate, 'savage' nations. But the cost of these advantages has been the evils released by writing in its alternate role as 'Pandora' of humanity – the theological dissensions, useless learning, bookish insolence, philosophical scepticism, and the general loss of the intimacy and directness of living speech. The divided reactions of seventeenth- and eighteenth-century authors towards writing, the first 'technology' of communication, remains a permanent part of the Western outlook. In exploring the evolution of this alternating pride in and distrust of writing, we journey close to the heart of Western culture's perception of itself and the world.

As I will argue, perceptions of writing since the Renaissance must be described in this way – as ambivalent and conflicting, and not as uniformly reverent or hostile. Recent scholarship has tended to indicate that visual language has been historically either extolled or vilified. On the one hand, scholars of literacy and 'print culture' have delineated the energetic confidence of Western thinkers in the salutary influence of written language on the moral well-being of

1

society. Harvey J. Graff has rightly referred to a 'literacy myth' that
can be traced back to the Enlightenment – a confidence in literacy as
the triumph of light over darkness, and as the foundation of
democratic liberties.[2] On the other hand, Jacques Derrida's works on
'logocentrism' have drawn attention to an enduring legacy of
distrust towards writing in the Western tradition. From Plato to
Rousseau to Heidegger, philosophers have deprecated writing as the
faded supplement to speech, and have feared its nefarious en-
croachment on the self-authorising 'presence' of the living voice.[3]
Yet neither the 'literacy myth' nor 'logocentrism' can be taken as a
complete summary of attitudes towards writing in European thought.
Nor do these theories take into account the enormous changes that
have occurred in the understanding of writing, its origin and history,
and its relationship with speech. These changes were particularly
dramatic during the period from the Renaissance to the early
nineteenth century which laid the basis of modern philosophical,
linguistic and social thought.

During this period, I will contend, attitudes towards writing
developed in a dialectical pattern: an early enthusiasm for the powers
and benefits of written language was widely challenged in the mid
eighteenth century, but was subsequently reaffirmed in a new,
mediated form. In the Renaissance, occult philosophers venerated
hieroglyphics and ancient Hebrew writing as sacred scripts closely
connected with the nature of the universe. The high reputation of
writing continued throughout the seventeenth century, when projects
to institute a new written nomenclature for international communication became one of the most fashionable pursuits of the new science.
In the middle decades of the eighteenth century, however, philosophers and rhetoricians widely attacked writing for its allegedly
destructive influence on both language and morals. The Enlightenment was a time of intense debate concerning the advantages of
literate culture, as traditional praise for writing was confronted by a
new scepticism about the arts and institutions that writing made
possible. This debate was indeed more characteristic of the mid and
late eighteenth century than of the Romantic age. In that later
period we find a new willingness to reconcile the opposed opinions for
and against writing. In contrast with Enlightenment thinkers, who
tended to adopt extreme positions, poets and philosophers of the
Romantic age typically acknowledged and exploited the benefits of
writing while also remaining sharply conscious of its deficiencies and

potential dangers. Poets aspired to fashion a language that combined the permanence of writing with the immediacy of speech.

It cannot be said that the Romantic authors permanently resolved this debate: in our century, opinions about writing seem as divided and extreme as those in the time of Rousseau and Johnson. From the eighteenth century and the Romantic era, however, we have inherited a much clearer perception of how writing and speech differ as means of communication. According to the prevailing doctrines of seventeenth-century linguistics, all communication, whether written or spoken, consisted of 'arbitrary signs'. Although explorers had begun to encounter New World cultures without alphabetical writing, there was as yet no coherent concept of an 'oral tradition' that could preserve history and laws without written records. It is in the eighteenth century that we find grammarians and philosophers discriminating carefully between linguistic capacities of writing and speech, and between their differing functions. The same age gave us our modern understanding of an essential difference between 'literate' and 'oral' societies and styles of language.

Awareness of the disparity between writing and speech derived in large part from the increasing recognition that written language lacks the means of recording the full range of sounds at the disposal of the speaker. In fundamental ways, writing is a more limited and less flexible form of communication than speech, lacking its fine semiotic differences, and its resources of intonation and gesture. Such insights helped to bolster the intense antagonism to writing that we find in the works of mid-century authors such as Rousseau and Sheridan. Yet, during the same decades, other scholars described the influence of literate culture on language as highly beneficial, and as crucial to the creation of a 'cultivated' language for the use of philosophy and art. As Johnson, Priestley and others argued, writing provides a solid basis for the gradual improvement of speech towards greater variety and precision. It also facilitates the achievement of logically organised discourse and of intensive reflection on the nature of language and the operations of the mind itself. Both critics and advocates of written language recognised, most important, that alphabetical writing is not *merely* a copy of speech. They anticipated some of the insights of modern scholars of written language, such as Josef Vachek and William Haas, into the inaccuracy of viewing alphabetical writing as ideally a 'phonetic' transcription of speech sounds. Alphabetical writing contains a large component of non-phonographic devices; it performs functions that cannot be duplicated by speech; it heavily influences how educated people in literate societies understand spoken language; it can be learned without much knowledge of corresponding speech sounds, as in the case of people who read but cannot speak a foreign language. Contrary to the extreme position often expounded during the first half of our century, as notably in the work of Saussure and Jakobson, writing is a legitimate language system in its own right, designed to achieve ends quite distinct from those of either speech or phonetic transcription.[4]

It was in the eighteenth century, moreover, that scholars took the first crucial steps towards a comprehensive and accurate knowledge of the history of written language. In earlier centuries, writing was considered to be among those gifts bestowed on humanity at the creation. This doctrine was widely challenged by orthodox writers in the seventeenth century. Not until the eighteenth century, however, did the historians Nicolas Fréret and William Warburton develop the thesis that writing had evolved over many centuries from primitive pictographs to modern alphabets. As always, this position did not go unchallenged: there was a conservative backlash against the new histories of writing during the middle years of the eighteenth century, along with a rejuvenation of belief in the divine origin of letters. Nonetheless, it was the work of the 'conjectural historians' that led to the ground-breaking research of Young and Champollion in the early nineteenth century. These scholars, translators of the Rosetta Stone, lent the weight of empirical evidence to the speculative histories of the Enlightenment. They showed that while phonographic marks of some kind have existed almost from the inception of written records, fully developed alphabetical systems are the product of centuries of innovation and trial and error. The alphabet is among the most arduous and complex of human achievements.

In the following book, therefore, we will consider how ideas about writing have developed through a vigorous process of inquiry and debate. But this process cannot be detached from the changing social conditions of the seventeenth and eighteenth centuries. Of particular significance is the growth of literacy in Europe during this period. In Britain, and throughout northern Europe, the number of literate people increased dramatically from the Renaissance onwards. The progress of literacy was not uninterrupted or universal: it tended to be more marked in the city than in the country, among men rather than women (though women were catching up in the eighteenth century), and made few significant inroads below the middle classes. Nevertheless, signatures on marriage registers and other documents provide strong evidence that at least half of the British population could both read and write by the middle of the eighteenth century – writing being traditionally a later and more advanced accomplishment than the ability to do simple reading. The principal factors promoting literacy were Protestantism, which encouraged individual reading of the Bible, and the rise of the commercial middle class, a segment of society that prized literacy for its worldly advantages. Renaissance Humanism, it might be added, popularised educational ideals that pointed to writing as the first step in training virtuous and useful citizens. While the growth of literacy lagged behind somewhat in Catholic Europe, even there the capacity to read was encouraged by many Church leaders as a means of meeting the challenge of Protestantism. In France, literacy doubled during the eighteenth century, rising to over fifty per cent in some areas of the more urbanised and commercially developed north.[5]

These were the changes that permitted the expansion of the printing industry during the same period. People became literate to read the Bible or to do their business; but their newly acquired literacy gave them access to books of all kinds, from almanacs to novels, from printed sermons to works of free-thinking philosophy. The more efficient retailing and distribution of books, the development of new literary forms such as the newspaper, and the institution of circulating libraries gave ever widening access to printed materials. In assessing the social and psychological impact of 'print culture', however, we must be wary of over-simplification. It may seem plausible to conclude, with some modern historians of print culture, that as more people learned to read, European culture became more oriented to vision rather than to sound, more likely to think of language in specifically 'spatial' terms, and less sensitive to the nuances of the living voice.[6] But an examination of linguistic developments between the Renaissance and the nineteenth century reveals quite a different pattern. European intellectuals of the late eighteenth century were generally *more* attuned to the powers of speech, and more sceptical of the capacities of writing, than were their predecessors of a century before. Why should this be so?

One major factor was the more detailed and accurate understanding of language promoted by two centuries of linguistic research.

The deepening knowledge of speech sounds and intonation made ever clearer that no imaginable system of alphabetical writing could duplicate the expressive range of the living voice. We also find the progressive 'demystification' of writing. For the Medieval person, a book was a rare and precious object, worthy of painstaking illumination, and frequently enshrouded in an aura of mystery and sanctity. Even in the late Middle Ages, as scholars have recently shown, the book was losing its hallowed status as the written word became the mundane vehicle of bureaucracy and commerce.[7] Yet the venerated, even magical status of the written mark in the occult philosophy of the sixteenth century reveals that the Medieval out-look on writing disappeared only slowly. The Renaissance was still a time when only a small segment of society, largely its priests and aristocracy, could either write or read. The central place of hieroglyphics and emblems during this period is consistent with the authoritative role of such symbols in predominantly oral societies.[8] But as writing became a far more common and ordinary ac-complishment, spreading massively to the merchant middle class, it lost much of its previous mystique. By the Age of Enlightenment, European intellectuals were in a position to reflect with cool scepticism on the impact of widescale literacy on their world.

The fruits of literacy, inevitably, had failed to live up to the hopes raised in the seventeenth century. In that age, the worldly and heavenly benefits of the written word were widely sounded from the tribune and pulpit, especially in Protestant countries. But in the works of Rousseau, Sheridan and others of the mid eighteenth century, the living voice took its place among the 'natural' alternatives to a coldly rational, unnatural and sceptical age swamped with books and the idle, delusive theories of the literati. 'Always books! What a mania,' declares Rousseau's Savoyard Vicar. 'Because Europe is full of books, Europeans regard them as indispensable, without thinking that in three-quarters of the earth they have never been seen.'[9] Developing perceptions of written language thus reveal the complex, and often unexpected relationship between social and ideological change. Authors came to appreciate the powers of speech and the virtues of oral culture at the very time that writing was beginning to dominate their world. Against the nostalgia for a lost world of oral purity, in turn, other authors rose to the defence of writing. The traditional-minded continued to extol writing as the foundation of civilisation, and as a distinctive mark of the intellectual superiority of the West over a world generally benighted by the ignorance and barbarity of pre-literacy. Even today, this debate continues. The celebration and the distrust of writing represent two sides of a post-Enlightenment tradition that is deeply uncertain of whether its own technologies and skills have benefited or cursed humanity.

Behind my examination of these changes is this important assumption: the statements of individual authors are understandable only if they are situated in the specific context of their time. Particularly common in studies of Western 'logocentrism' has been the tendency to construct sweeping theories around the statements of a few 'Great Men', and to present single authors, even single texts, as representative of whole eras. We need to avoid dismissing the opinions of less prestigious writers as historically unimportant. We need also to keep in mind that no era in Western history has been free from profound and basic dissension on all issues. The direction of ideological change has never been from one universally held position to another. Certain opinions may gradually achieve pre-eminence, pushing previously dominant positions into the periphery of what the intellectual establishment deems sound or orthodox. But intellectual history – particularly in areas devoted to the human rather than the physical sciences – is seldom characterised by the complete or sudden eradication of previous outlooks. Proponents of traditional and innovative ideologies may battle for ascendancy over many decades, and their encounters inevitably produce hybrid ideologies that seem neither entirely old or new. Individual authors will display both attachments to the past and leanings to the future. And their statements always form part of an ongoing dialogue with other authors past and present, or even with the author's own changing and indecisive ruminations.

To do justice to these complexities and ambiguities, yet also to provide a coherent picture of the past has been the greatest challenge of this study. My approach is basically chronological. I will begin by tracing the 'demystification' of writing from the seventeenth to the late eighteenth century. European authors increasingly rejected the Renaissance preoccupation with the sacred and mystical status of ancient writing, emphasising instead the strictly practical functions of written language to preserve and to disseminate knowledge as efficiently as possible. In presenting this line of development, I focus throughout the first half of the book on changing ideas concerning the history of writing and the differing advantages of ideographic and alphabetical scripts. In the second half of the book, I move from these issues to discussion of the difference between writing and speech. The relative powers of writing and speech were vigorously debated during the mid and late eighteenth century, and remained a key theme in the work of poets and philosophers in the Romantic era.

Throughout this entire period, writing was a prominent issue in European thought. It is quite inaccurate to claim, as some have, that writing has been a historically ignored or marginalised theme. My purpose is, in part, to alert readers to the great richness and breadth of this field in the era that laid the foundations of modern thought. The active discussion in twentieth-century scholarship about the social and linguistic influence of writing has, in fact, continued a tradition of scholarship that dates back to the Renaissance. In the course of this study, we will find scholars of the seventeenth and eighteenth centuries formulating, with increasing distinctness, a conclusion that we are too apt to mistake as the peculiar illumination of our own wiser times – that writing, fountainhead of all that we do as literate individuals, has transformed speech, established a new social order, and nurtured the modern age of literature and science, with all its virtues and hazards.

CHAPTER I

Sacred and occult scripts in the Renaissance tradition

From Florence of the fifteenth century sprang the occult fascinations of the late Renaissance, a 'churning turbid flood of Hermetic, cabalistic, Gnostic, theurgic, Sabaean, Pythagorean and generally mystical notions that broke over Europe... carrying everything before it'.[1] This deluge did not stop at the border of the sixteenth century, but flowed strongly into the next, carrying with it the characteristic attitudes of occult philosophy to writing. In this tradition writing held a central and honoured place. It was venerated not for its clarity or contribution to public communication, but rather for its capacity to disguise hallowed truths from all but an elite group of philosophers and theologians, the inheritors of an ancient tradition of sacred knowledge. Writing was thought to have been created by God at the beginning of the world, and to have a close relation with the nature of the universe. Both socially and physically, writing was a source of power, a means to protect the privileged knowledge of a scholarly elite and to illuminate and control the forces of nature.

Modern concepts of writing, with their ideals of clarity and public literacy, were already beginning to emerge in the sixteenth century. Humanist educators such as Vives, Ascham and Mulcaster regarded writing not as an elitest skill, but as the very cornerstone of the instruction needed to produce useful and virtuous citizens.[2] But these pragmatic values would begin to predominate the study of writing only in the seventeenth century – partly in reaction against the veneration for sacred and secret scripts in the mystical sciences. The transformation of attitudes to writing from the Renaissance to the nineteenth century was indeed a process of demystification, the gradual diminishment of the once hallowed position of the written mark, and a growing perception of writing as an ingenious, socially beneficial, but highly imperfect product of human endeavour. To understand this process, we must begin with a close scrutiny of the doctrines and attitudes that were being abandoned. In this chapter, I will concentrate on the two major branches of the Renaissance study of occult scripts, the fascination for 'hieroglyphs' typical of hermetic science, and the closely associated fashion for the Jewish mystical philosophy of cabalism. Both these movements can be traced to Florence of the quattrocento. But my major concentration will be on the scholars of the seventeenth century who inherited many of the values and assumptions of what Francis A. Yates called the 'hermetic-cabalist' tradition, such as Athanasius Kircher, Robert Fludd and Jacob Boehme.[3]

THE SACRED CHARACTERS OF EGYPT: ANCIENT ACCOUNTS

Renaissance philosophers most valued writing in the form of mystical symbolism, rather than in the form of what we would call 'language'. It was the profound significance of the individual glyph or emblem, not the assembled meaning of letters or marks, that commanded their interest in the study of ancient scripts. Central to Renaissance studies of writing was the belief that the most ancient and learned nations had distinguished sharply between alphabetical writing, designed for the prosaic needs of common life, and a 'hieroglyphical' symbolism for the use of priests and philosophers. This was a division that Renaissance scholars found described in the classical works that provided virtually all their information concerning the history of writing.

The earliest of these reports was by Herodotus, writing in the fifth century BC. In his great account of his travels through Egypt, Herodotus remarked that the natives 'use two kinds of writing, one called sacred, the other common'.[4] This information was confirmed some six centuries later by Diodorus Sicilus, whose account of Egyptian writing was much fuller and more detailed. Diodorus noted that 'of the two kinds of writing which the Egyptians have, that which is known as "popular" (demotic) is learned by everyone, while that which is called "sacred" is understood only by the priests of the Egyptians, who learn it from their fathers as one of the things which are not divulged'.[5] Hence arose the assumption that the Egyptians and other ancient peoples used special, enigmatic characters for sacred subjects, while 'profane' writing – usually assumed to be alphabetical script – was reserved for 'vulgar' purposes.

This basic distinction between sacred and profane characters took a more elaborate form in the work of later classical authors. In the *Life of Pythagoras*, written in the third century AD, Porphyry observed that his subject went to Egypt to be instructed in 'three sorts of writing: epistolographic, hieroglyphic, symbolic'.[6] And in a longer and more detailed passage in the *Stromata* (Miscellanies), Clement of Alexandria distinguished between the 'epistolographic', 'hieratic' and 'hieroglyphic' scripts of the Egyptians:

Now those instructed among the Egyptians learned first of all that style of Egyptian letters which is called Epistolographic; and second, the Hieratic, which the sacred scribes practise; and finally, and last of all, the Hieroglyphic, of which one kind is...literal (Kyriologic), and the other Symbolic.[7]

This third-century Father went on to make even further subdivisions of 'symbolic' hieroglyphs, which he indicated could be either 'figurative' or 'quite allegorical, using certain enigmas'.[8] It was not totally clear what Clement meant by these distinctions between various kinds of hieroglyphs. And the very obscurity of his account gave room for much imaginative speculation about Egyptian scripts, as in William Warburton's influential history of writing in the eighteenth century. In the Renaissance, however, scholars favoured the relatively clear bi-partite division between 'sacred' and 'profane' writing found in Herodotus and Diodorus Sicilus. They paid little attention either to the 'hieratic' writing mentioned by Clement, or to his classification of the various kinds of symbolic hieroglyphs. It was, in part, this neglect of Clement's account that hindered the true understanding of Egyptian writing, for Clement was the most accurate of all ancient sources. He was right to point out that the Egyptians possessed three rather than two kinds of writing: the hieroglyphs, used on monuments, and two abbreviated and cursive forms of the same marks – the hieratic and demotic ('epistolographic') scripts. Fifteen hundred years would pass before Clement's division was confirmed and fully understood by Young and Champollion in the early nineteenth century.

Meanwhile the division between 'sacred' and 'profane' served as the primary basis for conceiving Egyptian and other ancient scripts, even well after the Renaissance. This division appealed to a traditional sense of social hierarchy, where the priest and the scholar were in exclusive possession of divine mysteries. It was considered sacrilegious and even dangerous to expose these sacred truths to common knowledge. Hence, Clement of Alexandria had praised the Egyptians for contriving a special form of cryptic writing intended, as he thought, to hide knowledge from the vulgar.[9] And this praise was echoed by scholars of the fifteenth and sixteenth centuries who regarded themselves as inheritors of an ancient scholarly tradition, the *prisca theologia*, dating back to the Egyptians. According to a legend attributed to Manetho, an Egyptian priest of the third century BC, the greatest of Egyptian philosophers, Hermes Trismegistus, had recorded all his secrets in hieroglyphs inscribed on steles.[10] Some classical reports, such as those of Manetho and Eusebius of Cæseria, even made Hermes the inventor of hieroglyphs.[11] Hermes, legendary author of the *Asclepius*, *Divine Pymander* and the works of the *corpus hermeticum*, exercised a profound influence on Renaissance thought. His fame helped to establish the high reputation of hieroglyphics as the form of writing most suitable to recording the most profound and sacred truths of philosophy.

According to Marsilio Ficino (1433–99), the Florentine neoplatonist who first translated and interpreted the *corpus hermeticum*, Hermes and the ancient priests had used hieroglyphics in imitation of God. Just as God has knowledge of things by immediate intuition, not by means of discursive thought, so the priests expressed themselves by means of single concrete images, not discursive prose. 'The Egyptian priests did not use individual letters to signify mysteries,' wrote Ficino, 'but whole images of plants, trees or animals; because God has knowledge of things not through a multiplicity of thought processes but rather as a simple and firm form of the thing.'[12] Indeed, God could be said to have written in 'hieroglyphs' throughout nature. Many plants and herbs bore some outward sign or 'signature' of their medicinal properties, a Renaissance doctrine well described by Michel Foucault in *The order of things*.[13] These 'signatures' were intended for the general guidance of humanity. But God also possessed an occult symbolism decipherable only by the philosophically enlightened or divinely inspired. The need for special inspiration to interpret nature, as well as the Bible, was emphasised by Sir Thomas Browne in *Christian morals*, a seventeenth-century work influenced by Renaissance ideas of nature and writing: 'The Hand of Providence writes often by Abbreviatures, Hieroglyphicks or short Characters, which ... are not to be made out but by a Hint or Key from that Spirit which indited them.'[14] Like the Egyptian priests described by Clement, God had contrived a 'double language' (*lingua duplex*), bearing different meanings for the vulgar and the enlightened, and meant to divide the commonality from the priests, the profane from the elect.

In a brilliant discussion of visual imagery in the Renaissance, E. M. Gombrich linked the cult of hieroglyphs with, in particular, the neo-platonist theories of Ficino and the philosophical movement he inspired. The neo-platonists sought a 'supra-sensible' realm beyond the sensible world. All physical objects bore a 'symbolic' relation with metaphysical forms, and by duplicating these natural symbols in 'hieroglyphs', the philosopher could harmonise his own symbolism with the cosmic network of affinities and correspondences.[15] Contrary to what might be gathered from Foucault's account of the Renaissance, scholars of this age usually placed little importance on any actual 'resemblance' between language and the world. They did not believe, for example, that Egyptian priests depicted a sun with a picture of a sun, or even any round shape. Rather, the priests always referred through their symbols to higher metaphysical realities that could be discerned by the intellect but not the eye.[16]

The decline of neo-platonic epistemology, with its characteristic split between physical and metaphysical realms in nature, contributed to the diminishing interest in hieroglyphical writing during the seventeenth century. This decline was also induced by changing ideas about the role of the scholar in society. Particularly as literacy increased, becoming the rule among merchants as well as theologians, the notion that truths must be carefully disguised from popular knowledge fell into disrepute. New importance was attached to the ideal of general legibility and clarity in all written communication. By contrast, as Gombrich has remarked, little value was placed on clarity in Renaissance iconography, where 'symbols... seemed to become more obscure the triter the meaning they were supposed to hide and to reveal'.[17]

HORAPOLLO AND RENAISSANCE IDEAS OF THE HIEROGLYPH

Ideas about the kinds of symbolism used by the Egyptians were strongly influenced by a single work from the fifth century AD, Horapollo's *Hieroglyphics*, first discovered in 1419 on the Greek island of Andros. This work purported to be by a real Egyptian sage, knowledgeable in the ancient symbols. In fact, as George Boas has argued, there were at least two authors writing under the name 'Horapollo', one of them a Greek who knew little of Egypt or its scripts.[18] Consisting of numerous explanations of supposed hieroglyphs, the *Hieroglyphics* is largely informed by folk tales and beast fables, many of them highly idiosyncratic and exotic. According to Horapollo, for example, 'a man concealing his inferiority' was portrayed by the Egyptians by the symbol of 'a monkey urinating' for 'when [a monkey] urinates, he conceals his urine'.[19] Similarly, 'when they would wish to depict a man prevented from committing suicide, they draw a beaver. For that animal when hunted, bites off his testicles and throws them at the hunter.'[20] There is little here in common with the imagery of the Renaissance. Nonetheless, fifteenth-century scholars such as Marsilio Ficino were fascinated by the *Hieroglyphics*, which circulated in scholarly circles in manuscript. And after the *Hieroglyphics* was translated and printed in the early sixteenth century, it became one of the most popular and influential works of the era. 'Commentaries' on Horapollo, such as G. P. Valeriano's massive work of 1556, greatly expanded the list of hieroglyphs, staying close to images of beasts, but reverting to the more familiar associations of European bestiaries, where lions stand for royalty and foxes for cunning.

It is certainly possible to exaggerate the influence of Horapollo. Indeed, the *Hieroglyphics* seems to have exerted a much stronger influence on the emblem tradition of the sixteenth and seventeenth centuries than on the actual study of ancient scripts. Nor did the *Hieroglyphics* seem to have any impact on occult philosophers like Henry Cornelius Agrippa or John Dee, who clearly saw 'hieroglyphics' as profoundly erudite symbols, not emblemised folk tales. It is important to note as well that the original manuscript of *Hieroglyphics* was not illustrated. Renaissance artists were free to imagine the symbols described in this work as they wished. Hence, the 'hieroglyphics' found in illustrated works such as Francesco Colonna's *Hypnerotomachia* (1499), a dream-vision about some vaguely 'Egyptian' ruins, bear only the slightest resemblance to real Egyptian writing. Colonna's dreamer finds such emblems as 'An Anchor and a Goose' and 'A Dolphin and an Arke close shut', all of which contain hidden meanings of a moral rather than a metaphysical nature.[21] 'Hieroglyph' thus became among the vaguest and most adaptable labels of the Renaissance, denoting virtually any kind of obscure symbolism. Before Kircher's studies of real obelisks

and artifacts, scholars were not especially interested in the decipherment of actual Egyptian inscriptions, to which they had no easy
access. More typically, they invented their own.

A famous example of such an invented 'hieroglyph' is John Dee's
'hieroglyphical monad', unveiled in a treatise in 1564 (see Plate 1).
Dee claimed that his mind was 'pregnant' with this symbol for seven
years, though the actual delivery took only twelve days.[22] Despite this
long gestation, the basic structure of Dee's monad is fairly simple,
combining the zodiacal sign for Mercury [☿] changed slightly, with
the sign for Aries [♈], one of 'the fiery triplicy' along with Leo and
Sagittarius. Dee's sign thus refers to two of the main ingredients of
alchemy – mercury and fire. The adjustments to the upper portion
of the monad form the signs for the moon [☽] and the sun [☉].
Together, these symbols also suggest the movement of the moon and
the sun around the earth, indicated by the point in the middle of the
circle. The cross in the middle section, 'the most consummate hieroglyphic sign',[23] stands most obviously for Christianity, but its four
radii also indicate the four elements. Dee dwelled on the numero-
logical significance in the cross: a cross joins two Vs, the Roman
numeral for 5, to make a sum of 10. As Pythagoras had shown,
the sum of 1, 2, 3 and 4 (the four points of the cross) is 10. And
of course the entire cross forms the Roman numeral for 10. The cross
can additionally be said to combine two Ls, the number 50, making
a sum of 100, or 10 times 10.

The beauty of the monad, in Dee's mind, was that it compressed
innumerable truths of the universe in a simple arrangement of lines
and circles (the constituent shapes of all nature), reducing the
principles of many sciences to unity and harmony. It expressed at
once, though only to the enlightened, what took many pages to
describe in words, a virtue that reflected the superiority of 'hieroglyphical' symbolism to ordinary alphabetical prose. Furthermore,
Dee apparently believed that his symbol had actual physical powers,
though he does not mention this most awesome truth in his treatise.[24]
Other philosophers of the sixteenth century were more forthright
about the magical powers of written symbols. The latent power of
'Hyerglyphicall, or sacred letters' was, for example, an important
theme in Henry Cornelius Agrippa's *De occulta philosophia* (1530).[25]
Agrippa dwelled in particular on the special 'efficacy' of Hebrew
writing, which possessed an inherent sympathy with the objects it
signified by divine institution.[26] Like Agrippa, the Swiss alchemist

Plate 1 Frontispiece of John Dee's *Monas hieroglyphica* (1564)

Paracelsus believed that 'signs, characters, and letters have their force and efficacy'.[27] He developed an elaborate science of inscribed shields which, applied directly to the skin, would cure a variety of ailments from heart pains to impotence. Most crucial for Paracelsus was that his characters always be used in harmony with the other forces of the cosmos, 'the nature and proper essence of metals, the influence and power of the Heavens and the Planets, the signification and disposition of the characters, signs and letters'.[28] The magus must always await the 'propitious' moment when all these forces were conjoined, for only then would the inscriptions serve as a kind of lightning rod for the accumulated powers of nature.

Paracelsus's emphasis on the concentration and harmonising of various powers is comparable with Dee's effort to compress the truths of all the sciences into a single monad. According to both philosophers, the written sign gained its special meanings and powers by virtue of the exact positioning of elements or materials that were themselves quite common and powerless. Like other scholars of this era, they wrenched the term 'hieroglyph' from its original context in Horapollo and the lore of the Egyptians. It became a general term for any kind of mysterious and enigmatical symbol, replete with hidden significance and reacting in powerful sympathy with the forces of the cosmos.

ATHANASIUS KIRCHER'S STUDIES OF HIEROGLYPHS

The weighty volumes of Athanasius Kircher mark the beginning of serious research into the origin and history of writing. Unlike previous students of hieroglyphics, Kircher attempted to decipher actual Egyptian writing, and to construct a history of writing by amassing empirical evidence. A German Jesuit renowned for his wide-ranging scholarship, Kircher had been summoned to Rome to serve as Professor of Mathematics at the Roman College. Pope Innocent X was restoring the Pamphilian Obelisk, a first-century imitation of an Egyptian monument, and Kircher was commissioned to interpret its inscriptions. In fulfilment of this task, Kircher produced *Obeliscus pamphilius* (1650), which was followed by his grandest work, the four volume *Œdipus ægyptiacus* (1652-4), and other works concerned in whole or in part with ancient and exotic scripts.[29]

Kircher was a Renaissance scholar in the Age of Science. He believed unquestioningly in the genius of Hermes Trismegistus even at a time when the very existence of this personage had been thrown into doubt, and when the value of his supposed teachings was widely denied. The most significant challenge to the existence of Hermes was in *De rebus sacris et ecclesiasticis exercitationes XVI* (1614) by Isaac Casaubon, who furnished evidence that 'Hermes' was actually the name taken by a number of Egyptian authors in the first century AD. Although Casaubon's influence was less revolutionary than modern scholars have tended to assume – even in the eighteenth century, many reputable historians remained convinced of the real existence of an Egyptian sage named Hermes – contemporaries were widely convinced by Casaubon's demonstration that the doctrines of the so-called 'Hermetica' were in fact a bastardised combination of Christianity and platonism.[30] Like Marsilio Ficino more than a century before, Kircher saw the line of precedence in reverse. He believed that Thrice-Great Hermes had anticipated both Plato and Christianity. Kircher's whole method of decipherment was founded on the search for cryptic expositions of Hermes' doctrines.

As an illustration of the method of decipherment that Kircher would use throughout his career we might consider his reading of the east face of the monument, as set out in *Obeliscus pamphilius* (see Plate 2). Kircher read these hieroglyphs from top to bottom as portraying the descent of things from an inconceivable God, through the intelligible archetypes and successively to the physical objects of the world. Kircher's major intellectual source was platonism, with strong elements of both cabalistic and Christian teachings. The top object, a serpent emerging from a winged globe, was construed by Kircher as a symbol of 'the incomprehensible, inseparable, and eternal nature of God', the serpent signifying God's creative fecundity and the wings his power as the prime mover. Kircher thought of God as an omnipresent Being, constantly animating all nature, as symbolised by the female figures in the next section. The deity in the centre, flanked by two genii, is half naked to show the purity and simplicity of God, but her lower half is clothed to show that God is the source of occult knowledge. Only one foot of the central figure is shown, to suggest the permanence and fixity of God, while the attending figures are drawn with both their feet, indicating the readiness of heavenly agents to fly at the Deity's command. The hawk in the next section, symbol of the sun, represents the sky and the descent of the archetypes into the realm of particulars, the basket of fruit on the hawk's head referring to divine wisdom. Finally, the bottom section portrays the

Plate 2 East face of the Pamphilian Obelisk as reproduced in Athanasius Kircher's
Obeliscus Pamphilius (1650).

earth, consisting of various four- and three-sided shapes referring to the four elements and the difference between inanimate, vegetable and sensible bodies. Along with this descent of divine archetypes to the physical world, Kircher discerned various patterns of three: for instance, there are three female figures, and the top hieroglyph consists of three separate elements. The number three was significant to Kircher as reflecting the triune nature of God, for he believed that Hermes had espied the Trinity even before the Christian revelation.[31]

Kircher believed that Hermes had developed hieroglyphics for specifically philosophical purposes. For their ordinary affairs, the Egyptians used an alphabetical writing that predated the hieroglyphs. In Kircher's history, therefore, the order of scripts was just the reverse of that described by eighteenth-century historians such as Warburton, who argued that the alphabet was the last and most sophisticated development in the evolution of scripts. Kircher insisted on the inherent superiority of hieroglyphical to alphabetical writing. This superiority lay, in his view, in the capacity of hieroglyphs to communicate a complete philosophical meaning at once, rather than gradually and cumulatively, in the manner of speech or alphabetical writing. Like Dee, Kircher particularly valued the *compression* of a complex, abstruse significance in a single image.[32] In keeping with the whole Renaissance tradition, indeed, Kircher thought of hieroglyphs less as a kind of 'language' than as a system of discrete images, all with self-contained meanings.

For the enlightened, however, even the 'profane' alphabet of the Egyptians had a hidden significance, thought Kircher. Relying on the erroneous assumption that the Egyptians used the Coptic alphabet as their 'profane' script (in reality, Coptic is a relatively modern script largely derived from Greek), Kircher analysed all the letters into the shapes of ibises, hawks, oxen, dogs, as well as some natural objects such as water, the sun and the moon (see Plate 3). He claimed, for example, that the letter A originally showed the beak of an ibis across its out-spread legs. Other letters were construed as beasts in similarly unlikely postures. Hermes had formed these letters, wrote Kircher, with the double purpose of giving an alphabet to the vulgar and also of conveying truths to the illuminati. Each shape had a cryptic significance in Hermes' theosophical system.[33]

As a Jesuit, working near the heart of the Counter-Reformation, Kircher totally approved of the supposed Egyptian practice of concealing their most sacred truths from the vulgar, who would wrest

Primæva literarum Ægyptiarum fabrica, & inſtitutio faſta à Tauto ſive Mercurio Trifmegifto.

Charaſter Zoographus.	*Figura literarum vulgaris.*	*Græcorum ad eas affinitas.*
I.	**ₐ** ᴀᴦ**ᴧꞵꝺꞒ ᴧꞒᴧꞒꝺꞚ** *dicitur, id eſt,* Bonus Dæmon.	A
II.	**ᴦ** **ᴦᴧꞒꞒᴧᴦ** *dicitur, id eſt,* Norma.	Γ
III.	**ᴧ** **ᴧᴧᴧᴦꞚꞄ** *dicitur, id eſt,* Bonus ager.	Δ

Z   III.

Plate 3   The origin of Coptic and Greek letters, as developed by Hermes Trismegistus from the shapes of ibises. From Athanasius Kircher's *Turris Babel* (1679).

such knowledge to their own destruction. Nor were the Egyptians the only ancient people who used writing to record their theology in a form legible only to the pious and adept: this was also the method of the ancient Jews, as revealed by their mystic science of letters, cabalism.[34]

CABALISM AND HEBREW

The fascination with hieroglyphics represents one branch of the study of writing in the late Renaissance, particularly connected with the mystic doctrines of Hermes Trismegistus. A second, major branch was the study of Hebrew, which few in the Renaissance doubted was the earliest form of writing, learned by Adam in the Garden of Eden. For philosophers of the Renaissance, Hebrew exemplified the same features of ancient writing that Kircher found in hieroglyphics. Beneath the 'literal' significance of Hebrew characters lay abstruse philosophical meanings legible only to an elite group of illuminati. And like the hieroglyphics, Hebrew letters were also thought to bear a direct though occult relation with the nature of the universe.

The primary source for these doctrines was the medieval Jewish philosophy, cabalism, which became immensely popular in the Renaissance. As was the case with hermeticism, the well-spring of this interest was late fifteenth-century Florence. Ficino's friend Giovanni Pico della Mirandola (1463–94) studied cabalism in the belief that its doctrines confirmed the truths of Christianity, even declaring, to the indignation of orthodox contemporaries, that 'there is no science which makes us more certain of the divinity of Christ than magic and cabala'.[35] Pico's enthusiasm for the cabala was communicated north by the German diplomat and Hebraist Johann Reuchlin. In the early decades of the sixteenth century, 'every corner of Europe knew of and talked of cabala ... For a brief time the Hebrew cabala was one of the themes of the moment, and the Christian interpretation of cabala was born'.[36]

A central illumination of cabalism was that Hebrew letters were ordained by God at the time of creation, and even constituted, in a mysterious sense, the very substance of the created universe. God 'drew them, hewed them, combined them, weighed them, interchanged them, and through them produced the whole creation and everything that is destined to be created'.[37] So instructs the *Sefer yetsirah* or Book of Creation, the most ancient cabalist text and the major source of its teachings about the mystical significance of Hebrew letters. One possible implication of this doctrine, explored by Medieval cabalists, was that Hebrew letters possessed magical powers, and could be used to direct the forces of nature.[38] More influential in the Renaissance were the cabalistic arts of Scriptural interpretation, which instructed that every letter and punctuation mark of the Torah contained some hidden wisdom. Through the transposition and recombination of letters, and by calculating their numerical values, those versed in the secrets of cabalism uncovered layer upon layer of sacred truth beneath the literal meaning of the Torah.[39]

In their quest to unlock the hidden wisdom or *hokhmah* of the Torah, the cabalists looked particularly for the seventy-two names of God, all of which derived mystically from the greatest of all names, the Tetragrammaton – YHVH ⟨יהוה⟩. In both Judaic and Christian versions of the Bible, vowels were added to these four consonants to form 'Yahweh' or 'Jehovah'. But Judaic tradition held that the Tetragrammaton, pronounced by God on Mount Sinai (Exodus 20:2), was too sacred to be articulated by human breath, and that its true sound was consequently unknown. The inference of some Christian authors was that cabalism gave a decided advantage to written language over spoken language. In one of the earliest works devoted specifically to the history and nature of language, *Thrésor de l'histoire des langues de cest univers* (1613), Claude Duret cited the authority of the 'sages hebrieux' (Hebrew sages) that 'l'escriture est plus spirituelle que la parole' (writing is more spiritual than the spoken word). 'L'escriture, selon qu'alleguent les Cabalistes,' he explained, 'a cest aduantage sur la parole, que beaucoup de secrets de diuinité se representent par escrit, qui ne scauroyent s'exprimer de bouche.' (Writing, according to what is alleged by the Cabalists, has this advantage over speech, that many secrets of divinity can be represented by writing, which cannot be expressed by the mouth.) Duret was thinking in part of the distinction in Judaism between the Written and the Oral Torah. The Oral Torah is the tradition of commentary on the Scriptures, and can thus be seen to be dependent on the Written Torah. In Duret's mind, therefore, writing precedes speech in the transmission of divine truth. In his more colourful phrase, the mouth is 'le temple & tabernacle de la loy escrite' (the temple and tabernacle of the written law).[40] This interpretation is particularly significant as an indication of how inclined Renaissance authors were to give precedence to written over spoken language. Whether Duret was justified in calling on the authority of cabalism to support this opinion is more difficult to say. While it is true that the Written Torah precedes the Oral Torah, the cabala is itself an essentially *oral* tradition of commentary passed down from teacher to student in confidence.[41]

Other authors of the early seventeenth century dwelled with enthusiasm on the divine origin of Hebrew letters and their close relationship with the created world. In *The oliue leafe: or, universal abce* (1603), Alexander Top calculated that God performed twenty-two acts in the first week of creation – a number that corresponded exactly with the twenty-two Hebrew letters also invented by God during this time. Top's conclusion was that 'euery of these seuerall *Hebrew* letters ... signifie or import some speciall workmanship of the Lordes Creation'.[42] Thus, Top was interested not in the transposition of letters in Scripture or in the names of God, but in the individual significance of the Hebrew letters, which he called 'the true *Hagiography* [*sic*] or *Hieroglyphs* of our first Fathers'.[43] Top's main concern was evidently to refute the claim that Hebrew was invented by humans like all other forms of writing, a sceptical view that was already becoming common in his time. He argued that Hebrew had endured too long to be the work of fallen mortals: it was too 'memorable', to use his curious expression.[44] Moreover, he claimed that all alphabets derived from Hebrew, which was a truly 'universal abce'.

Unhappily, Top was very sparing of illustrations to support these sweeping claims: the slim *Oliue leafe* is not the work of an accomplished scholar. It nonetheless shows the existence of a popular interest in the origin of writing, and the spread of a kind of vulgarised cabalism even among the semi-literate. Hebraic musings would be fashionable, for example, among the radical sectaries of the Civil War and Commonwealth. But there were weightier and more knowledgeable adaptations of the cabala among Christian authors. In *Œdipus ægyptiacus* and other works, Kircher wrote at length on the hidden significance of Hebrew letters. Like Egyptian writing, he believed, Hebrew had both 'sacred' and 'profane' forms: the sacred form was the familiar square Hebrew, while the character used for non-sacred purposes was the similar, but much simpler Samaritan character. Only square Hebrew, he insisted, possessed the virtue of making sense no matter how its letters were rearranged, a sign of its sacred origin and its conformity with the nature of worldly objects.[45] This conformity between Hebrew and the cosmos was explored in even greater depth by Kircher's contemporary in England, Robert Fludd, one of the most prolific and unbending adherents to the philosophical pursuits of the Renaissance.

ROBERT FLUDD

The Rosicrucian philosopher Robert Fludd is best known as the vigorous defender of the geocentric universe against Kepler, and of hermetic science against the French empiricists, Mersenne and Gassendi.[46] He was also deeply versed in the cabala. His ruminations on the origin and nature of Hebrew letters, in the second volume of the titanic exposition of his world system, *Utriusque cosmi, maioris scilicet et minoris, metaphysica, physica* (1617–21), are basically a rehearsal of cabalistic ideas, interpreted from a Christian point of view. This part of his work is particularly worth considering as an example of cabalistic ideas in the work of a Christian author, and as a vivid illustration of that great though declining doctrine of the Renaissance – the divine origin and sacred character of Hebrew writing.

Like Top, Fludd was anxious to uphold the divine origin of Hebrew from attacks by contemporary sceptics. The Hebrew letters were 'non ab homine inventæ, sed ab ore Tetragrammati in mundi primordi formaliter & characteribus igneis in hyle ventrem inscupltæ fuerint' (not invented by man, but engraved formally and in fiery characters in the womb of the *hyles* by the mouth of the Tetragrammaton in the primordial world).[47] He thus imagined the Hebrew alphabet emblazoned on the *hyles* or primal substance of the universe, a mystic vision that closely resembled descriptions of the creation in the *Sefer yetsirah* and other cabalist texts.[48] Fludd went on to narrate, in great detail, the creation of the universe by means of a commentary on the occult significance of each Hebrew letter and of their order in the alphabet. At the centre of this commentary were the three letters that make up the Tetragrammaton ⟨יהוה⟩ – *jod, he* and *vau*. (The reader should keep in mind that Hebrew is read from right to left). In Fludd's view, it is significant that the Tetragrammaton actually contains only three different characters, for this suggests the triune nature of God. Each letter stands for a member of the Trinity. The first letter, *jod*, represents the Father, embracing the entire meaning of the Tetragrammaton on its own. This truth is evidenced by the position of *jod* as the tenth letter of the Hebrew alphabet, for 1, 2, 3 and 4 (that is, the four letters of the Tetragrammaton) add up to ten. The letter *he* signifies the Holy Spirit, for it is an aspirate letter, produced by the breath (*spiritus*). Finally, *vau* is 'Messiæ hieroglyphicum' (the hieroglyph of the Messiah).[49] In the Tetragrammaton, this letter is located between the two *he*s, indicating the Son's role as an intermediary or 'vinculum spiritualis' (spiritual bond) between the world and its Maker. The first or 'He Superius' (upper *he*) is closest to *jod* or the Father, indicating the heavenly realm above the firmament. The final or 'He Inferius' (lower *he*) signifies the earthly realm below the firmament. *Vau* is thus the firmament, the threshold between heaven and earth, for no one goes to the Father except through Christ. In the accompanying illustration (see Plate 4), *vau* is portrayed as a scale, held by the Father (*jod*), and balancing the two realms signified by the two *he*s. The repetition of *he* in the

Tetragrammaton, it might be added, makes the divine name circular after *jod*, showing that all things proceed from and return to the Father.[50]

In *Monas hieroglyphica*, John Dee challenged grammarians to give some explanation for 'the shapes of letters, for their position, for their place in the order of the alphabet, for their various ways of joining, for their numerical values, and for most other things'.[51] This was the goal that Fludd set out to achieve in his descriptions of the Hebrew alphabet. He found a parallel between the ten *sefiroth*, the aspects by which God is revealed to this world, and the first ten letters of the Hebrew alphabet, from *aleph* to *jod*. He saw mystical significance in the order of the Hebrew alphabet, and gave a complex symbolic meaning to each of the letters. For instance, since *aleph* was symbolic of the beginning of the world and of the manifestation of God in the created world, it seemed to follow that the next letter, *beth*, should stand for knowledge of the creation and for the Messiah. The sacred nature of Hebrew was also revealed by the presence of hidden meanings in its written words. For example, the Hebrew word for 'sun' ⟨שֶׁמֶשׁ⟩, *shin-mem-shin*, was perfectly appropriate because *shin* was symbolic for light, and this light seemed to surround and submerge the central *mem*, symbolic of the material body.[52] Every Hebrew word thus told the story of its own nature, though only, of course, to those 'adepts' acquainted with the secret key to its interpretation.

In Fludd's system, nothing about Hebrew writing was random: its every characteristic reflected and confirmed his insights into the nature of God and the structure of the universe. It should be noted again that Fludd had little interest in any actual visual resemblance between Hebrew letters and worldly objects. The correspondences that he detected were of a highly esoteric nature, disguised from the human eye, and revealed particularly in the order and numerical value of the letters. It was a somewhat later tradition, influenced by empiricist demands for visible evidence, that searched for physical similarities between letters and objects.[53] For most authors of the hermetic tradition, too evident a similarity between Hebrew characters and objects would contradict the role of Hebrew as a holy script fully meaningful only to guardians of the sacred knowledge, such as Fludd and his fellow brethren of the Rosy Cross.

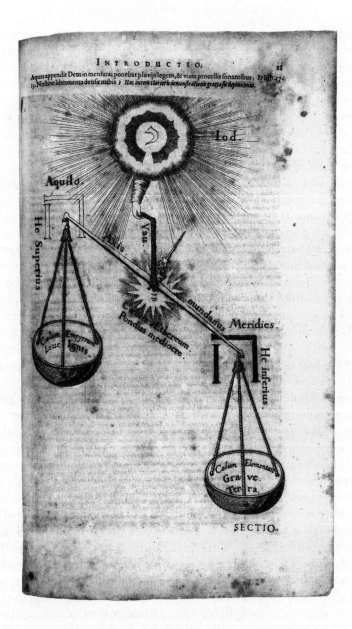

Plate 4 The sacred meaning of the Tetragrammaton, as illustrated by Robert Fludd in *Utriusque cosmi, maioris scilicet et minoris, metaphysica, physica* (1617–21).

JACOB BOEHME AND 'POPULAR CABALISM'

To this point, we have considered doctrines of occult and sacred writing largely as they appeared in the highly esoteric and learned books of authors such as Kircher and Fludd. The obscurity of sacred scripts was, to these authors, a great virtue, for it kept dangerous truths from the eyes of the ignorant masses. Paradoxically, as Gershom G. Scholem pointed out, the same obscurity could be valued by the masses as a means of challenging and undermining scholarly elitism. To groups whose beliefs are dismissed as worthless by the learned in the established institutions, secret languages and symbols give a sense of shared purpose, privileged insight and renewed authority.[54]

The mystic theology of Jacob Boehme illustrates how roughly 'cabalistic' doctrines were advanced as a popular alternative to the learning of Church and university. Boehme's prime targets were the narrow and literal interpretations of Scripture, and the empty disputes of learned clerics, which he believed were stultifying the spirit of modern Christianity. In *Mysterium magnum* (1623), his commentary on Genesis, he condemned the theologians who 'wrangle and jangle about the meer *Husk, viz.* about the *written* word and Letter, and they have *not* the *living* word of God dwelling in them'.[55] The breaking of the unified spoken word into alphabetical parts is closely related by Boehme to the disintegration of Christianity into competing factions, and the division of the original Adamic language into mutually incomprehensible tongues. Babel, he contended, was 'born of the spirit of letters'.[56] Boehme acknowledged that the Scriptures were the '*Cabinet*' of 'Christ's voice'. Nevertheless, just as God 'played upon' the dumb 'signatures' of nature, so 'there must be a true and right *breath*' to awaken the silent letters of the Bible into sound and meaning.[57]

Boehme was referring in part to his own allegorical readings of the Bible, which attempted to go beyond the literal meaning to some deeper, mystical sense. But he also had in mind a cabalistic transposition of letters in the Scripture to reveal its 'hidden Mystery'. To cite a typical example, Boehme argued that the name 'Methusæl' allegorised the religious ascent from selfishness to submission to God, for it begins with the syllable 'me': 'this Angels Name in divine Power doth first forme it selfe in the fleshly Selfehood; for the syllable ME which beginneth the word of the Name doth first forme in the *outward* words birth.'[58] In cabalistic fashion, he also disclosed 'the *Hidden* Name of God'.[59] But he rejected the usual inference in cabalistic literature that the name of God could be written but never pronounced. His version of the Holy Name was distinctively oral, consisting solely of the five vowels or what Boehme called the 'breathing' or 'sounding' letters. Properly arranged, and with the mere addition of an aspirate H, the vowels I, E, O, U, A spell 'Jehova'.[60]

This, then, was writing that really 'breathed', that had real 'life': Boehme shows how mystical doctrines of written language were often adopted in opposition to literal interpretations of the 'dead letter'. As we have seen, scholars in the hermetic-cabalist tradition often portrayed occult symbolism as a superior alternative to alphabetical writing. Ordinary writing, after all, is a translation of the voice, but mystical scripts seem to speak directly to the soul in the bodiless and heavenly voice of pure intellect. Boehme's version of this doctrine differs from that of other mystical thinkers in his emphasis on the need not for learning, but rather for divinely bestowed inspiration. Dismissive of priestly erudition, his views had tremendous appeal among the popular religious sects that flourished in the lower middle classes of the seventeenth century. Members of these groups were relatively unlearned, even semi-literate. But Boehme gave them a powerful answer to the scholars who, by virtue of their erudition, claimed to have the sole authority to interpret Scripture.[61]

The desire to undermine the power of a lettered elite helps to explain John Webster's advocacy of hieroglyphics and cryptology in *Academiarum examen* (1654), an attack on the curricula at Oxford and Cambridge. Modern historians of science have taken a particular interest in Webster's tract, and in the aggressive reply by Seth Ward, Savilian Professor of Astronomy at Oxford, because these works pit some of the major ideals of the old occult science against the principles of the new inductive and materialist science of the Royal Society.[62] For our purposes, the Webster–Ward debate is significant because it also highlights contrasting beliefs about writing. The Renaissance fascination with occult scripts clashed directly against the ideals of public information and historical philology favoured by Ward, advocate of the new science.

Like Boehme, whom he praised, Webster hated the tyranny of lettered theology, and began his polemic with a lengthy attack on the forms of Scriptural exegesis used in the universities. The ascendent approach to Scripture at the universities was highly erudite and literal-minded: its predominant goal was to establish an authoritative edition of the Bible through a comparison of various versions in many different scripts, including Latin, Hebrew, Greek, Chaldean, Samaritan, Syriac, Arabic, Persian and Ethiopic.[63] The implication of this polyglot method was that one needed to be skilled in all the 'Oriental' languages to reach authoritative interpretations of Scripture. To many Puritans, seeking inspiration from their humble family Bible, this was a threatening suggestion. As the Puritan Webster protested, citing Seneca: 'Nostra quæ erat Philosophia, facta Philologia est' (that which was our philosophy is made philology.)[64] He went on to argue that the most learned reading of the Bible was useless without the inspiration of the Holy Spirit: 'So that he that is most expert, and exquisite in the *Greek* and *Oriental* tongues, to him notwithstanding the language of the holy Ghost, hid in the letter of the Scriptures, is but as *Hiroglyphicks*, and *Cryptology*, which he can never uncypher, unless God bring his own key, and teach him how to use it.'[65]

Webster's reference to Scriptural language as a form of 'Hiroglyphicks' or 'Cryptology' was not entirely facetious. It signified his conviction that, in the historic fashion of sacred writings, the true meaning of the Bible was 'hid' beneath its literal meaning. So instead of learning Greek and Hebrew, he went on to argue, students at the universities should learn about hieroglyphs and other cryptic emblems: 'How probable, pleasant and useful is the *Hieroglyphical, Emblematical, Symbolical* and *Cryptographical* learning... Was not the expressions of things by Emblems, and *Hieroglyphs*, not onely antient, but in and by them what great mysteries have been preserved and holden out to the world?'[66] Webster perpetuated the traditional belief, central to Kircher's studies, that the hieroglyphics were designed to preserve the knowledge of religious mysteries. But Webster's admiration for hieroglyphics differed from Kircher's in at least one significant way. Kircher, the Jesuit, found great merit in the supposed purpose of the hieroglyphs to disguise religious mysteries from the vulgar. Such hoarding of religious knowledge by a priestly elite was abhorrent to Webster, the radical Protestant. He portrayed the hieroglyphs as a means by which religious truths were 'holden out to the world', even if, as he previously made clear, the 'key' for unlocking sacred mysteries was received from God.

Seth Ward's reply to Webster, *Vindiciæ academiarum* (1654), demonstrates how attitudes to hieroglyphics and writing in general were changing in line with other important shifts in the intellectual climate of the age. In the words of John Wilkins, who wrote the preface to Ward's pamphlet, the elements of Boehme's theology and of cabalism in Webster's work showed that he was a 'credulous fanatick Reformer'.[67] Ward even indulged himself with a ludicrous parody of cabalistic jargon. Defending the goal of scholars to determine the literal meaning of the Bible through the comparison of its various translations, Ward pointed out that an understanding of the literal sense was necessarily antecedent to the search for a deeper, allegorical sense. As for hieroglyphics, they were 'uselesse', for they were 'invented for *concealment* of things, and used ... in mysteries of Religion which were *infanda*'.[68] Ward's curt dismissal of hieroglyphics was reflective of the rising culture of scientific thinkers who had lost interest in Hermes Trismegistus and the magical secrets inscribed on Egyptian obelisks. Most important, Ward stressed the ideal that writing and the learned arts of the universities should have public information and general benefit as their governing aims. Written language, he urged, should 'serve for *explication* of our minds and notions', not 'the Art of *Concealment*'.[69] As we will go on to consider, this belief in the need for the clear and public dissemination of knowledge was one of the distinctive principles of the new science, differentiating this intellectual movement from the occultism and emblemology typical of the hermetic tradition.

The principles of openness and clarity help to explain why advocates of the new science and new philosophy showed much less interest in hieroglyphics than their predecessors. Bacon, Galileo, Comenius and other reformers were more apt to praise alphabetical writing, which they heralded as the most ingenious and useful of human inventions. In some respects, opponents to the hermetic tradition added little to the actual knowledge of the history of writing. It was the conservative Kircher who did most to stir practical investigation of ancient scripts. Yet the demystification of ancient scripts and visual symbols was a necessary step towards the major histories of writing in the eighteenth century. Before Warburton and Barthélemy could undertake their progressive work on the history of writing, previous scholars had to discredit the belief that hieroglyphics and Hebrew were sacred characters bearing, in cryptic form, the mystical illuminations of the *prisca theologia*.

CHAPTER 2

The demystification of writing in the seventeenth century

The seventeenth century, an age of philosophical and scientific revolution, was also a time of changing ideas about the nature and function of writing. Most notable was a sharp decline during the seventeenth century of belief in the occult significance of hiero-glyphics, Hebrew and other ancient scripts. Scholars became far less prone to believe that single images could serve the purposes of science, philosophy and communication. In contrast with John Dee, for example, rationalist scholars did not see the benefit of packing all the knowledge of the universe into a single image like the *monas hieroglyphica*. Influenced in part by the dialectical logic of the French Protestant philosopher Ramus, who abandoned pictorial imagery in favour of the orderly tabulation of data, leaders of the new science preferred the discursive presentation of knowledge in letters, numbers and other abstract symbols. As Frances A. Yates has summarised in *The art of memory*, 'above all, gone in the Ramist system are the images, the emotionally striking and stimulating images, the use of which had come down through the centuries from the art of the classical rhetor. The "natural" stimulus for memory is now... the abstract order of the dialectical analysis.'[1]

Protestantism helped to promote a second and closely interrelated change in the philosophy of writing. This was the new importance placed on the public dissemination of knowledge. The idea that 'dangerous' secrets had to be disguised from the masses, and thus hidden in some form of cryptic language or mystical symbolism, was anathema to scientific and educational reformers like Bacon, Galileo, Comenius, or Wilkins. These scholars were committed to the Humanist demand that knowledge be publicly useful. Urged by this ideal, they championed what a recent historian has called the 'ideology of openness',[2] valuing written language not as a means to hide, but as a means to communicate knowledge over the distances of space and time. This emphasis on the public nature of writing helps to explain the enormous admiration for alphabetical writing that all these authors express. Whereas Kircher and Fludd dismissed alphabets as 'vulgar', Galileo portrayed the alphabet as 'surpassing all stupendous inventions', an opinion re-echoed through the work of rational-minded, Protestant authors of the seventeenth century.

THE DECLINING PRESTIGE OF HEBREW

Of all the changes occurring in attitudes to writing, none was so significant as the gathering consensus that Hebrew was not divinely bestowed and may not even have been the first writing. From the late sixteenth century on, a series of prominent scholars claimed that the first form of writing was not Hebrew but rather a related and similar script, Samaritan. The position of these scholars, who included Joseph Scaliger, Geraldus Vossius, Brian Walton and Edward Stillingfleet, marked an important step forward in histories of writing: as evidenced by the relative simplicity of its characters, Samaritan is indeed an earlier version of the more familiar square Hebrew.[3] Such a challenge to the primacy of Hebrew was nonetheless bound to meet with sharp resistance, even among those who were generally sceptical of cabalism and the Renaissance fascination with mystical writing. In *An essay towards a real character* (1668), for example, John Wilkins argued that belief in the primacy of Hebrew was important to refute atheists and infidels who denied that any version of the Scriptures was original or uncorrupted by translation: ''Tis amongst rational arguments none of the least, for the Truth and Divine Authority of Scripture, to consider the general concurrence of all manner of evidence for the Antiquity of the *Hebrew*, and the derivation of all other Letters from it.'[4] In Wilkins's case, however, this orthodox view no longer entailed some special veneration for Hebrew as a script with occult meanings or the marks of divine origin. Though he defended the primacy of Hebrew, he also criticised it as a highly primitive script surpassed in completeness and accuracy by later forms of writing.

This was the position taken earlier in the century by the Dutch Jesuit Hermannus Hugo in *De prima scriblendi origine* (1617). Hugo's book was the first devoted entirely to the history and nature of writing. *De prima scriblendi origine* also signals important changes in attitudes to writing in his time, for Hugo gave scant attention to the hermetic and cabalistic ideas about writing that were popular in the Renaissance. In Hugo's mind, writing had the strictly practical function of recording and preserving speech: it is defined in his first chapter as 'vocem aut vocis partes ob oculos ponere per literas' (putting the voice or parts of the voice before the eyes by means of letters).[5] He rejected claims concerning the magical powers of writing, and filled his tract with dry, factual accounts of the evolution of writing instruments and paper, and the different ways of opening and closing epistles. Hugo agreed that Hebrew was the first form of writing, 'nam prima lingua fuit Hebraica' (for the first tongue was Hebrew).[6] But he left unresolved whether Adam received Hebrew characters from God or invented them himself, or even whether they were contrived by his youngest son, Seth. Whatever the origin of Hebrew writing, it was far from being the most perfect in existence. The Jesuit particularly criticised the direction of Hebrew writing from right to left as evidence of its 'rude' and 'uncultivated' state. Writing from left to right, the direction later adopted by the Greeks, was more 'commodious', he claimed, because the right-handed writer moved away from the body and could more easily see his letters. Hugo also suggested that the Hebrews began with only ten letters, a number that increased to twenty-two as need required over the centuries.[7]

A consistent and important premise of these observations was that writing has generally *improved* over the ages. This belief departed significantly from the assumption of most Renaissance authors that writing and other arts have declined since their pure, and divinely inspired origins. Fludd, Kircher and others studied writing in the light of their conviction that all human knowledge was possessed in perfection by Adam, who was instructed by the angels. Hugo, on the contrary, reflected a new optimism about human endeavour, and believed that all arts develop naturally from crude beginnings towards increasing perfection. This was also the forward-looking premise of Wilkins's *Essay towards a real character*. The very crudeness of Hebrew, in Wilkins's mind, was good evidence that it was the most ancient of scripts: 'The *Imperfection* and Defects of any Invention, do rather argue the *Antiquity*, than the *Novelty* of it; there being much time and experience required to the perfecting of any invention.'[8] Wilkins's view was that Adam himself had *invented* the first writing during his exceedingly long life.[9] Roughly the same argument had been made by Brian Walton at the beginning of his 1659 *Biblia sacra polyglotta*, though Walton, more daringly, claimed that Adam's letters were Samaritan rather than Hebrew.[10]

The demystification of Hebrew spelled the end of cabalism as an authoritative field of study for Christian authors. What secrets could be lodged in such a primitive and badly made script? The very term 'cabalistic' became a pejorative term to describe the superstitious veneration for Hebrew characters and fanatical interpretations of the Bible: in 1678, for example, the French Hebraist Richard Simon charged that Brian Walton was 'Cabbalistick' for suggesting that Adam even invented Samaritan characters.[11]

The discussions by Hugo, Walton and Wilkins also represent an important step towards the histories of writing in the eighteenth century. The central premise of later authors like Fréret and War-burton would be that writing has evolved towards ever more efficient forms, culminating in the European alphabets. In order for this kind of history to have legitimacy, it had to be authoritatively argued that Hebrew was a human invention rather than a divine gift, and that the history of writing had been marked by constant progress rather than decline from a perfect origin.

CHANGING ATTITUDES TOWARDS HIEROGLYPHICS AND THE ALPHABET

The same rational-minded scholars who questioned the primacy and perfection of written Hebrew were sceptical of the supposed genius of Egyptian hieroglyphics. These authors still assumed, inaccurately, that Egyptians had used two kinds of writing, hieroglyphics for the priests and alphabetical writing for the 'vulgar'. But whereas Renaissance authors generally praised this segregation, proponents of the new science were more apt to grumble democratically about the elitism of the ancient priests. Increasingly, the effort to disguise knowledge in mysterious symbols was regarded as a political ploy to protect power and self-interest. In *The history of the Royal-Society of London* (1667), for example, Thomas Sprat criticised the custom of 'Wise men' in Egypt and other ancient nations 'to wrap up their Observations on Nature, and the Manners of Men, in the dark Shadows of *Hieroglyphicks*; and to conceal them, as sacred *Mysteries*, from the apprehension of the vulgar'.[12] This concealment of knowledge was in stark contrast with Sprat's ideal of 'plain, undeceiving expressions',[13] and his praise of the printing press as the great stimulus to learning.[14] In *Origines sacræ, or a rational account of the grounds of Christian faith* (1662), a work with large sections on the history of writing, the Anglican divine Edward Stillingfleet made the same charge against the rabbis, who, he claimed, spun fictions about the occult wonders of Hebrew to keep the faithful in awe. Their primary design was 'to maintain a *Meum* and *Tuum* between their own Character and the vulgar, for hereby they prohibited all prying into their mysteries by any, but those who had the same *Interest* with themselves, and therefore were unlikely to discover any thing that might lessen their reputation'.[15]

The occult symbolism so relished by Kircher or Fludd as the very insignia of deep philosophising was thus re-interpreted as an instrument of political and religious oppression, typical of backward and superstitious peoples. Furthermore, advocates of intellectual change condemned hieroglyphics as insufficient for the practical needs of science and a civilised nation. Not only did these characters represent things imperfectly, wrote Comenius, but 'facilé ... quid repræsentarent, in oblivionem venire potuit, nisi creberrimâ iteratione' (what they represented easily fell into oblivion unless it was frequently reiterated).[16] In order to remain legible, in other words, hieroglyphics needed the support of an oral tradition in which the esoteric meaning of each symbol was passed from generation to generation. Did not this requirement defeat the very purpose of written records? Edward Stillingfleet agreed that hieroglyphics were insufficient for the purposes of preserving laws or historical records, being 'both *obscure, ambiguous, and unable* to *express* so much as to give any certain light to *future ages* of the *passages* of the *precedent*'.[17]

Only alphabetical writing, Stillingfleet went on to argue, enabled humans to preserve their history and laws, and thus to achieve a truly organised society. Alphabetical writing, dismissed by the hermeticists as a 'profane' script bereft of mystery, gained a new prestige among the rationalist scientists and philosophers of the seventeenth century. All *existing* alphabets, it was widely agreed, were inaccurate records of speech, filled with irrationalities and redundancies: projects for a new, reformed orthography were undertaken by numerous scholars from the mid sixteenth century onwards, in both Britain and France. But the *principle* of alphabetical writing was widely applauded as among the most brilliant discoveries in history.

Seventeenth-century scholars were not the first to extol the genius of the alphabet, which was frequently praised by classical authors.

According to Cicero, the genius of the alphabet revealed the divinity of the human spirit, an opinion reiterated by John Wilkins in *An essay towards a real character*. The invention of the alphabet was 'a thing of so great Art and exquisiteness', wrote Wilkins, that it gave evidence of 'the divinity and spirituality of the humane soul', for 'it must needs be of a farr more excellent and abstracted Essence then [*sic*] mere Matter or Body, in that it was able to reduce all articulate sounds to 24 *Letters*'.[18] In Wilkins's opinion, the genius of alphabetical writing lay in the reduction of the apparently innumerable range of vocal sounds to some two dozen basic elements. Other authors praised the miraculous bridging of sight and sound, a physical accomplishment unmatched by less sophisticated systems such as hieroglyphics.[19] The primary virtue of alphabetical writing was, however, its capacity to make knowledge permanently and reliably available to an unlimited audience. It was this benefit that stirred Galileo to describe the alphabet as the greatest of inventions in his 1632 *Dialogo sopra i due massimi sistemi del mondo*. The following eulogy concluded a long disquisition celebrating human genius and accomplishments:

But surpassing all stupendous inventions, what sublimity of mind was his who dreamed of finding means to communicate his deepest thoughts to any other person, though distant by mighty intervals of place and time! Of talking with those who are in India; of speaking to those who are not yet born for a thousand or ten thousand years; and with what facility, by the different arrangements of twenty characters upon a page!
Let this be the seal [*sigillo*] of all the admirable inventions of mankind ...[20]

It may surprise some readers that Galileo 'sealed' his discourse on human genius with this praise for alphabetical writing, rather than for the printing press. The opinion that the alphabet was a more significant achievement than printing was, however, by no means unusual at that time. As Thomas Hobbes wrote in *Leviathan* (1651), 'the Invention of *Printing*, though ingenious, compared with the invention of *Letters*, is no great matter'.[21] In the minds of many seventeenth-century authors, the alphabet was the primary and most remarkable invention because it had, after all, enabled the technology of the movable type to occur in the first place. They thought of the printed book as a more widely available manuscript rather than a medium with special linguistic functions and a quite different social impact.

Galileo's panegyric for alphabetical writing was widely quoted by English Protestant scholars such as Stillingfleet and Walton, for whom the Pisan astronomer had become the hero of scientific enlightenment, persecuted by the dark forces of Popish superstition.[22] For these authors, as for Galileo, the alphabet was an important symbol of the ideals that they most valued – openness and clarity, practicality, human genius and the capacity for continual progress. The alphabet was also associated metaphorically with the atomistic physics of the new science. Atomism, the previously vilified doctrine of Democritus, Epicurus and Lucretius, increasingly became the accepted scientific alternative to the metaphysics of Aristotle and the schools.[23] According to an ancient image – central, for example, to Lucretius's *De rerum natura*[24] – all objects in the world consisted of indivisible corpuscles, variously arranged, just as all words consisted of various combinations of a limited number of speech sounds or 'letters'. The inventor of the alphabet had thus established a principle that was fundamental to the physical sciences as well as to the study of language. Things of apparently endless complexity could in fact be reduced to a relatively small number of basic components, combined and recombined in innumerable ways. The 'alphabetum naturæ' became one of the standard images of the new science, used by Bacon, Boyle and others to describe their materialist vision of the world.[25] The same image was extended by Leibniz, Locke, Berkeley and Hartley to describe human thought, which, they argued, consisted similarly of basic units or 'simple ideas'. A great aim of philosophy, proclaimed the young Leibniz, was to determine the 'alphabetum cogitationum humanarum' – the alphabet of human thought.[26]

The image of nature or the mind as an 'alphabet' stands in sharp contrast with the image of nature as a great page of 'hieroglyphics', common in the neo-platonic philosophy of Ficino, Bruno and other Renaissance thinkers. According to that fading tradition, Hermes and the ancient priests had formed their hieroglyphics in imitation of God, whose sacred mysteries were adumbrated throughout the cosmos by means of 'signatures' or 'hieroglyphs'. Declining interest in hieroglyphics in the seventeenth century, accompanied by the much higher status of alphabetical writing, thus manifests a fundamental change in European thought, affecting a whole range of interrelated fields. Intellectual reformers preferred the alphabet because it served the ends of openness and social utility that they valued. The alphabet also exemplified their understanding of the physical universe. In every way, alphabetical writing was intimately associated with the social, intellectual and scientific outlook championed by the new philosophy.

In this age of exploration, pride in the alphabetic writing was further bolstered by a much stronger awareness that no nation outside of Europe had developed such a complete and efficient system for transcribing speech. The humble ABC, practised by the child in the schoolroom, became an important mark of the superiority of European civilisation over the illiterate 'savages' encountered around the globe.

WRITING AND CIVILISATION: EARLY ACCOUNTS OF NON-LITERATE CULTURES

The early travellers to the New World believed that most native peoples in North and South America were entirely without any system of writing. And it was this supposed illiteracy that they seized on as the distinctive mark of the 'otherness' of New World peoples, 'setting them apart', as Michael Harbsmeier has argued, 'not only from the people of Europe, but also from those of Asia and Africa'.[27] Writing became the very badge of 'civilisation'. The early travellers had virtually no concept of an 'oral tradition'. They denied that pre-literate cultures in the New World had any history, government, laws or literature. These peoples were considered barely social, even barely human, because of their lack of written language.

This is not to say that the explorers considered all the peoples of the New World to be illiterate. Indeed, in the view of Europeans, writing was the achievement that distinguished the different American peoples among themselves, as well as from the Europeans. The Aztecs were known to have picture-writing, referred to by some historians of the Spanish conquest, such as José de Acosta and Antonio de Solis y Ribadeneyra, as 'hieroglyphics'. The Incas had 'quippu', a system of recording by means of knotted strings. Unlike Stillingfleet and others who distrusted the efficiency of hieroglyphics – a scepticism which was increasingly the rule by the end of the seventeenth century – Acosta and Solis did not restrict the idea of true 'literacy' to the knowledge of alphabetical writing. They demonstrated a basic faith in the reliability of non-alphabetical writing to preserve the history and laws of these nations. Acosta recalled talking with an old Inca woman who, consulting her quippu, made 'a generall confession of all her life...as well as I could have done it in written paper'.[28] Similarly, Solis y Ribandeneyra described the Aztecs as a literate people with secretaries to record the deliberations and acts of the emperor Montezuma. They also had a written history of their nation taught to children in public schools.[29]

The 'writing' of the Incas and Aztecs qualified them as at least minimally 'civilised' peoples. But quite a different judgement was made of the many other peoples who appeared to lack any writing whatsoever. The first people met by Columbus, the islanders of the Caribbean, were portrayed by Francisco Lopez de Gómara as brutal, devil-worshipping savages, 'having no history except for songs'.[30] It was 'a great praise' of the Spanish conquerors of these people, proclaimed Gómara, that they had 'shown them letters, which are a thing so necessary to men that without them they are like true beasts'.[31] Citing a similar assessment by Samuel Purchas, in his famous catalogue of explorations *Hakluytus posthumus, or Purchas his pilgrimes* (1625), Stephen Greenblatt has summarised the view expressed in many of these early accounts: 'For Purchas...as for many other Europeans, those who possess writing have a past, a history, that those without access to letters necessarily lack. And since God "speaks to all" through writing, unlettered cultures (as distinct from illiterate individuals) are virtually excluded by definition from the human community.'[32] Samuel Purchas was among those who regarded writing as the definitive mark of a 'civilised' people: 'amongst Men, some are accounted Ciuill, and more both Sociable and Religious, by the Vse of *letters* and Writing, which others wanting are esteemed Brutish, Sauage, Barbarous.'[33] Purchas agreed that some New World peoples, like the 'Mexicans' and 'Hondurans', possessed 'Hieroglyphicall characters' or other marks by which 'they kept their Records'.[34] But wholly illiterate peoples in the New World lacked any sense of religion or history, and could hardly be said to belong to 'societies' at all. Some travellers, such as Thomas Hariot, were more willing to grant illiterate peoples a few rudiments of religion and social organisation: but a people without writing was, almost by definition, ignorant, childish and superstitious.[35]

The wonder elicited by the writing of the Europeans became among the most conventional themes in early accounts of the New World. And that wonder was a potential source of power, as recognised by Francisco Lopez de Gómara. Gómara proposed that the art of writing could be used to convince savages of the divine forces commanded by the Holy Church. He recounted the story of a Carib who ate some fruit that he had been ordered to carry to a neighbour along with a letter explaining the gift. When the neighbour learned of the theft from the letter, the Carib went back to his people, warning them against the magic 'speaking papers' of the white men.[36] In another story, told by Defoe in his 1726 *Essay upon literature*, an Indian in Virginia delivers a letter to the governor. Amazed that 'the Governor could tell him all his Errand before he spoke one word of it to him', he falls to his knees. The governor 'was a Deity and to be Worshipp'd', he cried, 'for...he had Power to make *the Paper speak*'.[37]

Little wonder that writing was reputed to be the greatest of human inventions in this era. Travellers were reporting that they were actually *worshipped* for their literacy. It is clear, as well, that writing was lending legitimacy to the colonial ambitions of the Europeans. The wonder of the American aboriginals demonstrated the vast technological superiority of the Europeans, and the supposed benefits of their expansion in the new continent. Accounts of New World travellers were also changing how people understood the history of writing. Evidence mounted that 'hieroglyphics' were not the exclusive invention of crafty Egyptian priests, but predated the alphabet in many parts of the world. Alphabetical writing, it increasingly appeared, was extremely rare, the end-point in the development of writing from 'primitive' to more sophisticated and 'civilised' forms. The use of written symbols for purposes of divination and magic – as in parts of western and southern Africa, where Islam had spread the knowledge of letters – seemed increasingly 'barbaric' to Europeans, who considered themselves the torchbearers of truth in a world of darkness.[38]

PROJECTS FOR A 'UNIVERSAL WRITING'

Encounters with nations without alphabetical writing helped to convince many Europeans both that writing was invented by humans and that it had 'progressed' towards ever more efficient forms. Released from the assumption that any form of writing was divinely ordained, philosophers were free to imagine how writing could be improved even further and made to serve an even wider range of

functions. The seventeenth century thus became an age of enthusiastic experimentation with written language. There was truly
an explosion of projects for shorthand, codes for secret messages, and
written languages for the deaf.[39] Most exciting of all, scholars of
language produced numerous plans, of varying completeness and
detail, for a totally new international language. Many of these
languages were intended not only to facilitate international communication, but also to provide a more accurate, 'philosophical'
(scientific) form of denotation than any 'vulgar' tongue in existence.
These projects for a universal or philosophical language, which have
dominated recent scholarship on seventeenth-century linguistics, are
of interest to us here primarily for what they reveal about attitudes to
writing at that time. For there seemed little question among the
inventors that both the linguistic and philosophical purposes of their
new languages could be achieved just as well in a written as in a
spoken form.

For example, when Marin Mersenne told his friend Descartes
about a new language in 1629, Descartes responded that 'toute
l'vtilité ... que ie voy qui peut reüssir de cette inuention, c'est pour
l'écriture' (all the utility which I see might enable the success of this
invention is for writing).[40] This immediate interest in the potential of
a new written language reflects, in part, the practical objectives of
Descartes and other philosophers of his time. In an age before
telecommunications, it was obviously more useful to institute a
language that could be transmitted internationally in books, and
translated into any spoken language whatsoever. The same motive of
international accessibility seems to have been foremost in the minds
of the many later authors – including Cave Beck, Francis Lodwick,
and John Wilkins[41] – whose energies were devoted primarily to
creating a system of visible symbols. Some of these authors, such as
Descartes and Wilkins, hoped that the written language might
eventually be given its own spoken form. And others, such as
Urquhart, Dalgarno and Newton, attempted to contrive a language
that could be both spoken and written from the start. They based
their plans on an alphabet of speech sounds, with each sound and
letter given a complete meaning according to an overall scheme.[42] In
contrast with philosophers in the eighteenth century, however, none
of these authors suggested that written language was inherently
inferior to speech in its capacity to signify with accuracy and clarity.

According to some recent scholars, indeed, the visible sign

generally dominated over the way the seventeenth-century authors imagined language. As Murray Cohen has observed of grammatical theories in that age, 'speech and knowledge emerge from what we see or can visualise'.[43] Language was envisioned as an aggregate of discrete signs, each denoting a mental image, which in turn mirrored a natural world of separate physical objects. As the syntactical relations between signs could not be easily visualised, they tended to be neglected. The planners devoted themselves largely to instituting an accurate one-to-one relationship between individual signs and concepts. Richard W. F. Kroll has linked this understanding of language with atomism and materialism. In the 'somatic tradition' of the seventeenth century, writing and visual communication were valued for their close affinity with the body, source of all knowledge and the true foundation for phenomena of the mind and nature previously considered immaterial.[44] It might be added that the tendency to think of language in predominantly visual terms reached its peak when 'print culture' was still in its early stages. A century later, when Europe was more literate and books more widely available, speech and sound clearly dominated over writing and visual communication as the primary subjects of European linguistics.

The linguistic and cultural context described by Cohen and Kroll helps to explain why most of the language planners seem predisposed to envisage the new philosophical language as written rather than spoken. Indeed, according to the Scottish grammarian George Dalgarno, the language planners were unreasonably prejudiced towards a 'real character' or graphic symbolism. Setting out his own plan for a universal language in *Ars signorum* (1661), Dalgarno ascribed this bias towards writing largely to the powerful influence of Francis Bacon.[45] In *The advancement of learning* (1605), Bacon encouraged the invention of a new international language modelled on the 'characters real' of the Chinese. Exemplifying what Madeleine V.-David has called 'the Chinese prejudice' – the tendency to view Chinese and other foreign scripts solely through the lens of European ideas and objectives – Bacon wrongly assumed that Oriental nations used a common writing that denoted 'things or notions', not words.[46] This ideographic writing, he observed, had facilitated communication between people who spoke the many dialects of China. Could not a common writing be formed on the same principles for communication between scholars around the world?[47]

Like the many scholars who took up his proposal for a 'real

character', Bacon had particularly in mind the need for an improved, accurate nomenclature for use by scientists. Only written records and communication, he believed, could ensure the progress of science: as he asserted in the *Novum organum* (1620), 'no course of invention can be satisfactory unless it be carried on in writing'.[48] Throughout his scientific works, the ideal of 'literate experience', documented facts passed from scholar to scholar, is contrasted with the 'prattle' of the ancients, whom Bacon accused of being too reliant on rumours and windy public disputation.[49] 'Vulgar' speech, in Bacon's mind, was unstable and inaccurate, a primary source of errors of reasoning, 'the Idols of the Marketplace'.[50] A new written language, on the other hand, could be adjusted to reflect the most recent scientific observations on nature in a stable form.

Later in the century, similar considerations led Lodwick, Beck, and Wilkins to think foremost of a new written language. Chinese writing continued to stand as a model of what might be achieved: sixteenth-century accounts of China, such as those by Matteo Ricci and Juan Gonzales de Mendoza, portrayed the Chinese as a highly sophisticated people who preferred to converse by writing rather than by speech, even in ordinary situations.[51] Other sources of inspiration for a new international nomenclature were astronomical and alchemical symbols, and musical notes – all forms of written notation common to speakers of different tongues.[52] But the *philosophical* possibilities of graphic characters were best exemplified by mathematical notation, which improved dramatically during the seventeenth century towards its modern form.[53] One of the century's best mathematicians, René Descartes, was inspired by the insight that a person could construct all possible numbers, and could perform the most complicated mathematical procedures, by learning only ten basic digits. As he wrote to Mersenne, he hoped that scholars could discover an analogous set of 'simple ideas' of which 'all that [men] think is composed'. Simply by learning the characters for these relatively few ideas, the scholar could go on to determine all possible knowledge from the first principles of the human mind.[54] G. W. Leibniz, who studied a copy of Descartes' famous letter to Mersenne, also had in mind the model of mathematical symbolism.[55] During the 1660s and 1670s, he devoted himself with great enthusiasm to the invention of what he called a 'general characteristic', a notation for individual ideas that would give all mental calculations 'the same unanswerable clarity as arithmetic'.[56] He even argued that ancient

Chinese writing was a form of philosophical symbolism based on binary arithmetic.[57]

But did not speech have some important advantages over writing? This was Dalgarno's major objection to the dominance of writing in many previous schemes for a new language. He acknowledged that writing was more lasting and stable: *vox perit litera scripta manet*. But speech was quick and convenient, and much superior to writing for the needs of ordinary communication.[58] Dalgarno's desire, then, was to combine the permanence of writing with the quickness of speech. This was a very common ideal of this age, so interested in making all technologies more useful and efficient. Plans for shorthand or 'brachygraphy' were especially popular in England. During a visit there in 1641–2, Comenius gazed with amazement at common people busily scribbling down sermons in shorthand.[59] Dalgarno's 'art of signs' was initially planned as a better form of shorthand. And some other inventors of universal characters, such as Francis Lodwick, shared this interest.[60]

Even according to Dalgarno, however, the difference between writing and speech was largely functional. Considered purely as means of signification, neither writing nor speech was superior for the purposes intended by the language planners. Here we arrive at perhaps the most important reason why most seventeenth-century scholars believed that writing could fulfil the ends they had in mind for their languages. They assumed that both writing and speech consisted almost entirely of 'signs' which represented 'things' or ideas by means of an arbitrary convention. As Dalgarno wrote in his *Didascalocophus; or the deaf and dumb mans tutor* (1680), 'all signs, both vocal and written, are equally arbitrary, and *ex institutio*'.[61] For this reason, there was no important advantage in either a written or spoken language, beyond their differing virtues of permanence or speed. While admitting that speech had preceded writing in history, language planners widely rejected the assumption that speech had any precedence in 'nature'. As John Wilkins asserted in the grandest of the universal language schemes, the 1668 *Essay towards a real character*,

But though it be true, that men did first *speak* before they did *write*, and consequently writing is but the figure of Speech, and therefore in order of *time* subsequent to it; yet in order of *Nature* there is no priority between these: But *voice* and *sounds* may be as well assigned to Figures, as *Figures* may be to Sounds.[62]

Wilkins was justifying his plan to begin with a written language which could subsequently be given a spoken form. Initially, he proposed, every person could attach the words of his own language to the common script. Assuming that speech had neither any 'natural' precedence over writing, nor any particular superiority in communicating thoughts, Wilkins's only reasons for beginning with a written language were practical. He believed that 'a common *Character* or *Letter* ... will conduce more to that great end of *Facility*, whereby ... men are to be invited to the Learning of it'.[63] He observed that if he began with a spoken language, recorded in alphabetical script, the scholar would have to learn two new systems at the same time, written and spoken. But his 'real character' demanded initially only that the student learn a set of graphic symbols. Wilkins had strongly in mind the need to contrive a language that people would take the trouble to learn.

The language planners were not oblivious to the fact that speech possessed some means of expression lacked by writing. Speech contained some onomatopoeic words that lost their resemblance to things in a written form. Speech also gained emphasis and feeling from tone of voice, and from the gestures and facial expressions that naturally accompany oral dialogue. In his famous 'Apology for Raimond Sebond', Montaigne placed considerable importance on these factors in making language properly understood: 'The tone and inflection of my voice have a certain expressiveness and signification in conveying my meaning. It is for me to regulate it in a way to make myself understood.'[64] Montaigne's opinion was corroborated by oratorical teachings dating back to Cicero and Quintilian, who dwelled similarly on the importance of intonation in expressing the feelings of an eloquent speaker.[65] But the scholars who planned a new universal character were not generally interested in creating a more 'eloquent' language: they were interested primarily in forming a more accurate language for the purposes of science and business. For this reason, none of the language planners paid more than the most glancing attention to the role of intonation in language.[66] The same neglect is characteristic of much grammatical literature of this century. The study of prosody, though a traditional grammatical division, virtually disappeared from seventeenth-century grammars.[67] Grammarians generally confined their glancing discussions of 'accent' (pitch) and pause to sections on punctuation – that is, to sections relating specifically to the study of written language.

Intonation was not generally considered to contribute anything essential to meaning. In the Port-Royal *Logique* (1662), for example, Antoine Arnauld and Pierre Nicole called qualities such as intonation, gesture and facial expression mere 'accessories' to the principal signification of words.[68]

The plans for a universal or philosophical writing thus belonged to a linguistic and grammatical tradition that made little distinction between writing and speech for the purposes of communication. John Locke's famous discussion of language in book 3 of *An essay concerning human understanding* (1690) comes to mind strongly here. Locke defined words as 'external sensible Signs' which '*signify* only Men's peculiar *Ideas*, and that *by a perfectly arbitrary Imposition*'.[69] Whether these 'sensible Signs' were made of air or ink clearly made no difference to Locke. He gave no attention to intonation, gesture or means of expression exclusive to oral communication. Like most others of his time, he abandoned these features of language to the outer regions of 'Rhetorick' – the suspect use of language to raise the passions.[70] As we will see, rhetoricians and grammarians of the eighteenth century strongly disagreed with this narrow understanding of what is 'essential' to language. Giving a more central place to intonation in ordinary communication, they found little interest in projects for a new international writing. Locke's primary aim, on the other hand, was to discredit Renaissance ideas concerning the 'natural' relation between words and 'things.' All language, written or spoken, was 'arbitrary'. This was the linguistic doctrine behind most of the projects for a universal character – projects that, despite some superficial similarities, had little essential in common with Renaissance interests in hieroglyphics, cabalism and 'natural' signification.

UNIVERSAL CHARACTERS AND RENAISSANCE IDEAS OF
WRITING

Recent scholarship on seventeenth-century language schemes has often portrayed seventeenth-century projects for a 'real character' or universal writing as direct continuations of the Renaissance fascination with mystical symbolism, hieroglyphics and emblems.[71] In some cases, this lineage is indisputable. Determined adherents of the hermetic-cabalist tradition, such as Athanasius Kircher, were among those who devised elaborate plans for a new philosophical language.[72] But can the legacy of Renaissance philosophy and emblemology be extended as well to authors such as Wilkins or Dalgarno, despite their support for the principles of the Royal Society? Wilkins's 'real character', it is pointed out, resembled hieroglyphics in important respects: a single character stands for an entire 'genus' of objects or ideas, and is then varied systematically according to the particular 'species' and 'division'. Other methods, such as those of Dalgarno or Leibniz, seem to owe something to the cabalistic arts of manipulating letters to discover hidden meanings: these authors used letters, each symbolising some root concept, which were combined with other letters to produce larger concepts. Leibniz and others had studied the 'combinatory arts' of Ramon Llull, a fourteenth-century philosopher who was deeply influenced by the cabalists in his native Spain.[73]

Most significant, modern scholars have claimed that there are crucial links between the philosophical outlook of the language planners and the classical metaphysics that informed Renaissance discussions of language. In *An essay towards a real character*, which crowned the Royal Society's ambitions for a philosophical language, Wilkins declared his goal to establish a consistent relationship between his 'real characters' and natural 'species'. By learning the symbols for these species in an ideal language, he asserted, we would 'be instructed likewise in their *Natures*'.[74] Such statements recall how Renaissance scholars described Adamic language or the philosophical symbolism of the *prisca theologia*. From Ficino to Kircher, hermetic thinkers argued that Hebrew characters or the ancient hieroglyphs enlightened the interpreter concerning the 'intelligible species' or 'forms' of things.

But these philosophical and linguistic affinities are less substantial than a superficial comparison suggests. Hermetic philosophers such as Dee or Kircher valued the compression of entire philosophical truths into single images. This was not the goal of Leibniz, Wilkins or Dalgarno. Their languages were based on characters that denoted elemental concepts, and were of no philosophical significance until assembled into propositions. They devised languages that were meant to be read like prose, or combined as in mathematics, not scrutinised character by character. Nor was there really much in common between the hermetic view of nature and that of the new science. Neo-platonism, which was so central to the philosophy of Ficino, Bruno or Kircher, bears no resemblance to the inductive and materialist principles championed by the Royal Society: Wilkins, Dalgarno and others searched for truth in the empirical examination of nature, not in any direct mystical illumination or apprehension of 'forms' or 'ideas' distinct from matter. Rejecting the Renaissance ideal of natural signification, these authors insisted on the totally arbitrary relationship between signs and 'the notions of things' they denoted.

The realist tradition of the Medieval schools, with its language of 'essences' and 'universals' existing in nature, did exercise a lasting influence on scientific and linguistic thought in the seventeenth century. As M. M. Slaughter has rightly argued, Wilkins's division of nature into tables of 'genera', 'species' and 'differences' owes a great deal to the taxonomic principles of Aristotle and the schoolmen.[75] But this peripatetic vision of natural order should not be confused with mystical neo-platonism. Moreover, Wilkins echoed the generally approved view of his day in asserting that the essences were unknowable to human intelligence. Given the constraints of human perception, 'men should be content with such a description by *properties* and *circumstances*, as may be sufficient to determine the primary sense of the thing defined'.[76] The same limitation was drawn by Dalgarno in *Ars signorum*.[77]

Schemes for a philosophical language thus had little in common with hieroglyphics or other kinds of symbolism studied in the Renaissance. But this is not to deny that the language planners relied on a vision of language and nature that was becoming obsolete even as they wrote. Wilkins, Dalgarno and their predecessors leaned heavily on the assumption that, with careful study, scientists could achieve an accurate and permanent classification of nature. Only by means of this classification could the language planners hope to establish a fixed relationship between their symbols and nature. Yet, as Locke would argue at length in his 1690 *Essay*, if we could not know the 'real essence' of objects – that is, the underlying source of all their sensible properties – then we could have no certain basis for dividing nature into genera and species. In truth, Locke concluded, the 'Boundaries of *Species*, are as Men, not as Nature makes them'.[78] Particularly in the English and French traditions, where Locke's influence was most powerful, this denial that humans possessed an absolute standard for classifying natural objects helped to dispel the dream of a fixed philosophical nomenclature. Some interest in a new philosophical language remained in Germany, where Leibnizian rationalism, further developed by Christian Wolff, preserved confidence in natural classification and deductive logic.[79] But there were no significant attempts at contriving a universal language in either England or France until the last decade of the eighteenth century.

In summary, then, the invented languages of Wilkins, Dalgarno and others reflect a point of transition in intellectual history between ancient Aristotelian metaphysics, with its belief in a stable natural order, and the ontological scepticism of post-Lockean empiricism. To the hermetic-cabalist tradition, however, these language planners owed, at most, some rough impression of how single emblems or letters might be utilised for philosophical ends. Their philosophical and linguistic principles were quite alien to the visions of Athanasius Kircher or Robert Fludd. The mystic and rationalist traditions were similarly divided concerning the practical use of a philosophical language. And it is this opposition regarding the social role of science that most clearly explains why Wilkins and other advocates of the new science dismissed the study of hieroglyphics and cabalism as irrelevant to their purposes.

For these authors saw no value in concealing knowledge from the public or in restricting truth to a small elite of priests and intellectuals. Wilkins, it is true, wrote a book early in his career on cryptology, *Mercury: or the secret and swift messenger* (1641). Other leading advocates of the new philosophy, such as the mathematician John Wallis, showed a keen interest in the same subject. But these authors had a strictly practical interest in 'secret' writing. They did not set out to unlock the secrets of the cabala or the *prisca theologia*. Instead, they aimed to facilitate private communication between politicians and men of commerce, or, like Wallis, to provide a secure method of military communication.[80] Plans for a 'universal writing' or 'real character' were, similarly, motivated by pragmatic and public-minded goals. The specific needs of the philosopher and scientist were certainly uppermost in the minds of Bacon, Dalgarno or Wilkins. Yet the language planners also entertained the more general hope to furnish what Wilkins called a 'remedy... against the Curse of the Confusion'.[81] They believed that the evils introduced at Babel were not only linguistic. Failures of communication had also given rise to the civil and religious conflicts that so plagued their age. By instituting a new language, clear and accessible to all literate people, these scholars would reduce misunderstanding, and provide the means to achieve greater harmony between nations and individuals.

These utilitarian and irenic objectives explain why Wilkins's few allusions to hieroglyphics are so dismissive. In a thinly veiled criticism of Kircher in the introduction to his *Essay towards a real character*, Wilkins echoed the view of many contemporaries like Stillingfleet and Sprat that Egyptian hieroglyphics were only a means 'to conceal from the vulgar the Mysteries of their Religion'. He also observed that other societies, such as the Mexicans, used non-alphabetic forms of writing simply because of 'want of the Knowledge of *Letters*'. The same was probably true of the Egyptians: 'it seems to me questionable, whether the *Egyptians* did not at first use their *Hieroglyphicks* upon the same account, namely, for want of *Letters*.'[82] Wilkins had no interest in hieroglyphs because, like most of his contemporaries, he shared few of the objectives or values of Renaissance scholars: he did not wish to confine knowledge to an elite group of priests or to an inspired elect; he believed that language and all human arts had generally improved rather than degenerated over the centuries; he wished to make his new language as widely useful and practical as possible. These were central values in the rationalistic, scientific tradition that had inaugurated a new understanding of the nature and history of writing.

WRITING AS 'PHARMAKON' – REMEDY AND EVIL

Wider and clearer communication advanced both scientific knowledge and social harmony: this was a central belief among the seventeenth-century scholars who set out plans for a new universal writing. It could not be denied, however, that the spread of literacy had exerted a disruptive as well as a beneficial influence on society. Writing, though a major tool of progress, had also engendered useless disputes, learned vanity and dogmatism. The evidence of this consequence lay all around in an age of proliferating sects and schisms, sceptical doctrines and violent theoretical contentions.

The pernicious effects of literacy seemed to be confirmed by ancient myths. In one myth, told in Ovid's *Metamorphoses*, Cadmus the Phoenician sowed sixteen teeth of a dragon, which transformed into sixteen warriors. Erasmus interpreted this story as referring to Cadmus's introduction of sixteen letters into Greece, the beginning, according to legend, of both Greek learning and all the philosophical dissensions of the ancient world.[83] Another story, told by Socrates in Plato's *Phædrus*, describes how Theuth, the Egyptian name for

Hermes, offered his invention of writing to King Thamus. The king rejects this invention as dangerous to the welfare of his people: 'What you have discovered is a recipe not for memory, but for reminder. And it is not true wisdom that you offer your disciples, but only its semblance, for by telling them of many things without teaching them you will make them seem to know much, while for the most part they know nothing.'[84] In the ensuing commentary on this story, Socrates instructs that writing is a 'dead discourse' in contrast with 'living speech', referring to his own method of dialogue. This oral technique leads the student to an independent discovery of the truth, rather than the thoughtless rehearsal of empty verbiage.[85]

In the imagery of this dialogue, as Derrida has shown in his well-known essay 'Plato's pharmacy', the letter is *pharmakon* – a remedy but also a poison. Derrida presents this scene as a fearful condemnation of writing's poisonous effects re-echoed, in various forms, throughout the entire subsequent history of Western thought.[86] In the seventeenth century, however, scholars overwhelmingly agreed that the benefits of writing far outweighed its dangers. This was John Milton's opinion in his great defence of unlicensed printing, *Areopagitica* (1644), which alludes to the legend of Cadmus. 'I deny not', acknowledged Milton, 'but that it is of greatest concernment in the Church and Commonwealth to have a vigilant eye how Bookes demeane themselves as well as men ... I know they are as lively, and as vigorously productive, as those fabulous Dragon's teeth: and being sown up and down, may chance to spring up armed men.' But these dangers, Milton insisted, did not justify the suppression of books. Books were sometimes the source of evil because good and evil were inseparable consequences of the fall. That the written word was capable of disturbing the world proved, moreover, that it was not 'dead discourse', but carried on some of the spirit of the living author: 'Books are not absolutely dead things, but doe contain a potencie of life in them to be as active as that soule was whose progeny they are'.[87]

While conceding the dual evil and good of writing, therefore, Milton was far from sympathising with King Thamus's rejection of this invention. Other authors of this period directly denounced Thamus for his suppression of writing. 'It was but a barbarous Act of *Thamus*, the *Egyptian* King ... to forbid the Learning of Letters', wrote Wilkins in *Mercury: or the secret and swift messenger*. Wilkins conceded that writing had often been the source of evil – but could not the same be said of speech? 'We may as well cut out our Tongues', he protested, 'because that member is *a world of wickedness.*' Any human art, including speech, could be abused. Such dangers did not justify the halting of human progress, a sentiment widely shared by scholars in this vigorous age of experiment and idealism concerning the potential of human reason.[88]

The traditional inventor of writing, Hermes, portrayed as a cunning charlatan in Plato's dialogue, also had his defenders in the seventeenth century. He even enjoyed something of a rehabilitation. We will recall that belief in Hermes Trismegistus, author of philosophical works anticipating the doctrines of Plato and Christ, had been debunked by Isaac Casaubon in 1614. But Hermes, the Egyptian Theuth and Roman Mercury, remained a prominent figure in the classical pantheon – a god whose reputation was as ambivalent as that of his legendary invention. Messenger of the gods, Hermes was also the patron of thieves and a cunning trickster. These unattractive qualities, Wilkins argued, had been falsely attributed to Hermes. The 'Poets' had only 'feigned' that this god was 'chief Patron of Thieves and Treachery'.[89] Other students of this myth gave almost exclusive attention to Hermes' ancient reputation as the benefactor of nations, a Promethean figure who brought humanity the arts of the gods. In *Origines sacræ*, Edward Stillingfleet portrayed Hermes as himself an emblem or 'Hieroglyphick' of public utility and the rational arts. Hermes had been originally a '*useful person*', argued Stillingfleet, whom the Egyptians greatly venerated and so 'by degrees attributed the *invention* of all *useful things* to him'.[90] Stillingfleet suggested that many of Hermes' less appealing attributes, such as his associations with trickery and theft, actually referred to the crafty Phoenician traders who introduced letters into Greece.[91]

A similarly euhemeristic reading of the Hermes story was proposed by Sir Isaac Newton in his late work on Biblical history, *The chronology of ancient kingdoms amended* (1728). Newton did not believe that any one person invented alphabetical writing: he was indeed among the first to propose that writing, along with mathematics and astronomy, was actually developed for practical purposes by common people – Red Sea merchants who needed a system of marks to do their accounts.[92] He agreed, however, that ancient peoples were in the habit of emblemising their arts and values in stories of gods and heroes. The real Hermes, Newton argued, was actually the secretary to the Egyptian King Sesac. This venerable figure was deified after his death, and, in the manner of ancient societies, was celebrated as the author of all the various national achievements, including the alphabet.[93]

The interpretation of the legend of Hermes was thus changing along with the general shift of social and intellectual attitudes in the seventeenth century. Hermes the occult philosopher, venerated in the Renaissance, was eclipsed by Hermes the symbol of progress and invention, central values of the scientific revolution. But the reputation of this 'god or god-like man', as Plato calls him in the *Philebus*,[94] would never be as high again. Like his greatest and most useful invention, writing, Hermes would again be vilified by eighteenth-century authors who had become disillusioned with the ideals of progress and civilisation that had emerged from the previous century. No wonder this god had been viewed with such suspicion by the ancient world, remarked Jean-Jacques Rousseau in his prize-winning first *Discours* of 1750: his invention had made possible all the arts and sciences that had been 'inimical to men's repose'.[95] And other philosophers of the late eighteenth century found much wisdom in the objections of Plato's Thamus. 'It may be justly questioned', acknowledged Lord Monboddo, referring to the *Phædrus*, 'whether [writing] has upon the whole contributed to the improvement of knowledge.'[96]

But Rousseau and Monboddo were authors of a much different intellectual era. Their pronouncements cannot be taken as expressions of some permanent hostility to writing in the Western tradition, for they were really reacting *against* what they considered the excessive vanity of their culture in this marvellous invention and all that it had made possible. Authors of the Renaissance, as we have seen, often lauded writing – meaning cryptic ideograms and mystic codes – as more 'spiritual' than the spoken word. And leaders of the scientific revolution, while generally impatient with occult symbolism, continued to praise writing as a great example of human progress and European genius. It was they who established a link that endures even today – the link between writing, civilisation, progress and reason. But we are also the heirs of a later age, the age of Rousseau and Monboddo, which became more anxious about the poisonous effects of writing, *pharmakon*, bringer of both good and evil.

CHAPTER 3

' The uniform voice of nature' : conjectural histories of writing in the early eighteenth century

In the seventeenth century, even orthodox Christians were willing to abandon the traditional belief in the divine origin of writing. But these scholars found it much more difficult to doubt that alphabetical writing was the work of some single, mortal intelligence, either Adam or the clever Egyptian deified as 'Hermes'. The great orderliness and utility of the alphabet seemed the self-evident signs of some designing mind of great skill and beneficence. That no such mind existed, but that writing was the product of whole nations over many generations – this assumption seemed as implausible to them as Hermes Trismegistus seems to us. The thesis that writing gradually evolved towards its present European forms was the distinctive contribution of eighteenth-century 'conjectural histories'.

The most influential of these histories was William Warburton's dissertation on writing in *The divine legation of Moses* (1738–41). Some of Warburton's ideas were anticipated by earlier authors, notably by Nicolas Fréret. But it was Warburton who fashioned the most detailed, plausible case for the theory that writing slowly developed over many centuries from primitive to ever more sophisticated and efficient forms. His methodology in making this case was highly typical of eighteenth-century studies of language. Assuming that human nature was always and everywhere the same, Warburton conjectured about the probable course of linguistic development in the past on the basis of what he observed of human needs and abilities in the present. At all times and all places, he believed, the development of writing had been guided by 'the uniform voice of nature'.[1] As Hans Aarsleff has shown in his ground-breaking studies of linguistic thought in the eighteenth century, this was the same method later used by Condillac, Maupertuis, Adam Smith and others to trace the origin and history of speech.[2] All these authors attempted to isolate the drives that motivated the first, awkward efforts at communication. From this genesis, they traced the slow unfolding of language towards the contemporary flowering of developed speech and the alphabet.

By the end of the century, the reliance of these historians on informed guesswork had fallen into disrepute, superseded by the demand for empirical research. Indeed, the very term 'conjectural history', coined by the Scottish philosopher Dugald Stewart in 1794, was originally meant to be pejorative.[3] Yet it was Warburton and others of his time who had inspired the scientific research that Stewart admired, giving credence to an entirely new understanding of the history of writing. Early eighteenth-century historians broke decisively from many of the traditional prejudices that previously blocked the accurate understanding of ancient writing. They looked to the distant past not for the fires of Adamic wisdom, but for the nascent sparks of primitive insight. Inspired by reports of pictographic and 'hieroglyphical' writing in the New World, they speculated on the apparently intimate connection between levels of 'civilisation' and the gradual development of alphabetical literacy. A key theorist on the nature of this connection between civilisation and writing was Giambattista Vico. Though Vico almost certainly knew nothing of Warburton, he developed a closely parallel history of writing from pictures to letters. And far more than his English contemporary, Vico made explicit how this evolution was simultaneous with the rise of democracy and the improving capacity for abstract reason.

NICOLAS FRÉRET

Some of Warburton's major theories about writing were sketched out by a major historian of the early century, Nicolas Fréret. As Frank E. Manuel has observed, Fréret led a movement of historical thought that subjected old assumptions and old authorities to the cold scrutiny of reason.[4] Among other breakthroughs, this methodology directed him to a profoundly original understanding of the history of writing. In his 1718 *De la langue des Chinois; réflexions sur les principes généraux de l'art d'écrire*, this eminent historian, secretary of the Académie des Inscriptions et Belles-Lettres, constructed a short history of writing that relied in no way on the Biblical account of the origin of letters, or on any of the classical stories. Instead, he asked a simple question: how would primitive humans, guided only by the light of nature, first attempt to preserve their knowledge in a visual form?[5]

The most plausible answer was that they would draw pictures, a conjecture corroborated by the use of pictographs by the natives of North America and Mexico, as reported by many travellers since the sixteenth century: 'le moyen d'exprimer les pensées par des peintures ou représentations des choses dont on parle, est celui qu'emploient encore aujourd'hui les sauvages du Canada, et celui dont se servoient les Mexicains avant que les Espagnols eussent détruit leur empire.' (The expression of thoughts by pictures or representations of things about which one is speaking is still used today by the savages of Canada, and was used by the Mexicans before the Spanish destroyed their empire.)[6] Fréret's interpretation of pictographs as simply a primitive form of writing differed fundamentally from the inference of Renaissance authors that ancient emblems contained secret religious or philosophical meanings. Indeed, Fréret derided the Spanish conquerors who destroyed many of the pictorial books of the Mexicans, thinking that they were used for some kind of black magic.[7] Whereas authors of the Renaissance tradition generally assumed that all human arts were degenerating from the time of Adam – hence their search for enlightenment in the mysteries of early scripts – Fréret believed that human history was progressive, and looked to pictographs, hieroglyphics and other ancient scripts merely as early stages in the gradual improvement of writing towards its present forms.

The great motives for developing new kinds of writing after the pictograph were, in Fréret's view, convenience and economy. Pictures were difficult and time-consuming to draw, and took up too much room. Here again, he reflected a way of understanding the evolution of human arts that would become highly typical of studies of writing in his century. Historians increasingly abandoned the assumption that the improvement of human arts was usually driven by the 'genius' of single inventors. Rather, the evolution of scripts had been motivated in part by a communal desire to shorten and ease labour. Above all, according to Fréret, ancient peoples needed new forms of writing because there was so much that they could not say with pictures: 'Il y a ... un très-grand nombre de choses qui ne se peuvent exprimer distinctement par cette voie ... telles sont les actions de mouvement, les changemens de rapports et de qualités, mais sur-tout les passions et les sentimens des êtres vivans.' (There are

... a great number of things that cannot be expressed distinctly by this route ... such are the nature of movements, the changes of relation and quality, but especially the passions and sentiments of living beings).[8] Fréret was especially aware of the difficulty of depicting 'passions and sentiments' in visual language. The only kind of writing with the power to communicate non-visual experience was, he concluded, an 'écriture représentative' that relied on no resemblance for its signification. Such a representative writing could take two forms. First, qualities, movements, passions and so forth could be signified 'd'une manière symbolique ou figurée' (in a symbolic or figurative manner) through the use of an imagined rapport between such notions and visual signs. Second, these notions could be represented through entirely arbitrary signs, established by convention.[9]

The first kind of writing was used by the Egyptians. Fréret's view was that Egyptian hieroglyphics reflected an effort to signify non-visual ideas metaphorically. They were not, as most previous authors had claimed, a method to secrete religious truths from the vulgar. Chinese was the most important example of an arbitrary form of representative writing, used to denote ideas directly rather than indirectly through words. Thus, whereas previous authors had distinguished between only two forms of writing – ideographic and alphabetical – Fréret distinguished further between two sub-classes of ideographs, figurative and non-figurative. In addition, he identified a number of different phonographic scripts. Phonographic systems could be truly alphabetical, as in Europe; but they could also omit vowels as in Hebrew or Arabic (which Fréret conjectured was yet another form of 'real character', designed to provide a common script for various dialects); yet again, writing might mark whole syllables, as in Ethiopic and Indian scripts. Fréret even suggested that certain scripts, like the 'Tartar', fell somewhere between hieroglyphical and phonographic, with single characters compounded of marks for sounds. Conceiving of each script as an integrated system, based on a consistent method of signification, Fréret saw reason to challenge one of the most enduring legends about the history of writing – that the first Greek letters were introduced by Cadmus the Phoenician. It was very unlikely that the Greeks borrowed much from the Phoenicians, Fréret contended. These peoples used different kinds of writing systems, Greek being fully alphabetic and Phoenician consonantal.[10]

Fréret was thus willing to depart from traditional stories about writing, and to develop a modern history on the basis of reasoned conjecture about the probable course of human needs and abilities. But he made no attempt to explain the great diversity of scripts used by various nations. In his analysis, the different 'representative' and phonographic systems that developed over the centuries followed no particular order: they were merely different options adopted by different peoples for no reason that he tried to specify. Later authors, such as Warburton, were less willing to leave any development in the history of writing unexplained.

WARBURTON'S THEORY OF THE EVOLUTION OF HIEROGLYPHICS

Though he is now little studied, and is darkly overshadowed by contemporaries like Vico, William Warburton was an important figure in eighteenth-century thought. Besides being the Bishop of Gloucester, and a resounding voice in the century's theological controversies, he belonged to an elite literary circle, and is perhaps best known today as editor of the works of Alexander Pope and of Shakespeare. Among his contemporaries, he was particularly esteemed as the author of *The alliance of church and state* (1736), the century's definitive defence of the powers of the established Church of England. His dissertation on writing, first published in *The divine legation of Moses* was equally definitive, marking a watershed in the history of our present subject.[11] In the words of Maurice Pope, 'to ask whether or not the decipherment of hieroglyphs would have taken place without him is very much like asking whether or not the discoveries of modern science and technology would have taken place without the theoretical shelter for them erected by Francis Bacon'.[12]

The divine legation of Moses is in fact a work of Christian apologetics, though its theological ideas were considered convoluted and irrelevant even by many orthodox contemporaries. 'He carries you round and round', quipped Johnson to Boswell, 'without carrying you forward to the point'.[13] Against the infidels and deists spawned by modern rationalist philosophy, Warburton set out to prove that the ancient Jews really were the Chosen People, ruled directly by God. He also maintained that the ancient Jews had no belief in an afterlife of rewards and punishments, proving that this central doctrine could not be determined by reason, and was revealed to humanity only with the Christian revelation. The history of writing enters into his description of the events recorded in Exodus. He believed that the second commandment of the Decalogue, 'Thou shalt not make unto thee any graven image' (Exodus 20:4), was intended to prohibit the use of hieroglyphs, which were responsible for the idolatry of the Jews.[14] He also concluded that Moses had learned writing from the Egyptians, and had refashioned their letters into Hebrew characters.

But did Warburton really need an elaborate theory about the history of writing in order to fulfil his theological aims? This is very doubtful. He himself set an independent value on his history of writing. Much to the dissatisfaction of his bookseller, Fletcher Gyles, he distributed this section separately among his acquaintances even before the publication of the full *Divine legation*.[15] The section on writing was also separately translated into French – or rather adapted, with important changes and abridgements – by Léonard des Malpeines in 1744.[16] It was indeed in France that Warburton's essay was most widely admired. His theory harmonised perfectly with the interest of Enlightenment *philosophes* in tracing the history of language from its origin, and in determining the natural laws that had governed that history. The section on writing in Condillac's *Essai sur l'origine des connoissances humaines* (1746) rehearses Warburton's main theories, as does the article 'Écriture' in the *Encyclopédie*.[17] Chagrined that his ideas about writing were not so well received in England, Warburton used the notes of the 1765 edition to record the plaudits of his French admirers, and to castigate his opponents with great rudeness and bluster. He also made a number of significant additions to his history.

In the minds of his admirers, Warburton's greatest contribution was to debunk belief that hieroglyphics were first used by the Egyptian priests to disguise their sacred wisdom. Hieroglyphics, he argued, were simply an early and crude means of communication. His logic was, in important respects, much like Fréret's, though he showed no sign of knowing the French scholar's work on writing until the 1765 edition of *The divine legation*.[18] Like Fréret, he reasoned that primitive people started by drawing pictures, citing the description of Mexican pictographs by José de Acosta, as well as recently published reproductions of cave-drawings in Siberia.[19] Again like Fréret, Warburton remarked that 'the Inconveniences attending the too great Bulk of the Volume, in Compositions of this kind' would cause 'the more ingenious and civilized Nations' to find some way of abridging their pictographs.[20] Significantly, it was not until the 1765 edition that Warburton mentioned Fréret's main explanation for the invention of figurative hieroglyphs – the need to express abstract ideas and other non-visual conceptions.[21] This fact suggests again that Warburton had not read Fréret's essay when he first wrote his dissertation on writing. The two scholars, influenced by reports from Mexico and elsewhere, arrived independently at many of the same conclusions.

Though reasonably up-to-date with the discoveries in the New World, Warburton paid no attention to recent drawings and artifacts brought home by travellers to Egypt and the Middle East, cradle of literacy. He ignored important new reproductions of Egyptian and Persian writing by Montfaucon, Rigord and Chardin.[22] Instead, Warburton relied heavily on the old sources, especially the well-thumbed pages of Horapollo's *Hieroglyphics*, 'that admirable Fragment of Antiquity'.[23] And yet, despite the narrowness of Warburton's evidence, he constructed an original theory that would long influence antiquaries studying new archaeological evidence. The Bishop's contribution lay in his general map of how writing progressed. Horapollo's tract, with its extravagant symbols, suggested to him how the Egyptians progressed beyond pictures towards more sophisticated kinds of writing. Aiming to shorten their bulky pictographs, the Egyptians invented different kinds of tropes. Sometimes they used a method of substitution, making 'the principal Circumstance of the Subject stand for the whole', or 'putting the Instrument of the Thing, whether real or metaphorical, for the Thing itself'. Hence, 'two Hands, one holding a Shield, and the other a Bow' signified a battle, and 'an *Eye* eminently placed was designed to present *God's Omniscience*'.[24] At a later stage, the Egyptians denoted objects by 'any quaint Resemblance or Analogy', so that, for instance, 'the *Universe* was designed [*sic*] by a *Serpent in a Circle*, whose variegated *Spots* signified the *Stars*'.[25] Warburton thus classified hieroglyphics into three orders of images, corresponding to synecdoche, metonymy and metaphor. But his point was not that the Egyptians were being deliberately fanciful or mysterious. Rather, they were simply trying to make their form of writing less voluminous and time-consuming.

Given this explanation of hieroglyphics, Kircher's voluminous musings on their hidden philosophical significance seemed quite ridiculous. In Warburton's book, as in other works on writing in the eighteenth century, the learned Jesuit became a figure of fun, a sort of grammatological Don Quixote. Warburton scoffed at Kircher's reliance on the discredited legend of Hermes Trismegistus. He also mocked Kircher's 'deep' insights into the meaning of what were, in fact, only Roman imitations of hieroglyphics: 'it is pleasant to see him labouring thro' half a dozen Folios with the Writings of the late *Greek Platonists*, and the forged Books of *Hermes*, which contain a *Philosophy not Egyptian*, to explain and illustrate *old Monuments not Philosophical*.'[26] The only excuse allowed Kircher was that he was perpetuating the error of classical authorities, such as Manetho and Clement of Alexandria, who also seemed to believe that hieroglyphs were intended for sacred purposes. One of Warburton's notable departures from traditional approaches was, indeed, his willingness to challenge the accuracy of these classical accounts.

It is an ironic fact of Warburton's history, however, that he himself was more under the spell of traditional assumptions than he liked to pretend. Though he heaped ridicule on Kircher's 'visionary Labours',[27] Warburton raided the Jesuit's folios for evidence to support his own theories. And he did ultimately acknowledge that at least *some* hieroglyphs were designed specifically to secrete philosophical knowledge from the vulgar. Important sections of his dissertation examine 'how *Hieroglyphics* came to be employed for the *Vehicle of Mystery*'.[28] Mystery and intrigue were the main purposes of a special class of images that he called 'symbols'. These images differed from 'the *proper hieroglyphics*' in being more abstruse and 'enigmatical' than the strangest of hieroglyphs.[29] The oddness of these 'symbols' convinced Warburton that they could not possibly have had a popular use, and could only have been contrived by crafty philosophers to hide their secrets.

In this instance, as in others, Warburton vacillated between old and new ideas. He mocked Kircher's assumption that hieroglyphics contained philosophical mysteries only to endorse this belief later on. The general scheme of Warburton's history nevertheless remained original. The Egyptian 'symbol' was important to him not for the philosophical insights it might conceal: the evidence of Horapollo, he reasonably pointed out, suggested that the hieroglyphics recorded 'popular Superstition', not abstruse metaphysics.[30] The 'symbol' was significant to Warburton only as an intermediary stage between hieroglyphics and the alphabet, contributing to the movement of writing away from mimetic representation and towards increasing 'arbitrariness'. As we will see, however, he was not entirely successful in explaining the most crucial transition in the history of writing – the change from symbolising ideas to denoting speech sounds.

When the Egyptian priests created their 'enigmatical' symbols, they made writing so distant from mimetic representation as to be almost 'arbitrary'. The mimetic qualities were even further obliterated when they converted their symbols into a cursive or 'running-hand' script for quick writing.[31] These late forms of ideographic script signified by agreement as much as by resemblance: it was possible to learn that the hasty sketch of a wolf stood for 'aversion', or the image of a hare for 'openness', without recalling the logic that had given rise to this symbolism.[32] The Chinese went one step further in developing characters that lost all but the most remote similarity with physical objects. Though distantly related to hieroglyphics, Chinese characters signified solely by convention. And with these arbitrary marks, claimed Warburton, writing had finally evolved to 'the very Borders of *Letters*'.

Here then was the climax of Warburton's history. Chinese writing formed the bridge between hieroglyphics and letters, the end-point of the evolution of writing. 'Thus have we brought down the *General History of Writing*', he proclaimed, 'by a gradual and easy Descent, from a PICTURE to a LETTER; for *Letters* are the very next Step to *Chinese Marks*.'[33] This thesis exemplifies a principal inspiration in Enlightenment thought – that even an art of great order and utility, the apparent sign of some single intelligence, could in fact be produced by the unguided forces of 'nature'. Although alphabetical writing was so apparently the product of design, Warburton had supposedly done away with the need for some great genius to invent this most ingenious of human arts.

But had Warburton really shown the smooth, natural transition from the arbitrary ideograph to alphabetical writing? Even many of his contemporaries thought not: while he had explained how the marks themselves might become increasingly arbitrary, he had *not* explained why people would begin to use marks to represent speech sounds rather than 'things' or ideas. As the historian Francis Wise observed in 1758 of hieroglyphics and the alphabet, 'No two things can be more widely distant than these two arts: and therefore in our enquiries of this kind we ought never to lose sight of the distinction, between writing in general, and alphabetical writing.'[34] According to Wise, 'enigmatical' hieroglyphics and Chinese ideographs have nothing in common with alphabetical writing besides a lack of resemblance to physical objects. On this issue, both Warburton and his critics were hampered by a fundamental misunderstanding of Chinese and Egyptian writing. They all assumed, wrongly, that both of these scripts were fully ideographic, and provided no method for denoting sounds. In their minds, there was a clean separation between ideographic and alphabetical forms of writing. Given this assumption, the transition from ideographic to phonographic writing seemed unexplained in Warburton's general history of writing.

Warburton wrestled with this objection in his 1765 revision of the dissertation. He acknowledged that it seemed 'an immense leap' from Chinese characters to alphabetical writing, and he offered the following attempt to bridge the chasm. When writing became wholly arbitrary, he argued, attention was shifted from the thing to the word for the thing, forging the association between sound and mark:

> While the picture, or image of the thing represented, continued to be objected [*sic*] to the sight of the reader, it could raise no idea but of the thing itself. But when the *picture* lost its form, by being contracted into a *mark* or *note*, the view of this mark or note would, in course of time, as naturally raise, in the mind, the *sound* expressing the idea of the thing, as the idea itself.[35]

This is a thought-provoking passage. It suggests how the development of arbitrary marks might also have changed the very conception of written language. Non-mimetic marks might have drawn the mind away from 'things' and towards the sound of the word, making sounds rather than things the primary referents. From this change, ideographs might eventually have become alphabetical. One wonders, however, whether even Warburton found this logic fully satisfying. In both the first and second versions of the dissertation, he ultimately reverted to an old legend in order to explain why ancient people began to use writing to signify sounds rather than objects.

This was the legend of Hermes, inventor of writing. All the ancients agreed, Warburton observed, that the alphabet was invented by ' the SECRETARY *of an* Egyptian *King*'. He speculated that symbols and arbitrary characters had proved unfeasible for the king's communication with his generals and governors. The secretary therefore seized on the idea of using marks to represent sounds, a method that had the advantage of communicating with much the same clarity and precision possible in speech. Moreover, alphabetical writing was initially cryptic to everyone except the king's correspondents, preserving the secrecy of state affairs.[36]

Thus, at one of the most important stages in his new history of writing, Warburton returned to an old story which had been repeated from ancient times to the eighteenth century. His opponents, particularly in England, pointed to the sudden intrusion of this Egyptian secretary as an indication that neither Warburton nor anyone else could explain the origin of letters by natural means alone. God must have bestowed letters after all. As for the pugnacious Warburton, he was keen to show that he had in fact controverted traditional opinions once again. It was not hieroglyphs, he asserted, but rather letters that had been originally invented for secrecy: 'Thus the Reader at length finds that the very contrary to the common Opinion is the true; that it was the *first Literary Writing*, not the *first Hieroglyphical*, which was invented for SECRECY.'[37] This statement challenged the assumption of previous scholars, from Ficino to Galileo, that alphabetical writing was inherently public, designed for open communication rather than the concealment of knowledge. Admittedly, there is some interest in the proposal that alphabetical writing might first have been invented to conceal knowledge. But Warburton seemed to be disguising his failure of inspiration at this point, and his own retreat from conjectural history to traditional legends.

WARBURTON AND THE 'IDEOLOGY' OF WRITING

Warburton's fame as a historian of writing rested on his contention that hieroglyphics were initially invented only as a means of public communication, not to disguise the secrets of a priestly elite. As we have noted, however, Warburton did not break completely from traditional ideas. Ultimately, he did affirm that the wily priests developed especially 'enigmatical' hieroglyphics as a private cryptology. This thesis reveals the Bishop's understanding of the politics of ancient Egypt, a dimension of his essay examined in an ingenious essay on Warburton by Jacques Derrida, 'Scribble (writing-power)'.

Derrida points to the consistently 'ideological' nature of Warburton's analysis: 'Warburton proposes a history and a general system of writings, which he always analyzes according to an interpretation of "ideological" and politico-religious powers – of the ideological in general.'[38] According to Warburton, pictographs and early hieroglyphs were originally intended to communicate openly and publicly, and to serve the general good. It was a later 'abuse' of writing, as he called it, that turned this art into a mechanism for protecting the power and privileged knowledge of an intellectual elite. As Derrida writes, 'Naturally destined to serve the communication of laws and the order of the city transparently, a writing becomes the instrument of an abusive power, of a caste of "intellectuals" that is thus ensuring hegemony, whether its own or that of special interests.'[39]

Such, at least, is what Warburton would like us to think. In Derrida's reading, Warburton disguises the fact that the so-called 'abuse' of occult symbolism was in fact a natural and necessary stage in the development of the alphabet: the priests made their marks more enigmatical, and therefore more arbitrary, advancing writing closer to letters. Warburton's illogic is grist to Derrida's deconstructive mill. It shows the failure of Western thinkers to provide an adequate philosophical apparatus for demonstrating the reliability of language and the beneficence of 'nature'. For in Warburton's account, it was, in reality, 'nature' that was responsible for what he called an 'abuse' of written language. The use of marks to conceal knowledge and to consolidate tyranny was not, as he would like us to imagine, a regrettable deviation in the history of writing. It was rather an integral part of its natural evolution.

Derrida's analysis concerns the internal logic rather than the historical context of Warburton's argument. Of particular interest to Derrida is its constant vacillation between phases of publicity and secrecy – 'unveiling' and 'veiling' to cite Derrida's metaphors, borrowed from Léonard des Malpeines's adaptation. Can a knowledge of Warburton's intellectual context shed any further light on his 'ideology'? We might observe, first, that the oscillation between secret and public writing in Warburton's history reflects the conflict between Renaissance and Enlightenment ideologies about the ideal role of writing. Warburton's denunciation of secret hieroglyphs as an 'abuse' of the original function of writing was aimed at authors in the hermetic tradition from Ficino to Kircher who considered the concealment of religious knowledge by an elite priesthood to be both the original and the ideal purpose of hieroglyphics. That Warburton generally preferred the public use of writing reveals his rationalist outlook and his Protestantism.

We should also keep in mind, however, that Warburton himself was a priest – a conservative priest on political matters. He strongly advocated the continued 'hegemony' of the Anglican church in *The alliance of church and state*, arguing that while dissenting Protestants should be 'tolerated', only his church should be privileged with state support and protection.[40] Warburton's religious conservatism is evident in his choice of diction. It is true, as Derrida says, that he calls the use of secret writing an 'abuse'. But Warburton does not even come close to the kind of venomous language extruded by Derrida – 'a pathological depravation, an unjustifiable negativity', 'covered and twisted, concealed and devious, masked, hypocritical'.[41] Such terms are never used by the Bishop. As deployed by Derrida, they create the impression that Warburton feared and abhorred the craftiness of the Egyptian priesthood far more than he did. The Bishop of Gloucester was himself no political liberal or fervent democrat, for he believed strongly that his own 'caste of intellectuals', the priesthood of the Anglican church, should maintain its power over the vulgar.

Derrida is right to point out that the transformation of writing into 'the *Vehicle of Mystery*'[42] is an integral event in Warburton's history of writing, and not the mere 'accident' that Warburton sometimes indicates. But was Warburton really trying to disguise from himself and others that the 'voice of nature' was not so beneficent as he wanted to believe? In Warburton's view, it should be noted, the natural course of things has always been self-corrective. While writing often deviated into mystery, the inevitable outcome was always greater openness and legibility. Indeed, the priests were forced to create 'symbols' of increasing strangeness precisely because they had such difficulty keeping their secret writing secret. Their cryptic hieroglyphs ultimately engendered arbitrary signs, like those of the Chinese, which 'lie open to all'.[43] Similarly, the alphabet, invented for secrecy, ultimately became one of the most powerful tools of public communication. In an interesting reinterpretation of the famous story in Plato's *Phædrus*, Warburton indicated that the Egyptian king rejected Theuth's invention because he discerned its capacity to undermine royal and priestly power.[44] And when the alphabet eventually did become public knowledge, the priests were forced, yet again, to create a *new* secret alphabet, the '*Hierogrammatic*, or *Sacerdotal*' mentioned by the third-century Father, Clement of Alexandria, in his discussion of Egyptian writing.[45]

At every stage, in short, secret writing became public. The natural course of history has been consistently towards, not away from, greater openness and transparency. Whatever his logical confusions (the Bishop was no genius), Warburton shared the optimism of Enlightenment thinkers concerning the beneficent order of nature. And his conviction that 'the uniform voice of nature' had everywhere directed humans towards the improvement of writing and other arts was made even clearer in his 1765 revision of the essay.

WARBURTON'S 1765 REVISION

A great deal occurred in the study of writing in the quarter century between the first publication of *The divine legation* and 1765, much of it inspired by Warburton's dissertation. New and more accurate transcriptions of hieroglyphs had been made by Pococke, Norden and Caylus. The great French antiquarian, Jean-Jacques Barthé-lemy, became the first scholar to restore knowledge of ancient scripts, identifying most of the letters of two ancient Semitic alphabets, Palmyrene and Phoenician. These developments encouraged War-burton to make some changes to his arguments, and to contribute his now authoritative reaction to recent events in the study of writing.

Among the most revealing of his additions was a long note in response to the recently propounded hypothesis that Chinese characters actually derived from Egyptian writing. This conjecture was presented in 1761 by the English Catholic divine and scientist John Turberville Needham, who claimed that an Egyptian in-scription on a bust in Turin could be deciphered by comparison with Chinese writing.[46] A similar link between Egyptian and Chinese scripts was proposed by a well-known orientalist, Joseph de Guignes, in a lecture read before the Académie des Inscriptions et Belles-Lettres in 1758. Guignes's theory was prompted by Barthélemy's discovery of the values for nineteen letters in the Phoenician alphabet, which belongs to the same group as Samaritan and Hebrew. He also seized on Barthélemy's tentative suggestion that Phoenician was derived from Egyptian cursive writing and, at one further remove, from the hieroglyph. Examining a Chinese dictionary one day, Guignes thought he saw a startling resemblance between certain

Phoenician letters and the ancient form of some Chinese characters. Further examination seemed to reveal a correspondence between the meaning of these Chinese characters and the meaning of the Phoenician characters – for it was assumed that Phoenician letters, as in Hebrew, had individual meanings as well as phonemic values. Hence, the Phoenician character *daleth*, also meaning 'door', struck Guignes as remarkably like the ancient Chinese character for 'door'; the Phoenician *aleph*, which also has the numerical value of 'one', looked like the ancient Chinese character meaning 'one'. Largely on the basis of this evidence, Guignes leapt to the conclusion that the Egyptians had 'colonised' China, and taught their letters to the uncivilised inhabitants. The Chinese, for no very clear reason, used these letters as ideographs rather than phonograms.[47]

Guignes' theory marks the point where 'conjectural history' begins to blend with mild forms of scholarly madness. He was roundly refuted by fellow academician Leroux Deshautesrayes.[48] Significantly, Guignes thought that he was confirming the theories of Warburton, whom he praised. Had not Warburton theorised that hieroglyphs changed into Chinese characters? Here was proof that this had happened, though by means of the intermediary stage of Egyptian letters, originally derived, as Barthélemy had shown, from the hieroglyph.[49]

In his 1765 essay, however, Warburton clarified that he had not meant to suggest that Chinese characters had actually derived from Egyptian hieroglyphs. Fulminating in a long note against 'one of the strangest fancies, that ever got possession of the pericranium of an Antiquary',[50] Warburton pointed out that since all writing consists of lines and circles it was not surprising to find some similarity between the characters of different scripts. Moreover, writing had developed in the same way everywhere in the world not because of any communication between nations, but because 'human nature, without any other help, will, in the same circumstances, always exhibit the same appearances'.[51] Uniform laws of development had caused the Egyptians and the Chinese, quite independently of each other, to develop characters of an increasingly non-mimetic nature.

But why, then, had the Chinese not developed alphabetical writing when the Egyptians had? This fact caused Warburton to make a significant adjustment to his assumptions about the 'uniform voice of nature', particularly in the 1765 edition. In this edition, he added a passage comparing the Egyptians, who were 'extremely inventive', with the Chinese, 'known to be the least inventive people on earth'. Because the Egyptians 'were of a lively imagination', and were 'studious of natural knowledge', they delighted in mysterious analogies and occult symbolism, developing and retaining tropical hieroglyphs in preference to arbitrary characters or alphabetical writing. The Chinese, on the other hand, had little ability to create figurative images. Having no taste for tropical hieroglyphs, and insufficient genius to discover the alphabet, they adopted arbitrary characters.[52]

It will be noted that this explanation is not entirely consistent with Warburton's general history of writing. Elsewhere he described Chinese characters as an 'improvement' on hieroglyphs. But in his comparison of the Chinese and Egyptians, he indicated that the Egyptians reverted *back* to the use of hieroglyphics after developing arbitrary characters because they possessed an imaginative genius lacked by the Chinese. Moreover, this account leaves the impression that the uniform voice of nature is less important than variations in national character. Different nations have developed the kinds of writing most suitable to their differing personalities and abilities. Warburton did not use the word 'race', a term then used in English mostly to refer to family groups and horses. Nevertheless, his recourse to the belief that every people has its own innate characteristics clearly looks forward to the great importance placed on 'racial characteristics' by linguistic philosophers of the early nineteenth century. For example, Wilhelm von Humboldt would also blame an innate deficiency of imagination in the Chinese for their lack of alphabetical writing and for the monosyllabic nature of their spoken language. Languages were more or less 'successful', in Humboldt's view, depending on the strength or weakness of a race's innate linguistic sense.[53]

As so often in his dissertation on writing, therefore, Warburton was a figure of transition, a scholar with a highly traditional background who anticipated the dominant intellectual trends of later decades. He developed a 'conjectural history' before Condillac or Rousseau, but ultimately turned back to the story of Hermes, inventor of writing, to bridge the gap between ideographs and the alphabet. In modern style, he openly scorned the Renaissance fascination with occult and sacred characters. Yet one also discerns that he admired the imagination and inventiveness of the Egyptian priests. And although Warburton exemplified the Enlightenment confidence in the universality of human nature, he qualified this doctrine with a theory of national characteristics that anticipated linguistic doctrines of the early nineteenth century. Warburton himself was a highly ambivalent, even disorganised thinker. Yet it was this unlikely hero – blustering, vain, uncouth – who did most to stimulate the conjectural history of writing, and to inaugurate a new era in the study of writing and language.

THE HISTORY OF WRITING IN VICO'S *SCIENZA NUOVA*

Warburton was not alone in reasoning that writing had developed through a long process from pictographs to the modern alphabet. This was also the thesis of Giambattista Vico, a scholar who was virtually ignored outside Italy in Enlightenment Europe, though he has achieved considerable fame in the twentieth century. Vico's *Scienza nuova* is roughly contemporaneous with Warburton's *Divine legation of Moses* (1738–41), being first published in 1725 and then expanded in two subsequent editions of 1730 and 1744. Yet there is no evidence that either scholar knew of the other's ideas. Indeed, in his discussion of the history of writing, Vico mentions only Latin works by authors such as Hermannus Hugo, Geraldus Vossius and Olof Rudbeck who had long ceased to have much influence on scholarship. Nor did this Neapolitan scholar have much impact on later research. He is mentioned by none of the eighteenth-century scholars who are discussed in this book, with the exception of Antoine Court de Gébelin. Even this writer only briefly mentions Vico along with a number of other historians.[54]

Despite this apparent isolation from major scholarly currents of his day, Vico produced one of the century's most sophisticated and original histories of writing. Writing is not the chief theme of the *Scienza nuova*: he examines the origin of writing only as part of his comprehensive theory concerning the development of all human arts and institutions. Yet the breadth of Vico's history makes his study of writing all the more important. Far more than Fréret or Warburton, Vico situated the development of writing in the context of the whole development of modern civilisation. It was he who most illuminated the significance of writing in the evolution of reason and modern political economy.[55]

Like Fréret, Vico argued that humans originally developed figurative emblems as a way of communicating abstract or non-visual ideas. But Vico went much further than Fréret in suggesting that the first written marks played an important role in the psychology of primitive humans. Hieroglyphs, argued Vico, were a form of 'poetic character' that primitive humans used not merely to record or convey their ideas, but more fundamentally to make sense of the world. Because ancient people lacked the ability to form abstract concepts like 'authority' or 'ownership' or 'useful inventions', they made visual images, 'mute symbols', that stood for these concepts and could be presented whenever these people wished to recall or enforce the founding principles of their society. In Vico's words, 'the first men, the children, as it were, of the human race, not being able to form intelligible class concepts of things, had a natural need to create poetic characters; that is, imaginative class concepts or universals, to which, as to certain models or ideal portraits, to reduce all the particular species that resembled them.'[56] In at least one important respect, Vico had a quite different understanding of primitive peoples from that of modern scholars of oral cultures. Vico believed that primitive people are visually, not orally, disposed in all their ways of understanding the world. Hence, like a number of authors in the middle decades of the century, Vico experimented with the idea that some form of writing came before speech (though, in fact, he was extremely inconsistent on this point).[57] He imagined primitive wanderers *looking* up at the sky, and believing that it was the giant body of a god. They believed that the flashes of lightning, the stars, the birds and so forth were the signs or language of the massive sky-god.[58] These were the signs that they subsequently duplicated in order to signify that all their authority derived from Jove.[59]

Very much a philosopher of the Enlightenment, Vico suggested that this vision of nature as a great volume of hieroglyphs revealed the deficiencies of the primitive mind, and not, as Ficino or Kircher would have it, the mysterious wisdom of ancient magi. Early humans thought of visible nature as a grand expression of God because, 'immersed in the body', they were incapable of conceiving of the Deity in any but the crudest, most sensual terms. Those whom Vico considered to be at the lower end of the intellectual scale in modern society – children, the vulgar and women – still relied on a kind of 'hieroglyphic' understanding of the world, in so far as they always thought in concrete sensual images. Nevertheless, Vico also indicated that the alphabet and the spread of literacy had generally diminished the ability of modern people to imagine nature as a vast, animated body of signs: 'the nature of our civilized minds is so detached from the senses, even in the vulgar, by abstractions corresponding to all the abstract terms our languages abound in, and *so refined by the art of writing* ... that it is naturally beyond our power to form the vast image of this mistress called "Sympathetic Nature"' (my italics).[60] Vico thus drew a connection between the advent of alphabetical writing and the capacity for abstract thought. Furthermore, he argued that this event was important in the political evolution of humanity. The discovery of alphabetical writing instigated a political upheaval that overturned the social hierarchy of the ancient world.

In this discussion of the political history of writing, Vico developed the distinction between 'sacred' and 'profane' writing drawn by ancient writers. Vico's related distinction was between the hieroglyph or 'heroic devices' used by the ruling patriarchs of ancient society, and the 'epistolary' (alphabetical) writing developed by their slaves. The patriarchs controlled their household because they controlled its 'poetic characters' – the myths, symbols and sacred rites that embodied the authority bestowed by Jove. These poetic characters confirmed the authority of the patriarchs, who took the names of gods and heroes, and excluded the slaves or *famuli* from any rights or ownership. Vico's suggestion was that the *famuli* really had no choice but to believe the heroic myths. Suffering from a primitive incapacity for abstract thought, they were simply incapable of understanding the world except through the poetic characters supplied by their masters. The patriarchs held sway not only over their bodies but also over their minds.[61]

The slaves did, however, have an 'epistolary' language for entirely practical purposes. Their articulate speech, written in alphabetical characters, was the distinctive creation of enslaved labourers in ancient society: 'The epistolary speech of the Egyptians, suitable for expressing the needs of common everyday life in communication from a distance, must have been born of the lower classes of a dominant people in Egypt.'[62] The epistolary language of the plebeians was, moreover, an important source of class awareness, for it was their one activity over which their masters had no power.

In Vico's words, 'vulgar speech and writing are a right of the people'. All attempts by emperors and governments to introduce even a single new letter have been failures, for 'epistolary' language has been established by 'free consent' and the tacit agreement of the populace.[63] As Plato had suggested in the *Phædrus*, alphabetical writing was an essentially democratic medium, facilitating communication among ordinary people.[64] Vico went further, arguing that alphabetical writing also promoted the very capacity to conceive of popular rights. The vulgar isolated single sounds from words; they observed that these sounds had universal value throughout the whole language. In other words, the vulgar formed epistolary language by means of abstraction. They learned to recognise the component parts of language, rather than just entire words or symbols. Repeating the well-worn encomium, Vico called the creation of epistolary writing 'a feat of consummate genius'. But the real importance of this discovery – undertaken by a whole class of people, not some individual – was that it taught the vulgar to reason abstractly about all areas of knowledge. The linguistic practice of alphabetical writing laid the groundwork for abstract philosophy and for political rights: 'Hieroglyphics and heroic letters [or emblems] were reduced to a few vulgar letters ... By means of these vulgar genera, both of words and letters, the minds of the peoples grew quicker and developed powers of abstraction, and the way was thus prepared for the coming of the philosophers, who formed intelligible genera.'[65]

These 'intelligible genera' included those principles of law, justice, property and so forth that had previously been known only through visual characters and heroic myths, the 'imaginative universals'. It was by means of intelligible genera or 'abstract universals' that the vulgar established their identity and rights apart from the fables and hieroglyphs of their masters. For example, 'when intelligible universals had come to be understood, that essential property of law – that it must be universal – was recognised, and the maxim of jurisprudence was established that we must judge by the laws, not by examples.'[66] Freed from the necessity of conceiving authority only as derived from the commands and symbols of the patriarchs, the vulgar rose up to demand equal rights to marriage, ownership and all the privileges previously confined to the heroic families. The political liberation of the people corresponded with the rise of metaphysical philosophy (which is concerned with abstract truths) and with the ascendance of alphabetical writing over hieroglyphics.

Although Vico shared Warburton's conviction in the 'ideological' importance of writing, he did not believe that hieroglyphics had ever been used deliberately as a vehicle of secrecy by an elite group of priestly philosophers. Rather, hieroglyphics and alphabetical writing were the distinctive media of two social classes struggling for ascendance in ancient society. Moreover, the outcome of this struggle, the triumph of the plebeians and their popular languages, left Vico with deeply ambivalent feelings. While sympathetic to the struggle of the *famuli* to overcome their oppressors, he also regretted the dissolution of the stable and closely knit world of the ancient heroes, with its imaginative vision of 'Sympathetic Nature'. Just as the alphabet had broken speech into abstract units, so the democratic reforms of the plebeians had dissolved society into competing individuals, precipitating a movement back towards the wandering and dispersed state of humanity before the rise of civilisation.[67]

Vico's *Scienza nuova* exemplifies 'conjectural history' in a sophisticated and wide-ranging form that still seems stimulating today: he offered the century's most detailed analysis of the relationship between writing, reason, and ideology, strongly anticipating modern theories concerning the social impact of media. Vico's conclusions about the influence of writing on the capacity for abstract thought have been reaffirmed by modern scholars of print culture. But Vico was not just an isolated genius. He reflects an increasing awareness across Europe in his day concerning the important role of writing in civilisation. Historians of the eighteenth century were coming to see writing as far more than a form of visible speech. Writing, they concluded, was a powerful and shaping force in European life, fashioned though the joint efforts of whole nations over the course of many generations.

CHAPTER 4

Conservative reaction: the study of writing after Warburton

In the mid and late eighteenth century, the history of writing became a thriving branch of scholarship, though the direction of these studies was not always towards more modern theories. A surprisingly large number of authors rejected Warburton's conclusions, contending that writing could not have evolved without the direct intervention of God. There was also renewed interest in the hidden significance of hieroglyphics and letters, their resemblance to objects and sounds, and their concealed content of ancient beliefs. These lines of investigation seem, at first sight, more typical of the Renaissance than of the Enlightenment. But many conservative-minded scholars were dismayed by the erosion of traditional ideas in the study of language, as in other fields. They aimed to recover some belief in the beneficent intervention of God in human affairs. And many of the same scholars also sought to unearth a buried treasure of hidden significance and esoteric wisdom in the apparently 'arbitrary' shapes of modern letters. Alienated by the cold rationality of a sceptical age, a wave of scholars utilised the techniques of modern research to reinvigorate doctrines that had been out of fashion since the seventeenth century.

But this wave was short lived, and quickly dissipated on the hard shores of empirical research. Warburton's most enduring legacy was to stimulate the archaeological study and decipherment of hiero-glyphics and other early scripts. Scholars in this burgeoning field were strongly influenced by his theories concerning the gradual evolution of writing from pictographs to the alphabet. Their discoveries would confirm many of Warburton's conjectures, utterly discrediting belief in the divine origin of letters among reputable intellectuals. Nevertheless, scholars of writing also became dissat-isfied with Warburton's reliance on mere guess-work concerning the probable development of writing. Bending instead to the pains-taking examination of actual inscriptions, antiquarians achieved new insights into the enormous complexity and inefficiency of ancient writing, and the remarkably slow and unwieldy process that had given rise to the first literate civilisations. 'The uniform voice of nature' gave way to a less orderly history of scribes contriving inconsistent, patchwork systems of record-keeping to suit the needs of the present moment.

THE DIVINE ORIGIN OF LETTERS

Accounts of the divine origin of writing had never entirely disappeared. In *An essay upon literature* (1726), Daniel Defoe argued that God delivered the first letters to Moses on Mount Sinai, a position based on a rather loose interpretation of Exodus 31:18:

> Upon the whole, we are sure the two Tablets of Stone, were written by the Finger of God, that is to say, Divine Power impress'd, by what Method we know not, those Words on the two Tablets of Stone and at the same time no doubt instructed *Moses* in the reading of them, and in the Knowledge of their Sounds; so we have unquestion'd Authority to assign the Knowledge of Letters, and the Art of writing them to a Divine original.[1]

The objection to this account of the origin of writing had long been that an illiterate Moses could not have read the Ten Commandments. In anticipation of this response, Defoe mentioned that God also 'instructed' Moses how to read (a view that, some authors complained, degraded God to a kind of celestial school-master). Defoe's major reason for reaffirming the divine origin of letters was that this writing was simply too ingenious ever to have been invented by human beings: 'if God himself in Favour to his Creatures ... had not inspir'd them with this Knowledge, all the Power of Invention that was ever bestow'd on Man before, could not, nor would to this Day have been able to do it.'[2] God not only gave humans his Law, but at the same time delivered the key to an art indispensable to civilisation – an art that humans could never have invented themselves.

It was in part to offset this scepticism with the human origin of writing that Warburton presented his thesis that letters evolved naturally from hieroglyphs. And the popularity of Warburton's case was a source of concern to the many who viewed his history of writing as another threat to belief in the benevolent involvement of God in human affairs throughout history. As Francis Wise complained in 1758, the disbelievers in the divine origin of letters seemed to have silenced the opinions of the faithful: 'We live in an age and country; where a Christian is in danger of reprehension, who should affirm that Letters were discovered by a God or by some divine man, though a heathen might openly profess such an opinion.'[3] In the cause of reestablishing the importance of God in the history of civilisation, Wise and others renewed the case for the divine origin of letters. Indeed, these authors even seemed to flaunt a fashion for religious orthodoxy, provocatively out of step with Enlightenment philosophy.

An early example of the reaction against Warburton is David Hartley's interesting but much ignored discussion of writing and language in *Observations on man* (1749). Hartley suggested that God may well have first taught Adam some visual representations, which would have been more suited to his undeveloped capacities than either articulate sounds or alphabetical symbols. Adam and his successors would have been able to develop and extend a few initial hints from God about how to draw and record various objects. Given the vast variety of visible shapes, as compared with the relatively few number of sounds, writing would have increased and evolved much faster than any form of primitive speech ('language'):

If we suppose some Kind of Picture-writing to have been imparted to *Adam* by God, or to have been invented by him, or by any of his Posterity, this might receive more Alterations and Improvements than Language, from the successive Generations of the Antedeluvians. For the Variety of Figures in visible Objects would suggest a sufficient Variety in their Characters.[4]

Hartley's willingness to consider the possibility that writing was the origin of language, and that, in the beginning, 'Sound would be the Name of the Mark' was by no means unusual in the mid and late eighteenth century. Eighteenth-century authors often stressed the dependence of the primitive mind on visual representation. For this reason, it was easy for Hartley – along with others like Vico, Rowland Jones, Wachter and Court de Gébelin – to imagine a kind of original inscription developed at the same time or even before speech. Hartley also proposed that the alphabet might be traced to the Edenic pictures. If the sound came to signify the mark, the mark would reciprocally become 'the Picture of the Sound', leading after many ages to an alphabet.[5]

This was a promising theory. Hartley seemed to have found a plausible resolution to the difficulty that had stumped Warburton: how the ideographic mark had eventually become linked to sound and transformed into phonographic writing. In the apparent determination to avoid offending the church, however, Hartley did not follow this line of reasoning to its logical conclusion. Instead, he rejoined the path of orthodoxy, arguing, like Defoe, that the first alphabet was 'communicated miraculously by God to *Moses* at *Sinai*'.[6] His reasons for this conclusion are not terribly lucid, though they have something to do with the legendary difficulty of inventing an alphabet. As he explained, 'Mankind ... before the Invention of Letters ... must have been farther removed from all Conceptions of Letters than the most unlearned Persons amongst us, since they have at least heard of Letters, and know that Words may be written and read by means of them.' The supposed difficulty of inventing an alphabet, we should emphasise, was not the actual forming of the letters: Hartley seemed basically to agree with Warburton's account of how the shape of the primitive pictograph might have mutated into the shape of a letter. The difficulty was rather 'analyzing complex articulate Sounds into their simple component Parts'.[7] This procedure was allegedly far above the capacities of barbaric ante-deluvians or illiterate savages. Similarly, Defoe's argument had been that God communicated not the shapes of Hebrew letters – those might have been contrived by Moses himself – but rather the secret of how to divide articulate speech into parts.

This line of reasoning differentiates eighteenth-century theories on the divine origin of language from accounts of this sort in the late Renaissance, like those of Fludd, Kircher or Webster. Those authors had looked for significance in the very form of the letters communicated by God, which they believed bore some symbolic kinship with divine ideas or the essence of worldly things; eighteenth-century authors were willing to acknowledge that the shape of letters was entirely arbitrary, but insisted that only God could have bestowed the procedure of dividing speech into letters. For this reason, Defoe, Hartley, Wise and others argued for the divine origin of writing without wishing to claim that Hebrew or any other character was sacred or pre-eminent. Another way of understanding their view is to contrast it with the very ancient legend that writing was invented by some god-like genius. Philosophers like Cicero and Galileo had acknowledged the great difficulty of dividing speech into its parts, but that difficulty was all the more reason, they thought, to celebrate the brilliance of the person who invented letters: writing proved the innate potential of the human intellect, not its limitations. Many eighteenth-century scholars, on the other hand, denied that such an inventor could ever have existed. They echoed the widespread assumption that people in a savage, pre-literate state were incapable of any abstract thought or invention of the least difficulty. For such authors, writing was beyond the ken of humans in the state of 'nature', and could only have been revealed by God.

This was the reasoning adopted by the many authors who re-asserted the divine origin of letters during the second half of the century. As James Beattie wrote in his 1788 *Theory of language*, 'alphabetical writing, must be so remote from the conceptions of those who never heard of it, that without divine aid it would seem to be unreachable and impossible'.[8] In Germany, Johann Peter Süssmilch denied not only that letters, but even the distinct articulations later marked by letters, were possible without divine intervention.[9] These arguments militated directly against the theory of the natural evolution of letters, primarily as developed by Warburton. Beattie offered very little proof for his assertions concerning the divine origin of letters; his only apparent motivation was to stand fast against newfangled ideas that detracted from the glory of God.

Other authors seized on the alleged illogic and inconsistency of Warburton's thesis concerning the natural evolution of letters. Just at the point where he was to explain the evolution of alphabetical letters, as we will recall, Warburton suddenly changed course, and indicated that the alphabet was *invented* by 'the Secretary of an Egyptian King'. Conservative Christians pointed to this sudden shift in his argument as evidence that it was, in fact, impossible to construct an account of the natural origin of letters. As Francis Wise argued in 1758,

Men of very great abilities have attempted to give us the natural and rational grounds of [writing's] beginning; but their different schemes are sufficient to satisfy me, that it requires more than the talents of them all put together, to give us such as shall be free from exceptions; and therefore I take it to be a thing as inscrutable, as its author.[10]

Along with hinting that the invention of writing was too difficult for illiterate savages, Wise's implication was that there remained no coherent accounts of this event besides those in the Bible. Charles Davy made a similar claim in *Conjectural observations on the origin and progress of alphabetical writing* (1772). Davy was willing to allow

Warburton's argument that 'writing, in the earliest ages of the world, was a delineation of the outlines of those things men wanted to remember, rudely graven either upon shells or stones, or marked upon leaves or barks of trees'. He even acknowledged that some people, like the Chinese, had found a way to contract these pictures into '*symbolical* figures'.[11] But that, alleged Davy, was as much as could be convincingly attributed to human invention. Besides the account of God giving letters to Moses on Mount Sinai, we have only 'conjectures' to explain the existence of alphabetical writing: 'Upon a supposition that letters, properly so called, were not first taught by Moses, all that we are able to trace out from history concerning their invention, amounts to little more than some few plausible conjectures in what country they were earliest propagated, whilst the author of them is entirely unknown.'[12] Davy's own use of the 'conjectural' method was thus designed largely to demonstrate its limitations. In preference to such interesting but uncertain guesswork was the word of Scripture, which Davy believed gave infallible testimony of the divine origin of letters.

It is a revealing fact that treatises propounding the divine origin of writing were more common during the second half of the century than the first. If modern historians do not usually notice this phenomenon, it is evidently because it opposed the general direction of linguistic theory in the eighteenth century. This direction was away from Adamic theories of the seventeenth century and towards the rise of modern philology in the late eighteenth century. It seems a law of intellectual history, however, that every force of change creates a force in the opposite direction. In the field of language study, the reaction to new ideas took the form of a revival of divine origin theories. And during the same decades, there was also a rejuvenation of the old Renaissance interest in hieroglyphics as the ideal form of written expression. As the Chevalier de Jaucourt asserted in his 1755 article on writing in the *Encyclopédie*, the hieroglyph is 'le moyen le plus propre à faire connoître la pensée' (the most proper means of making thought known),[13] a statement that contradicted Warburton's argument that hieroglyphics were merely an obscure and inefficient script replaced by alphabetical writing in fully civilised nations.

Plate 5 The phonetic basis of the Hebrew letter *aleph* as illustrated by F. M. van Helmont in *Alphabeti vere naturalis Hebraici* (1657).

ALPHABETICAL LETTERS AS 'HIEROGLYPHS'

Eighteenth-century authors showed little inclination to revive the more abstruse speculations of Kircher, whose reputation had been devastated by Warburton and other reputable scholars of ancient writing. Nevertheless, mid and late eighteenth-century grammatology was marked by a new receptiveness to theories concerning the 'natural' basis of letters, as argued in the seventeenth century by Franciscus Mercurius van Helmont, son of the more famous alchemist, Jan Baptista van Helmont. In *Alphabeti vere naturalis Hebraici* (1657), Helmont had defended the old belief that Hebrew was the original script, bestowed by God on Adam. Even by Helmont's time this doctrine was being widely questioned, and his argument was designed to conform with the more rational and scientific demands of his age. Citing recent studies of phonetics, he attempted to prove that the Hebrew characters were actually diagrams showing the position of the speech organs in making the sound designated by each letter (see Plate 5). Hebrew letters were thus entirely 'natural', and could only have been designed by the infinite wisdom of God in order to teach Adam how to speak and to write at the same time.[14]

Caught up in the conservative spirit of the time, many scholars of the mid and late eighteenth century found Helmont's approach tremendously appealing. Many of the same authors who were reviving belief in the divine origin of letters were also turning with fresh interest to doctrines asserting the 'natural' significance of letters: imagined affinities between letters and objects were taken as faint vestiges of an Edenic world directly ruled by a beneficent Creator. In *Hieroglyfic: or, a grammatical introduction to an universal hieroglyfic language* (1768), for example, the Welsh grammarian Rowland Jones reaffirmed Helmont's thesis that God designed the first letters in imitation of the vocal organs in order to teach humans to speak and to write at the same time. This first writing, he declared, was actually carved by God on the trunk of the Tree of Knowledge. God's inscriptions on the Tree of Knowledge marked the birth of speech as well as writing, for the marks referred to the position of the vocal organs necessary to make articulate sounds. (Before the fall, Adam and Eve communicated telepathically.) Unlike Helmont, however, Jones believed that this original writing consisted of Latin characters. The letter ⟨i⟩, for instance, is really a diagram of the extended larynx needed to make the appropriate sound; the letter ⟨o⟩ shows the shape of the mouth needed to speak that vowel. In addition, these marks have symbolic significance. The letter ⟨i⟩ is 'an indefinite line, representing man in his primitive state of innocence'. Similarly, 'the letter o is an indefinite circle, signifying the universe'.[15]

According to Jones, therefore, the letters of the alphabet are in fact 'hieroglyfs': they are all little pictures, showing the vocal organs and referring to various truths about human nature and the universe. His overriding concern was to re-establish a natural rather than merely arbitrary connection between language and the world. In other ways, however, Jones was very much an author of the eighteenth century. He did not mean to suggest that God wrote in a deliberately cryptic writing that could be interpreted only by the philosophically enlightened or the elect. Nor is there any hint of neo-platonism in his system, or any reference to divine 'signatures' inscribed in nature. His aim was not to recover the vision of nature as a vast book of 'hieroglyphics', filled with occult truths, but rather to combine some traditional ideas about natural origins of writing and speech with a basically modern and scientific understanding of the world.

This desire to harmonise modern and traditional ideas helps to explain the renewed popularity of Helmont's thesis among authors between 1750 and 1800. Johann Wachter's 1752 Latin treatise *Naturæ et scripturæ concordia*, for example, also presented the argument that Latin letters were modelled on the various positions of the vocal organs. The elementary sound of speech, the open vowel ⟨o⟩, is suitably marked by a circle, referring to the open mouth of the speaker. On the basis of this principle, Wachter attempted to reconstruct the whole history of language with all the interrelated innovations of sound and marks. Speech and writing, he insisted, evolved in strictly analogous ways: just as the open vowel was gradually modified to form all the articulate sounds of language, so the basic circle was modified to form all the letters of the alphabet. After the open vowel, people began to use guttural consonants. This sound was marked with a kind of primeval ⟨g⟩, a straight line, representing the throat, descending from the basic ⟨o⟩.[16]

A later and even more eccentric version of this type of analysis is L. D. Nelme's *An essay towards an investigation of the origin and elements of language and letters* (1772). In the beginning, wrote Nelme, God created the line and the circle – the component shapes or *essential forms* of all objects in nature and of all letters.[17] The arrangement of lines and circles for symbolic purposes was evident in the earliest language, which Nelme claimed was Anglo-Saxon. This etymology, like Jones's thesis concerning the primacy of Latin letters, enabled Nelme to draw complex connections between sounds, letters and meanings on the evidence of a few English words. The 'Sac-sons', or 'sons of Saces', believed that 'the *symbol* c was perfect, determined, and unalterable; its form is the *symbol* of a receptacle, or a *ca-pacious* body: thence *ca-t*, an open-mouthed creature'.[18] Other linguistic groups, like the Chadians, used letters as little maps, portraying 'their migrations from place to place'.[19] Like Jones and Wachter, therefore, Nelme believed that the letters were all hieroglyphic, for 'every letter is a distinct *root*, and descriptive of a distinct *idea*'.[20]

Despite some differences in the way they traced the evolution of letters and sounds (Wachter liked ⟨o⟩; Nelme preferred ⟨c⟩), these authors were motivated by the same basic objectives. First, they wished to show that the realm of 'nature' extended even over the shape of letters: nothing was 'arbitrary' and everything followed a system of laws that they attempted to determine. As Wachter argued, referring to the alleged resemblance between letters and the vocal organs, 'natura, quæ sonos omnes in suis præformavit, hic etiam scripturæ suprema lex est' (nature, which preformed all sounds in their causes, hence is even the supreme law of writing).[21] For Wachter, Jones or Nelme, the very notion of an 'arbitrary' component in language was impossible. As Charles de Brosses wrote in his *Traité de la formation méchanique des langues et des principes physiques de l'étymologie* (1765), another work which speculated on the natural significance of letters, nothing in language is without some cause or reason: 'Quelques écartes qu'il y ait dans la composition des Langues, dans la fabrique des mots, quelque part que l'arbitraire puisse y avoir, la convention n'a pu s'établir qu'en vertu d'une raison effective, née de l'existence même et de la propriété des choses.' (Whatever be the divergencies in the composition of languages, in the making of words, whatever arbitrariness might be there, convention is only able to establish itself by virtue of an effectual reason, born of existence itself and the nature of things.)[22]

Jones, Wachter, de Brosses and others also wished to show that speech and writing developed together, and were therefore naturally interrelated and mutually supportive. As L. D. Nelme asserted, 'if we can ascertain *symbols* that are understood by all men, we may also ascertain sounds that are analogous to those symbols'.[23] The work that crowned studies of this interrelation between speech and writing was the third volume of Antoine Court de Gébelin's *Monde primitif, analysé et comparé avec le monde moderne* (1777–93). Court de Gébelin's grand theme would have been very familiar to his readers by that time: 'l'Écriture ALPHABETIQUE est... composée de caractères Hiéroglyphiques' (alphabetical writing is... composed of hiero-glyphical characters).[24] There was no essential difference, he insisted, between alphabetical and hieroglyphic writing. Court de Gébelin differed from his predecessors, however, in tracing the origin of writing to a special kind of society, rather than to a particular nation or to primitive humanity in general. Only in agricultural societies, he argued, would people have any use for graphic marks. In agricultural economies alone, people would have property and engage in trans-actions; a farming society would be concerned about the weather and the seasons, and would therefore chart the skies. All these tasks require some kind of inscription to make records. Writing is thus an inevitable component in such agricultural societies, the first stage of civilisation.[25] It followed from this reasoning that all civilized societies are literate: 'il n'est aucune Région policée où l'on ne fasse usage de l'Écriture' (it is no civilised region where writing is not made use of).[26]

In closely linking the origin of letters and civilisation, Court de Gébelin was perpetuating a well-established tradition in post-Renaissance thought. Nevertheless, he differed from previous authors in describing writing as just one of a number of closely interrelated pursuits – agriculture, property, astronomy – that gave rise to pol-ished society. Writing was not the foundation of civilised life, as believed by many earlier authors, but just one of its many early manifestations. In addition, he did not believe that writing was 'invented': it evolved as naturally as speech, and according to regular laws which he attempted to determine. 'Ces deux Langages', he observed, 'l'un écrit, l'autre parlé, durent nécessairement suivre les mêmes loix' (These two languages, one written and one spoken, must necessarily follow the same laws).[27]

The great law governing both speech and writing was 'imitation'. The sound /m/, for example, begins the word for 'mother' in almost all languages because it has a natural though obscure relation with the idea of maternity. Analogously, the basic shape of the letter ⟨M⟩ is like a tree – the universal image of fruition and nourishment: 'Il est incontestable que M désigne, dans toutes des Langues, l'idée de *Mere*, de *maternité*, d'être productif & fructifiant... On a donc représenté l'intonation M en caractère hiéroglyphique, sous la figure, d'un arbre, d'une plante, d'une personne qui élève les bras pour porter son nourrisson ou pour cueillir du fruit.' (It is incontestable that M denotes, in all tongues, the idea of *mother*, of *maternity*, of something productive and fruitful... The intonation M is thus represented in hieroglyphical character by the shape of a tree, a plant, of a person lifting its arms in order to carry its infant or to pick fruit).[28] Reading Court de Gébelin's discussion of letters is sometimes like trying to imagine various objects in cloud shapes. Nevertheless, on the basis of this kind of analysis, he reconstructed an original natural alphabet wherein, as in the natural alphabets of Jones, Wachter and Nelme, sound and mark and object were all united in a complex network of relations. We should note carefully that Court de Gébelin did not regard the letter as the 'copy' or even the substitute for speech: letters and sounds were linked because they had evolved together according to the overarching laws of nature. Writing and speech are parallel forms of language. His purpose was to reintegrate the graphic mark into the organic process of linguistic history, and to reconnect sound and sight as mutually supportive and equally natural means of communication.

Much literature and art during the second half of the eighteenth century reflects the desire to reinstitute the hieroglyph as the primary form of graphic communication, and to reunite speech and writing, sound and sight, in a single, homogeneous medium. The illustrated poems of William Blake spring quickly to mind in this context, for there, very often, language and pictures interrelate to constitute a complete meaning captured by neither poem nor visual image alone. In the poems themselves, Blake often paid little heed to the difference between writing and speaking. The 'Introduction' to the 1789 *Songs of innocence*, for example, draws specific attention to the activity of writing: 'And I made a rural pen, / And I stain'd the water clear' (17–18).[29] But these lines lead directly to the image of a poem that is *heard*, rather than read: 'And I wrote my happy songs / Every child may joy to hear' (19–20). In 'London', 'the hapless Soldier's sigh, / Runs in blood down palace walls' (11–12): sound seems to coagulate into another 'mark' of modern unhappiness, an image reminiscent of the tumble of verbal and graphic imagery in the works of Jacob Boehme. Indeed, the works of this seventeenth-century mystic exercised an important influence on Blake's ideal of 'natural' language.[30] In his engravings, Blake's human figures are often posed in shapes that call to mind alphabetical letters – Os to suggest mourning, Xs to intimate prohibition, U to denote 'Urizen' (Blake's deity of reason and restriction) as well as states of fear, pain and entrapment.[31] Everywhere in Blake's work, in short, we see evidence of the desire to reanimate the graphic mark, to make phonemic writing more like hieroglyphs, 'speaking pictures'.

It would nonetheless be an exaggeration to identify later eighteenth-century studies of writing totally with the kind of theories found in the work of Antoine Court de Gébelin and the other rather lesser authors that we have mentioned. Revealingly, the Bodleian Library's copy of Nelme's treatise is filled with the mocking scholia of an eighteenth-century reader who considered it 'one of the most extravagantly ridiculous works that have issued from a disordered intellect'.[32] Many tracts on writing during this period, like those of William Massey and Thomas Astle, were merely dismissive of the thesis that letters resembled objects.[33] Most important, the conjectural histories of writing were being discredited by new archaeological research into the history of writing. Conjectures about the probable origin and progress of writing were increasingly replaced by the empirical study of ancient inscriptions and the painstaking reconstruction of old alphabets. By 1794, Dugald Stewart was already referring to 'conjectural history' as the defunct phenomenon of a previous age, overtaken by the concern of a new era to build knowledge through the study of facts.

DECIPHERMENT AND ITS INFLUENCE ON PERCEPTIONS OF WRITING

'Depuis environ vingt ans, un nouvel esprit agite de toutes parts les ruines de l'antiquité' (For about twenty years, a new spirit has everywhere shaken the ruins of antiquity).[34] So wrote Jean-Jacques Barthélemy in 1757, referring to the recent investigations of ancient monuments and inscriptions by Pococke, Norden, Caylus and himself. All these authors knew and generally accepted Warburton's theories about writing. They were particularly impressed by his theory that writing had evolved gradually from the pictograph to the alphabet. But unlike Warburton, whose 'egyptian learning', as he himself admitted, was 'conceived at home',[35] this new breed of antiquarian examined recently discovered artifacts rather than relying on the works of Clement of Alexandria and Horapollo. Moreover, their concerns shifted from the origin of writing towards the actual decipherment of ancient inscriptions. Barthélemy became the first scholar to restore knowledge of a lost script when, in 1754, he established the alphabet of Palmyrene. Later decades brought new knowledge of other ancient scripts such as Sassanian Persian and Persian cuneiform. In 1822 came the most famous breakthrough of all, Champollion's decipherment of the hieroglyphics and cursive inscriptions on the Rosetta Stone, which had been found in 1799 on the Nile delta by a soldier in Napoleon's army. The Rosetta Stone was of such monumental significance because it offered a trilingual script in hieroglyphics, demotic cursive and Greek, giving scholars the first direct translation of Egyptian characters. Yet so deeply engrained were many old misconceptions about Egyptian writing that it took almost a quarter of a century for scholars to capitalise on this new opportunity.

The methods used by scholars to decode these ancient writings have been well described in a number of previous books devoted to the history of decipherment.[36] For our present purposes, the emergence of this science is important principally as it affected perceptions of the nature, history and social function of writing. This effect was, in part, to lend factual support to some of the most controversial claims of Warburton's history of writing. Most important, the new evidence gleaned from ancient monuments confirmed Warburton's observations on the slow and natural evolution of written language. Insights made by Young and Champollion in their study of the Rosetta Stone helped to solve a crucial problem in Warburton's theory that, as we have seen, was exploited by some orthodox scholars to argue that letters could only have been bestowed by God. This was Warburton's failure to explain how ancient writers could have discovered the use of marks to denote sounds rather than things or ideas. Nineteenth-century decipherers determined what had only been suspected by a few scholars before – that hieroglyphics themselves denoted sounds as well as ideas. Young believed that hieroglyphs were occasionally used to denote syllables; Champollion determined correctly that the phonographic system of Egyptian writing was almost entirely consonantal.[37] Moreover, as Champollion concluded, it was probable that some characters denoting sounds had always been necessary in ideographic scripts to denote the names of monarchs and places. And it was from these first, crude efforts to denote sounds that a full alphabet might have been developed over many centuries.[38]

The gap between ideographs and the alphabet was, therefore, much less of 'an immense leap' than Warburton and others had imagined, for the various stages of development – pictographic, ideographic, phonographic – had overlapped to a considerable degree in the first, awkward attempts to form a written language. No God was needed to intervene to inspire humans with the secret of alphabetical writing; no ingenious inventor was needed to discover how to use marks to symbolise sounds rather than ideas. The decipherers also ratified Warburton's argument that the original purpose of hieroglyphics and other ancient scripts was not to conceal religious secrets, but merely to preserve and communicate information for public use. The inscriptions on ancient monuments did not disguise the secrets of crafty priests. Instead, they generally contained public proclamations and decrees, memorials to battles and records of laws. The Rosetta Stone, for example, bears a decree in praise of Ptolemy V.

Empirical research of ancient inscriptions thus completed the process that we have traced from the work of Kircher and others in the hermetic-cabalist tradition – the demystification of writing, which was increasingly viewed as a human technique rather than a divine gift, a practical tool rather than a magical art. But the science of decipherment did more than close one era in the study of writing; it also opened another. While confirming some of Warburton's most important theories, the decipherers also cast doubt on the central premises of the conjectural method. As the Scottish philosopher Dugald Stewart observed, conjectural historians had attempted to 'ascertain the progress that is most simple' rather than 'the progress that is most agreeable to fact'.[39] They assumed that the development of language and of writing followed a regular and consistent course, one step in the process leading smoothly to the next. In fact, argued Stewart, the course of linguistic history is often highly irregular and unpredictable, depending on 'the accidental lights daily struck out in the innumerable walks of observation and experiment'.[40] As Young and Champollion confirmed, early scribes did what they could to meet the needs of the moment. They used marks to denote sounds when necessary, mixing them with their ideographs, and frequently deviating from their own former practice and the practice of other scribes. When their marks were ambiguous, as often happened, they invented additional characters, 'determinatives', to make their meaning clearer. What they produced in the end were complex, unwieldy systems such as the Egyptian hieroglyphics or Persian cuneiform, which was partly deciphered by the Danish scholar Grotefend near the end of the eighteenth century.[41] These systems contained little of the order and regularity imagined by Warburton or later conjectural historians. The early scribes demonstrated little individual 'genius' and were generally guided by chance and momentary expedience rather than 'nature'.

In this slow and awkward way, writing was introduced to humanity, and the literate arts spread throughout Asia and Europe. But had this process been beneficial to humanity? Vico, as we will recall, had questioned the ultimate benefits of literacy, and looked back with some nostalgia to the more closely knit, pious and poetic world of the ancient heroes. While his doubts were rare in the early eighteenth century – a time when most scholars still admired alphabetical writing as the well-spring of all beneficial arts – a new wave of scholars of the mid and late eighteenth century was less inclined to regard the birth of letters as the beginning of a better, happier age for humanity. We will now proceed to examine this period of heightened scepticism about the benefits of writing and literacy. As we will see, an increasing number of scholars rejected the opinion, widespread since the seventeenth century, that the evolution of writing was a progressive and enlightening event. In their minds, the discovery and proliferation of writing and books had severely damaged humanity's original, innocent state of impassioned eloquence and natural wisdom.

CHAPTER 5

Writing and speech: the debate in Britain

Writing, long admired as the greatest of human inventions, and the mark of 'civilisation', became the target of numerous attacks from British and French scholars of the mid eighteenth century. In France, Rousseau deprecated writing in his *Essai sur l'origine des langues* and other works. In Britain, the elocutionist Thomas Sheridan became well known for his denunciations of writing's allegedly detrimental effect on the powers of speech and the moral health of the nation. These criticisms were echoed throughout the latter decades of the century by Lord Monboddo, Thomas Reid, Hugh Blair and many others. The disparagement of writing was by no means unopposed. Samuel Johnson vigorously advocated the benefits of both writing and literacy throughout his works, particularly his 1755 *Dictionary of the English language*. But the view that writing was incapable of the expressive powers of speech, and that its dominance had undermined the happiness and morality of people in modern society, was a prominent and fashionable opinion in the 1760s and 1770s.

What factors were behind this outburst of 'logocentrism', so different from the praise of writing common since the Renaissance? We have already noted the conservative tendency of history and linguistics in this era, and the dislike of the irreligious and sceptical principles propounded in recent scholarship. As part of this conservatism, many European scholars increasingly valued 'nature' over human ingenuity, and sought to trace all arts back to a natural or divine origin. Expressions of hostility to the 'dead letter' during the same era reflect the same conservative distrust of human technology and modern change. Here again we find a celebration of 'nature', as represented by the purity and directness of 'living speech', along with a dislike of what is human-made. Writing, 'letters', had made possible those learned arts that had allegedly corrupted European morals and promoted impiety. Among the social factors affecting ideas in the eighteenth century was a significant rise in literacy and the growth of the printing industry.[1] Writing and reading became more familiar, widespread skills, and less the accomplishments of a small segment of society. As writing became more common, and its effects on society more widely apparent, it lost much of the glamour associated with rare and difficult arts.

The diminishing reputation of written language was also an effect of changing ideas in linguistic thought. A key theme in linguistic scholarship of the mid and late eighteenth century was that the dominance of writing and literacy in modern culture had enervated the vigorous, natural 'tones' of living speech. Subordinated to writing, the voice had lost its energy and expressiveness, and was unable to serve the purposes of the orator, preacher or poet. Scholars of language and rhetoric in the mid century became far more aware of the special powers of speech – powers that could never be fully captured in a written form. To understand how this new aural sensitivity emerged, we will need to journey back briefly to the late Renaissance. It was in that era that grammarians began to envisage the possibility of making writing a perfect copy of speech. By the eighteenth century, however, this dream seemed increasingly far-fetched.

ORTHOGRAPHIC REFORM IN THE LATE SIXTEENTH AND SEVENTEENTH CENTURIES

For many authors of the sixteenth and seventeenth centuries, especially among advocates of the new science and philosophy, the alphabet 'surpassed all stupendous inventions'.[2] But it was also conventional to complain that alphabetical writing had not achieved its full potential, and provided an extremely flawed picture of speech. Current orthography, as Sir Thomas Smith quipped in *De recta et emendata linguæ anglicæ scriptione* (1568), was often as dark and mysterious as Egyptian hieroglyphics.[3] Thus, the same ideals of clarity, efficiency and reason that spurred intellectual reform in this era inspired numerous plans to make writing a more accurate and complete transcription of the speaking voice. Grammarians were also spurred by a new desire to perfect their native language, for English, like the other vernaculars of Europe, was increasingly supplanting

Latin as the language of philosophy, education and commerce.[4] Unhappy that some single sounds are denoted with two symbols, such as ⟨th⟩ or ⟨sh⟩, Sir Thomas Smith and John Hart urged the introduction of new letters, such as the defunct Anglo Saxon symbols eth ⟨ð⟩ and thorn ⟨þ⟩, and a special long ⟨ʃ⟩ to replace ⟨sh⟩. The same kind of reforms were proposed by several grammarians of the early seventeenth century, such as Alexander Gil and Charles Butler, when the fashion for orthographic change reached its height.[5] Others advocated even more radical reforms. In his 1617 *The art of pronunciation*, Robert Robinson offered an entirely new set of symbols, based on a painstaking analysis of the vocal organs. Vowels and consonants were classified according to whether they were produced by the 'outward', 'middle' or 'inward' regions of the mouth. Short vowels were given the same symbol as long vowels, except inverted.[6] John Wilkins and Francis Lodwick later invented forms of syllabic writing, influenced by Hebrew, each symbol representing the combination of a consonant and a vowel.[7]

The case for wholesale orthographic reform was not without opposition. In *The first part of the elementarie* (1582), an important tract on educational reform, Richard Mulcaster contended against Smith and Hart that orthography should be adjusted by 'custom' and 'reason' as well as by the criterion of sound.[8] In the following century, Mulcaster's practical and moderate attitudes would prevail among those who truly regulated orthography – printers, teachers, lexicographers and private individuals. Yet many grammarians continued to be intrigued by the possibility, at least theoretically, of creating a form of spelling that matched pronunciation with considerable accuracy and comprehension. Robinson and Lodwick were particularly optimistic about what their new scripts could accomplish: they expected that their systems could be used to transcribe any language whatsoever, and would enable the learner to pronounce any foreign language quickly and easily merely by examining the new marks.[9] According to William Holder in his *Elements of speech* (1669), all languages consisted of a 'natural alphabet' of separate sounds, greatly exceeding the number of symbols of all existing alphabets. He counted exactly thirty-six consonants and thirty-nine vowels,[10] describing these as the permanent 'store-house of Nature'.[11] At the bottom of these projects, therefore, was an understanding of language that many modern linguists consider highly naive. The reformers thought of language as composed of a limited number of distinct articulations, added up to form all possible words in the world.

This is what David Abercrombie has called a 'building-block' model of language. The model is, as Abercrombie pointed out, strongly visual, for it assumes that the sounds of language form separate units like the symbols that make up a word on a page.[12] The movement for wholesale reform of English spelling thus reflects a phenomenon of particular importance to our present study. For many centuries, both before and after the invention of the printing press, scholars were powerfully influenced by written language in their discussions of speech. It was not, indeed, until the mid eighteenth century that scholars of language became clearly conscious of this misleading habit, so common among literate people.

A major indication of this confusion between speech and writing was the use of the term 'letter' to describe both written marks and speech sounds. In the earliest studies of grammar, such as those of Aristotle and Plato, the terms 'stoicheion' (element) and 'gramma' (mark) were used to mean either a written letter or the corresponding speech sound.[13] Later grammarians tried to be more careful in distinguishing written marks from speech sounds. For example, the sixth-century Latin grammarian Priscian began his *Institutionum grammaticarum* by distinguishing 'elementum' (speech sound) from 'litera' (symbol). But Priscian, still influenced by old habits, mixed up these terms in the treatise that followed.[14] In the seventeenth century, even careful grammarians were strongly influenced by the written alphabet in their study of speech sounds. John Wallis, though highly regarded by contemporaries for his analysis of articulation, referred to ⟨x⟩ (as in 'box') as a single sound, despite his remark elsewhere that the symbol signified the combined sound /ks/; he assumed at one point that ⟨ch⟩ and ⟨sh⟩ were diphthongs.[15] These errors indicate that Wallis, like most grammarians of his day, was still thinking about speech through the medium of alphabetical writing, and had considerable difficulty banishing written symbols from his mind when he analysed articulations.

A similar confusion between letters and speech sounds would persist throughout the eighteenth century among some of the most accurate scholars. Even the great lexicographer Samuel Johnson had not fully separated marks and sounds in his mind. He defined 'letter' in his 1755 *Dictionary* as 'one of the elements of the syllables'.[16] This definition identified letters specifically with speech sounds. But

Johnson's illustration for this definition, Luke 23:38, identified 'letters' with written *marks*: 'A superscription was written over him in *letters* of Greek, Latin, and Hebrew.' Johnson elsewhere defined 'to write' as 'to express by means of letters', again presenting letters as marks rather than 'the elements of syllables'. At the bottom of Johnson's confusion between marks and sounds was the continuing dominance of the old 'building-block' model of language, which portrays speech as made up of vocal atoms, strung together just as letters are combined to make written words. This model can be useful as a rough guide to pronunciation, as shown by the international phonetic alphabets developed since the nineteenth century. But if taken too literally (so to speak), this model can also obscure the true nature of vocalisation.

Speech does not really consist of a number of vocal atoms; rather, as Roy Harris observed, 'it is essentially a continuous series of infinitely numerous sounds'.[17] No alphabet, not even our International Phonetic Alphabet, records discrete units of speech. Alphabetical writing instead denotes characteristic points in the transformations of vocal sound and the fluid movements of the vocal apparatus from position to position. Moreover, each symbol of the alphabet corresponds not to a single sound, but to a range of sounds recognised by speakers of a language to be 'significant'. The American linguist Edward Sapir pointed out that indigenous people of North America, faced with the task of inventing an alphabet for their languages, show an intuitive sense of the sounds that 'count', and those that are linguistically negligible.[18] In short, alphabets are not meant to be a complete transcription of all the vocal sounds in a language; they record, imperfectly, those kinds of sound that speakers identify as important to meaning.

In the vocabulary of our time, alphabetical letters refer to 'phonemes'. For example, while there are innumerable variations of any sound like /e/ or /d/, even in the speech of a single person, these variations are of no importance so long as they fall within the range of the relevant phoneme. The idea of the phoneme was, however, alien to linguistics of the seventeenth century. Most grammarians of this time – with a few notable exceptions such as Richard Mulcaster – believed that the alphabet could and should be a complete transcription of all possible speech sounds. Note, for example, how Robert Robinson defined writing as an ideally complete transcription of individual speech sounds: 'Writing is an artificiall framing of certaine markes and Characters different in forme and shape for euery seuerall sound in mans voice, whereby each simple sound hauing a proper mark appointed to it selfe, may by the same be as apparently scene to the eye, as the sound it selfe is sensibly discerned by the eares.'[19] Only vaguely aware of how much speech sounds do vary – from speaker to speaker and from language to language – grammarians denounced current alphabets for failing to render a complete and exact account of all the components of speech, Holder's 'natural alphabet' of human speech. Only gradually did it become apparent that the demand for a perfect alphabet could never be met. With the increase of research into the nature of speech, scholars of language became more aware of the tremendous complexity of spoken language, and of the impossibility of ever capturing its full range of sounds and intonations in written language.

DIMINISHING CONFIDENCE IN ORTHOGRAPHIC REFORM

Seventeenth-century scholars did not finally establish any new letters. Nevertheless, a remarkable consensus grew among grammarians, printers and educators about the need to make written English more regular and consistent. As D. G. Scragg has shown in *The history of English spelling*, orthography in printed books had achieved basically its modern form by 1700.[20] In the eighteenth century, there were numerous adjustments, but largely of a minor nature. Yet this standardisation did not generally entail making written English an exact copy of speech. The moderate views of scholars like Mulcaster, who believed that custom, analogy and etymology were as important as sound in adjusting orthography, finally prevailed over the determination to make sound the *only* criterion, and to restyle orthography into a complete and accurate copy of speech. This was less so in France, as we will later examine. But in Britain, even scholars who proposed radical reforms were increasingly pessimistic that their new letters and spellings would be commonly adopted.

Even the most illogical spellings, it was conceded, were protected by popular custom: 'Custom hath so rivetted this incongruity and imperfection in all Languages', observed John Wilkins in his 1668 *Essay towards a real character*, 'that it were an hopeless attempt for any man to go about to repair and amend it.'[21] Doubtful that he could ever change popular spelling, Wilkins presented his own extensively remodelled alphabet largely for speculative purposes. His doubts about the possibility of changing popular spelling were later elaborated by the grammarian Guy Miege, who observed ruefully in 1688 that 'the *Newness* of the Thing, the *Nakedness* of such Words as should be stript of their usual Letters, and the *Ambiguity* which should result from them in some Cases, are three great Discouragements from a further Attempt'.[22]

Wilkins and Miege were clearly disgruntled by the intransigence of orthographic custom: they still sympathised with the reforming zeal of Hart and Smith, optimistic humanists who were fully convinced that people were rational enough to abandon old habits once they were shown good reasons to do so. In the eighteenth century, however, some authors found inspiration in the refusal of ordinary people to change their habits of writing. 'Vulgar speech and writing are a right of the people', wrote Giambattista Vico, noting that even the Roman Emperor Claudius had failed to introduce three new letters into written Latin.[23] In the opinion of a later author, the Scottish philosopher James Beattie, there was something unpatriotic about attempts to change spelling in radical ways. In *The theory of language*, he repeated the long-standing concern that a new orthography would render all former books and documents, the heritage of the nation, illegible and obsolete: 'we have no laws to warrant the annihilation of property in books and manuscripts: nor is it in the power of lawgivers, far less of philosophers, to make a whole people renounce the written language of their fathers.' Orthographic custom, he pronounced solemnly, was 'the basis of British learning, as our laws are of the British government'.[24]

A second reason for the flagging interest in orthographic reform was a better knowledge of the real nature of speech. As Abercrombie has observed, a more detailed and accurate knowledge of speech was, ironically, perhaps the most lasting benefit of the endeavour to improve writing.[25] Aiming primarily to contrive new letters, grammarians from Hart to Robertson studied the sounds and the mechanics of articulation, achieving significant new insights. Indeed, they invented the science of phonetics, which ultimately seemed more interesting than orthographic reform. Progress in phonetic science also showed the inevitable deficiency of any possible alphabet. Even in the late sixteenth century, Mulcaster objected that the reformers were wrong to think of written letters as merely visual representations of discrete sounds: 'letters resemble the ioyntes in *sound*, but ar [*sic*] not the same with the things resembled.'[26] And later grammarians, such as John Wilkins, conceded that their spelling systems could do little more than provide rough guides to the real nature of speech. This was because, as Wilkins recognised, vocal sound did not consist of individual units or 'letters', but 'must be like a continued quantity, *divisibilio in infinitum*'.[27]

The few eighteenth-century scholars who proposed major orthographic reforms were more tentative about their proposals because they realised that human speech sounds are widely diversified. In *Vocal sounds* (1773), for instance, Abraham Tucker (writing under the pseudonym 'Edward Search') proposed the introduction of six new written letters into English. But Tucker acknowledged that even 'the best speakers' did not agree 'in their manner of sounding the same words'.[28] No form of writing could give more than a generalised impression of speech sounds. Partly for this reason, he denied that 'I mean to alter the common manner of writing'. He claimed that he was simply clarifying the nature of pronunciation for those who were interested.[29] What Tucker wished to clarify, above all, was that even the scholarly understanding of language continued to be dominated by writing. 'We in this country take in more strongly by the eye than by the ear,' he remarked, conscious of what Roy Harris has called 'the tyranny of the alphabet', the constant influence of alphabetical writing on our thinking about speech.[30] Tucker decried the habit of even the best scholars, from Aristotle to his own time, to consult writing, rather than the sound or the mechanics of speech, in their analysis of pronunciation. This awareness of how writing has influenced the analysis of speech reflects a significant advance in linguistic thought in the eighteenth century. Like many contemporaries, Tucker was far more aware of the differences between writing and speech, and was determined not to confuse them.

Samuel Johnson, as we have remarked, was rather less careful to discriminate between the written letter and the sound it denoted. Nevertheless, Johnson was fully a scholar of his time in his scepticism about major orthographic reform, for he was convinced that writing could never be made an accurate copy of speech. Having made this observation, however, Johnson came to a highly controversial conclusion. If writing could not be made the image of speech, he reasoned, speech could and should be made a more faithful reflection of writing.

JOHNSON AND THE WRITTEN STANDARD OF LANGUAGE

In the grammar appended to his 1755 *Dictionary*, Johnson described the 'very prevalent inclination to change the orthography' as the defunct phenomenon of the age of Charles I.[31] The grammarians who had wanted to reform orthography so that it perfectly reflected speech were, moreover, fundamentally misguided. They had 'endeavoured to accommodate orthography better to pronunciation, without considering that this is to measure by a shadow, to take that for a model or standard which is changing while they apply it'.[32] Pronunciation was too mutable and varied to be made a stable standard of orthography. Indeed, Johnson blamed the inconsistencies of English spelling not on the deficiencies and illogic of writing, but rather on the effort of people throughout the centuries to make writing into a copy of their speech. Without a fixed standard of pronunciation, people before the introduction of letters pronounced their words in innumerably different ways. And when the 'wild and barbarous jargon' of our illiterate ancestors was first recorded in writing, 'every penman endeavoured to express, as he could, the sounds which he was accustomed to pronounce or to receive, and vitiated in writing such words as were already vitiated in speech'.[33]

In Johnson's opinion, therefore, the orthographic reformers had understood the problem precisely the wrong way around. Writing should not be a copy of speech. Instead, pronunciation should be regulated as much as possible by orthography, for it was only writing that provided an acceptably secure and uniform standard: 'For pronunciation the best general rule is, to consider those as the most elegant speakers, who deviate least from the written words.'[34] Johnson had one predominant concern as a lexicographer – *stability*. The worst danger, in his view, was that language was in constant flux, particularly speech. While dictionaries could never *stop* linguistic change, they could help to retard and control this natural movement. He was also concerned that orthographic reformers tended to elevate a popular standard of pronunciation, as used by the uneducated, over the pronunciation of educated people who aimed to communicate with distinctness and clarity. In a passage much quoted in the eighteenth century, he complained that previous grammarians had failed to see that all living languages have two forms of pronunciation, 'one cursory and colloquial, the other regular and solemn'. Most orthographic reformers, he alleged, had attempted to make writing conform with the 'cursory' rather than the 'solemn' idiom, establishing 'the jargon of the lowest of the people as the model of speech'. 'Regular and solemn' speech, on the other hand, was the pronunciation of the literate classes. This was the speech that should be enshrined in guides to pronunciation because it conformed most closely to writing.[35]

This preference for a written standard for pronunciation did not imply that Johnson rejected the efforts to regularise orthography. Indeed, his *Dictionary* includes hundreds of modifications to English spelling.[36] But these changes were not designed to make writing a better copy of speech. They were governed by quite different criteria. As the grammarian Robert Nares later observed of his methods, he relied principally on the criterion of etymology, adjusting the orthography according to its ancient root. This etymological standard was supplemented by the principles of analogy and clarity of distinction. For example, he used ⟨cloth⟩ and ⟨clothe⟩ in analogy with ⟨breath⟩ and ⟨breathe⟩; he distinguished between the verb ⟨practise⟩ and the noun ⟨practice⟩. Johnson was professedly cautious about defying orthographic custom, even retaining the ⟨ck⟩ in words like ⟨musick⟩ and ⟨critick⟩. He nonetheless lent his considerable authority to some important changes – ⟨risk⟩ for ⟨risque⟩, ⟨ancient⟩ for ⟨antient⟩, ⟨entire⟩ for ⟨intire⟩, and many others.[37]

The overriding goal of all these changes was to make English orthography more consistent, and thus a more regular standard for pronunciation. Only a fixed, written standard, Johnson believed, would permit a language to improve. This principle was central not only to the *Dictionary*, but also to his understanding of the history and development of poetry.

WRITING AND THE IMPROVEMENT OF LANGUAGE

Johnson was always willing to defend his position that language could not improve without a secure, written standard. This conviction was, for example, central to his case against the 'Ossian' poems in *A journey to the western isles of Scotland* (1775). In the early 1760s, the young Scottish poet and scholar James Macpherson published what he alleged to be translations from the Gaelic of works by Ossian, a Highland bard of the third century. These works included two epics, *Fingal* and *Temora*. Macpherson claimed that he had reassembled Ossian's poems largely from the songs and verse of Highlanders, passed down through the centuries by oral tradition.[38] His reliance on the basic fidelity of an oral tradition is, in itself, a significant indication of how attitudes towards writing were changing at this time. By mid century, many reputable scholars were willing to entertain the possibility that the history and literary works of a people could be preserved without books. In 1769, the English traveller and archaeologist Robert Wood even advanced the first plausible and influential argument that Homer was illiterate, and that his epics were the product of an 'oral tradition'.[39]

But Johnson would have none of this. With his usual disdain for delicacy, he declared that Macpherson had merely forged the Ossian poems. His major evidence for this charge, much disputed in the subsequent controversy, was that 'the Earse never was a written language'.[40] It could not, therefore, have been the language of an epic or of any substantial poetry, beyond popular ballads. Other indigenous languages, he noted, such as Welsh and Irish, were 'cultivated tongues' because they had achieved a standardised orthography, precisely what he had aimed to establish for English. Indeed, 'the Welsh, two hundred years ago, insulted their English neighbours for the instability of their orthography'. 'Earse', on the other hand, 'merely floated in the breath of the people.' For this reason, it could 'receive little improvement'.[41]

Whatever the fairness or accuracy of Johnson's observations about Scots Gaelic or Macpherson, his arguments mark an important new stage in the study of literate culture. Johnson was among the first to describe how literacy promotes what he called the 'cultivation' of a language. A literate culture, he argued, demands greater effort and accomplishment from its scholars and teachers, who will 'set a proportionate value on their own thoughts, and wish to enforce them by efficacious expressions'. When speech becomes 'embodied and permanent', moreover, its 'modes and phrases are compared, and the best obtains an establishment'. Not only does writing facilitate the comparison of present words and expressions, but the present language can be compared with its past form. By this means, the speakers of a language gain an awareness of progress, and desire to improve language still further. Johnson's analysis is not so remote from what modern scholars have noted about the influence of literacy on language.[42] In his 1977 book *The domestication of the savage mind*, anthropologist Jack Goody commented similarly on the potential for detailed comparison between words and phrases opened up by writing. With the introduction of an alphabet, noted Goody, 'speech is no longer tied to an "occasion"'. It is made into an object available for comparison, improvement and scientific appraisal.[43]

It is no accident that the Ossian controversy occurred at a time when scholars were generally more aware of the difference between speech and writing, and between 'oral' and 'literate' forms of discourse. Johnson had strongly in mind a 'literate' style of language. And scholars of the same period, such as Joseph Priestley in his 1763 *Course of lectures on the theory of language and universal grammar*, were beginning to define what they considered a typical 'oral style'. In Priestley's view, this style was fragmented and discontinuous: 'it is not easy to conceive, that the language of any people, before the introduction of letters, could be otherwise than very incoherent and unconnected.'[44] The broken syntax of the Old Testament, he argued, was typical of a time when people were still unpractised in the art of composing their ideas in 'connected' discourse – discourse in which every idea was smoothly linked with what came before and after, a skill learned only by writing.[45] It was the same 'unconnected' quality of the Ossian poems that Macpherson's defenders pointed to as evidence of their origin in a primitive, oral culture. According to the Edinburgh Professor of Rhetoric, Hugh Blair, these qualities helped to prove that Macpherson had translated the genuine productions of an ancient rhapsode before the rise of letters.[46]

Indeed, not everyone agreed with Johnson that writing and literacy had *improved* speech – at least for the purposes of poetry. Macpherson's epics were admired by many for their fiery 'oral' style. And a new movement of rhetoricians and grammarians went so far as to claim that the modern dominance of writing had actually diminished the natural power of speech found in ancient verse and oratory.

THOMAS SHERIDAN, WRITING AND THE POWERS OF LIVING SPEECH

The most detailed and sustained analysis of the allegedly pernicious influence of literacy was by 'the Dublin Orator', Thomas Sheridan, now best known as the father of the more famous playwright, Richard Brinsley Sheridan.[47] In the middle and late years of the eighteenth century, Sheridan and Johnson came to embody the opposite extremes of opinion about written language. Indeed, the disagreement between Johnson and Sheridan on this issue seems to have contributed to a breach in their personal relationship shortly after the publication of Sheridan's most popular and successful work, *A course of lectures on elocution* in 1762. We are told by Boswell that Johnson 'thought slightingly of Sheridan's art', and had scoffed at the news that Sheridan had received a state pension: 'What! have they given *him* a pension? Then it is time for me to give up mine.'[48] Sheridan caught wind of this remark, and never forgave Johnson. Their falling out was thus immediately caused by an insult. But its original source, one suspects, was their sharply divergent opinions on language – particularly on the relationship between writing and speech.

In *A course of lectures on elocution*, first delivered to enthusiastic audiences in 1758 and 1759, Sheridan made a number of thinly veiled criticisms of Johnson's *Dictionary*. 'Our compilers of dictionaries,' he complained, '…as well as our grammarians, have never examined the state of the living tongue, but wholly confined their labours to the dead written language.'[49] Sheridan retained some of the early interest in making writing as much as possible like speech. He objected acidly that it was 'to the last degree weak and frivolous' to maintain anomalous spellings for the sake of preserving traces of a word's etymology.[50] Orthography, he argued, had been allowed to dominate over 'the nobler part of grammar', which was 'orthoepy', or right pronunciation:[51] 'This is the task on which I am now employed;…to make the spoken language, as it ought to be, the archetype of which the written language should be considered only as the type.'[52]

Sheridan's main objective was not, however, to reform English spelling. In order to re-establish the primacy of the living voice, he took quite a different approach: he set out to promote the arts of speech and elocution. Johnson, as we have seen, believed that the most 'elegant' speech was that which most resembled written language. Deeply antagonistic to this view, Sheridan worried that people in his literate culture already tended to speak too much as they wrote. He declaimed in particular against 'bookish men', who 'are generally remarkable for the worst delivery' (a remark that might well remind us of a certain talkative 'bookish man' of Sheridan's acquaintance). Sheridan's political outlook was little less conservative than Johnson's: his elocutionary ideal was court language as spoken in the age of Queen Anne, the heyday of Toryism. He nonetheless dared to suggest that even the illiterate vulgar had the advantage over the learned in the expression of passion. Because 'the man wholly illiterate ... has no other ideas of language, but what he has obtained thro' the ear', he conveyed his emotions with all the force of 'nature', untrammelled by the pernicious influence of writing.[53] Sheridan's *General dictionary* (1780) may well be seen as correcting the bias towards written language in Johnson's *Dictionary*. He included phonetic spellings alongside ordinary spellings to guide the reader's pronunciation, insisting that the standard of correct pronunciation must not be confused with the standard of orthography.[54]

But most important, his elocutionary arts were designed to re-invigorate spoken 'tones' and 'accents'. These were the very 'life, blood, and soul' of language, he argued, though they were 'utterly unnoticed in writing'.[55] By thus giving such importance to these prosodic qualities, exclusive to oral utterance, Sheridan exemplified one of the most significant trends in linguistic thought at the time.

As we have already noted, seventeenth-century grammarians had paid relatively little attention to the intonation of spoken language. Many ignored prosody altogether. Others touched on this traditional division of grammar only in connection with punctuation – that is, the correct writing of language. None of the inventors of a 'universal character' did more than mention tone or emphasis, or attempt to reflect these qualities in their new languages. They generally assumed that language consisted of 'arbitrary signs' for ideas, and that intonation was merely 'accessory' to the main meaning of language. It made speech more lively for 'rhetorical' uses, but played no *essential* role in communication.[56] Even in the seventeenth century, however, studies were afoot that ultimately brought greater awareness of the role of intonation in ordinary language. As grammarians, aiming primarily to reform writing, made a more careful analysis of speech, they became more attuned to the 'melody' of the voice. It is significant that the first discussion of English prosody was made by John Hart, the same grammarian who made orthographic reform his life's work.[57]

It was not until the eighteenth century, however, that prosody recovered its traditional place as one of the four main divisions of grammar. Even Johnson, though sceptical of the contemporary fashion for orality, expressed regret that prosody had been so scantily

discussed by seventeenth-century grammarians. He included a brief
discussion of prosody in the grammar appended to his *Dictionary*. But
his interest was in prosody as a quality of *poetic* language rather than
ordinary speech. He discussed metre rather than regular intonation.[58]

Tone, quantity and other prosodic qualities were nonetheless
foremost in the minds of many other grammarians of this period. By
far the most important of these qualities was 'tone'. The following
description of 'tone', taken from Daniel Fenning's *A new grammar of
the English tongue* (1771), was rehearsed in much the same words by
numerous grammarians of the middle and late decades of the
century. It focused in typical fashion on the role of tones as the
natural means to express the passions: 'each passion [is] expressed by
a *tone* peculiar to itself. Thus *Love* is expressed by a soft, smooth,
languishing tone; *Anger*, by a strong, vehement, and elevated one;
Joy, by a quick, sweet, and clear tone; *Sorrow*, by a low, flexible,
interrupted one...'[59] As used by more careful grammarians of this
era, such as Sheridan, 'tone' referred specifically to what a modern
linguist would call a change of pitch.[60] In Fenning's passage,
however, the word 'tone' referred generally to all the qualities of
pitch, pause, timbre, loudness and so forth that make up the
intonation of speech. Every passion, he assumed, induced a particular
manner of expression that was spontaneous and perfectly intelligible
to any listener in any language. 'Tone' of voice was a natural and
universal form of communication.

Vocal intonation was usually accompanied, moreover, by the
equally natural and universal language of gestures and facial
movements expressive of the same passions. For example, in the
following typical passage from James Burgh's *The art of speaking*
(1761), tone, gestures and facial movements combine in the complex
expression of 'desire'. (If my reader is alone, he or she might try
acting out this description as a private demonstration): '*Desire*
expresses itself by *bending* the *body* forward, and *stretching* the *arms*
toward the object, as to grasp it. The *countenance smiling*, but *eager* and
wishful; the *eyes* wide *open*, and *eyebrows raised*; the *mouth open*; the tone
of voice *suppliant*, but *lively* and *cheerful*.'[61] Like other scholars of
language in his time, Burgh thought of language as much more than
'signs' denoting ideas, the conventional view of seventeenth-century
grammarians. Instead, he regarded language as a network of
semantic, prosodic and bodily signals, both conventional and natural,
combined in the expression of both ideas and sentiments. Indeed, it

is in the eighteenth century, rather than before, that we can refer most accurately to what Richard R. W. Kroll has called 'the somatic tradition', for it was at this time that scholars began to describe language as an act involving the whole body.[62]

The resurgent interest in prosody is thus linked to the more careful scrutiny of the voice in grammars from the seventeenth century onwards. It also reflects other important changes in the late eighteenth century. We have considered that many historians of writing in the eighteenth century attempted to show that the alphabet possessed some original resemblance to objects in nature, and was not merely the product of human convention. It was the same goal of finding a *natural* basis for language that raised interest in intonation and gesture, widely portrayed as the spontaneous language of primitive humans and babies.[63] Scholars of language also increasingly considered the expression of passions as an essential part of language that had been too much neglected by previous grammarians and philosophers. Sheridan was among those who strongly criticised John Locke for confining his attention to the 'arbitrary signs' of ideas, ignoring the 'natural' means of expressing feelings. Locke's 'only object was, to examine the nature of words, as symbols of ideas', he observed, 'whilst the nobler branch of language, which consists of the signs of internal emotions, was untouched by him as foreign to his purpose.'[64] These 'signs of internal emotions' were 'tones, looks and gestures', the part of language instituted by 'God' rather than human convention.[65]

Sheridan's belief in the importance of these natural 'signs of internal emotion' thus reflects an extremely broad and vigorous movement in grammatical and linguistic thought of the mid eighteenth century.[66] He did not create the interest in prosody and elocution; it was *already* there, waiting to be marshalled into a deliberate campaign to re-invigorate the arts of speech. As Sheridan himself bragged, he attracted some 1,700 subscribers to the printed version of his lectures on elocution.[67] Closely associated with the importance given to powers of living speech was a proportionate scepticism with the 'dead letter' – even outright hostility towards the evil effects of this mute, toneless medium. The pernicious effects of writing were, moreover, social as well as purely linguistic. Just at the time when writing and print were beginning to dominate British society and its institutions, Sheridan and others were pointing to the damaging effects of these media on the moral health of the nation.

THOMAS SHERIDAN AND THE SOCIAL DANGERS OF WRITING

Most eighteenth-century scholars acknowledged that writing was an extremely useful invention, perfectly adequate for certain limited functions. But only speech, mother of all communication, could give full expression to the human soul. As Hugh Blair wrote in his influential *Lectures on rhetoric and belles lettres* (1783), 'though Writing may answer the purposes of mere instruction, yet all the great and high efforts of eloquence must be made, by means of spoken, not of written, Language.'[68] Sheridan generally agreed with this kind of division between the functions suitable to writing and speech. He did not deny that writing benefited society, so long as it was confined to its appropriate roles of sending messages and recording knowledge.[69] His major concern was that scholars had attempted to use writing for eloquence and moral instruction, purposes it could not fulfil nearly as well as speech. He scolded 'the vanity of ingenious men', who 'think, that they can do that by writing, which is beyond the power of writing to accomplish'.[70] Nor was this just a problem of rhetoric or lexicography. As the moral and political health of the nation relied on clear and eloquent communication, the tyranny of writing, vague and inexpressive, had undermined the welfare of the British people.

These social concerns were at the forefront of Sheridan's first work, *British education* (1756), where he contended that the almost exclusive attention given to written language in schools and universities was destroying the peace and orderliness of a nation. How could he prove this dramatic allegation? Readopting an argument made famous by Bernard Mandeville's *Fable of the bees* (1724–29), Sheridan observed that luxury was absolutely necessary to a nation's prosperity, but could be promoted only at the cost of increasing avarice and sensuality.[71] The only way to control these vices was to propagate religion through either the press or, much preferably, public oratory. Only effective oratory could reach the whole population since, as he pointed out, 'the bulk of the people are illiterate'. Moreover, the common people were far more susceptible to impassioned eloquence than to doctrine 'coolly offered to their understandings', a truth revealed by the remarkable popularity of the open-air Methodist preachers.[72]

At the most explicit level, therefore, Sheridan's social and political worries derived from his perception that the literate classes and their institutions – particularly the Anglican church – were losing control over the vulgar, religion and public morals. Sheridan was inspired by a conviction that may strike us as peculiar coming from 'an age of print': he believed that the *voice*, not printed materials, was the major instrument of ideological sway in his world. Literate people had lost their ability to move others with spoken language, and were therefore also losing their ability to control and govern society. Anarchy and Methodism loomed. Whatever the justice of these fears, Sheridan's criticisms of British education clearly struck a chord among his middle-class listeners and readers, many of whom shared his dismay with the viciousness of the times and with the soporific dullness of Anglican sermons. In his 1759 periodical *The bee*, Oliver Goldsmith ridiculed the dispassionate and literate style of Anglican preachers:

writing a discourse coolly in the closet, then getting it by memory, and delivering it on Sundays ... will not do. What then is to be done? I know of no expedient to speak; to speak at once intelligibly, and feelingly, except to understand that language; [to] be convinced of the truth of the object ... and to do the lot extempore.

Goldsmith seemed even to disapprove of the preacher reading from prepared notes, and urged clergymen to speak on the impulse of their spontaneous thoughts and emotions.[73]

It would be wrong, however, to assume that Sheridan and his admirers wished merely to release eloquence from any kind of training or regular method. In fact, Sheridan had little faith that speech could achieve its full potential without a rigorous education in oratory. He believed that such training was the source of the legendary greatness of oratory in ancient Greece. And the same instruction supported the high state of morals in that Golden Age.

Sheridan was among those daring scholars in the eighteenth century who challenged the traditional perception of ancient Athens as a highly literate civilisation. Among the Greeks of the Golden Age, said Sheridan, 'Writing was little known ... and by those who knew it, was made no other use of than to assist the memory.'[74] The scarcity of letters in ancient Greece was, moreover, a major reason for the political liberty and artistic greatness of that nation. Unlike British children, who were made to ply their books, Greek children learned to exploit the full potential of their voices, and to use all the tones, gestures and looks expressive of their affections. As the result, Greek orators like Demosthenes were able to move the public to action on any important issue before the state. Even in ordinary life, Greeks had the advantage of knowing the precise thoughts and feelings of others, for their ears were trained to perceive the slightest nuance of intonation. 'Hence arose their accurate knowledge of the human heart,' Sheridan concluded, 'which they studied in the original, in the great volume of society.'[75] With rise of writing and books in modern times, however, the ancient virtue and wisdom of the Greeks had been lost. As Sheridan lamented, 'nothing can contribute more to the propagation of selfishness in this country, than the ascendancy which the written language has obtained amongst us, over that which is spoken.'[76]

By reducing the influence of books, therefore, and increasing the role of eloquence, Britain would become a place not only of mellifluous orators, but also of more virtuous, orderly and insightful subjects. Indeed, confidence in speech and orality as forces of civic improvement gave rise to some remarkable effusions of optimism among Sheridan's contemporaries. 'Abolish ... writing among mankind for a century,' wrote Thomas Reid in his 1764 *Inquiry into the human mind on the principles of common-sense*, 'and every man would be a painter, an actor, and an orator.'[77] Perhaps predictably, there was also some exasperation with such assertions. Sheridan's fears were dismissed by many as exaggerated, his linguistic analysis as naive and inaccurate. Even in this time of radically changing attitudes, the case for the benefits of written language and literacy continued to have its strong advocates.

OBJECTIONS TO SHERIDAN

Those who criticised Sheridan's ideas often cited Johnson's opinion that writing ought to stand as the permanent model for pronunciation, which was diverse, changeable and endlessly prone to corruption. As John Rice wrote in *An introduction to the art of reading* (1765), 'With regard to the Difference between spoken and written Language, it may ... be not improper to observe, that the latter, having greatly the Advantage in Point of Universality, every Concession, in disputable or indifferent Cases, should be made to it by the former.'[78] Rice also censured many of Sheridan's precepts on impassioned elocution as 'mere declamatory Tricks, Clap-Traps for the Multitude'.[79] This statement reveals an important ideological dimension to this debate about oratory and language. Rice denounced what he believed was a pandering to the tastes of the

'Multitude', the superficial demands of a vulgar assembly. We may recall Johnson's similar criticism of orthographic reformers for elevating the speech of 'the lowest of the people' into a model of pronunciation. Both Rice and Johnson reacted against what they characterised as the vulgarity of linguistic ideas they opposed.

But we must be wary of oversimplifying the ideological divisions underlying this controversy. A scholar has recently portrayed Johnson, along with others such as James Harris and Lord Monboddo, as arch-reactionaries who aimed to suppress the idiom of the people by insisting on the supremacy of written language.[80] Yet Johnson was no mere foot-soldier for the privilege and power of the literate ruling classes. Against the popular argument that the poor were made proud and unruly by education, he argued consistently in favour of teaching 'the lowest of the people' to read and write. As he quite logically pointed out, no one would be vain of literacy in a society where *everyone* was literate.[81] Nor were advocates of oral language commonly the champions of the people. The Scottish philosopher Lord Monboddo, author of the five volume *Of the origin and progress of language* (1774–93), was among those who decried the bad effects of writing on modern culture. 'It may be justly questioned', he remarked, 'whether [writing] has upon the whole contributed to the improvement of knowledge.'[82] Yet Monboddo was also highly elitist on linguistic matters, denying that the common people had exercised any beneficial influence on the development of language. Modern language, he conjectured, had been fashioned by an ancient school of grammarians.

In short, we can draw no consistent equation between the elevation of writing and a conservative political philosophy, or between the celebration of spoken language and political liberalism. As Peter de Bolla has rightly pointed out, the radical Joseph Priestley was among those who promoted wider literacy and described the essentially positive influence of writing on speech. De Bolla takes this as a sign of Priestley's recognition that a more equitable society could be achieved only if the common people gained access to the media controlled by the ruling classes.[83] Yet Priestley, in turn, surely makes a strange bed-fellow with the Tory Johnson, who both promoted popular literacy *and* defended the virtues of 'subordination'. As for Thomas Sheridan, he was in most respects the stuffiest of conservatives, for all his preference for speech over writing. His major political concern, as we have considered, was to buttress the power of the ruling classes by increasing its ability to influence 'the bulk of the people'. He realised that a large proportion of Britain's inhabitants were still illiterate. For this reason, it was the *voice*, not the 'text', that was the true foundation of the moral and religious control being lost to popular movements like Methodism.

Hence, criticisms of Sheridan were not ordinarily of a political nature. This debate took place among middle-class authors who were largely of one mind concerning the need to protect their hegemony, whether by writing or speech. Criticisms of Sheridan focused, rather, on his claim that the salvation of political order was possible only by re-invigorating the powers of eloquence. According to John Rice, impassioned elocution had little of the religious, moral and political significance that Sheridan claimed for it. In his view, preachers and other public orators should 'labour to *convince*', rather than merely to 'persuade'. Impassioned rhetoric might move an audience for the moment. But only solid arguments, based on a proper literate education, could create the kind of *conviction* needed to have a lasting influence on the moral health of a nation. As Rice observed of one of Sheridan's elocutionary heroes, William Pitt, some orators stirred the passions while they spoke, but they as often lost the vote in the end.[84]

Neither Rice nor Sheridan's other critics disputed that speech was capable of greater passion and liveliness than writing. Sheridan had won this point. Most works on oratory and literary criticism stressed the need for both the public or private reader to supply the passionate tones omitted in a piece of writing. The ability to know and supply the appropriate tones was, as Lord Kames wrote in *Elements of criticism* (1762), the very essence of literary 'taste': 'The chief talent of a fine writer, is a ready command of the expressions that nature dictates to every man when any vivid emotion struggles for utterance; and the chief talent of a fine reader, is a ready command of the tones suited to those expressions.'[85] Not everyone agreed, however, that the lack of tones made written language inherently deficient or confusing. As Joseph Priestley argued in *A course of lectures on oratory and criticism* (1778), writing suffered from no serious deficiency in this regard, for an ordinary reader could not help but supply the appropriate tones to a literary text: 'because, if we feel the sentiment, we unavoidably do give the language the assistance we can from pronunciation, the powers of *written language* have been supposed to be as extensive as those of *language* and *pronunciation* together'.[86] Scholars were thus far more conscious than their predecessors in the seventeenth century that tones and other vocal qualities played an important role in language, and that these qualities could not be fully reproduced in writing. They pointed to the need for collaboration between the reader and the text. Nonetheless, disagreement continued on whether the need to contribute tones and other vocal qualities presented a serious difficulty or hinderance to the appreciation of literary art.

Sharper debate occurred on the question of whether speech was inherently clearer or more meaningful than writing. In *British education*, Sheridan argued that public orators were forced to be more precise than authors, since their language passed by the listener so quickly. On the other hand, 'clearness is not so absolutely necessary to the writer, for let his language be ever so obscure, his reader may stop, and take what time he pleases to find out his meaning'.[87] According to John Rice, however, Sheridan had greatly exaggerated the importance of tone and emphasis to the meaning of language:

One might be led to imagine, by the extravagant Manner in which the Importance of Emphasis is treated by some Writers, that written Language had really no determinate Meaning at all; but that all depended upon the oral Utterance of the Reader: I shall endeavour to shew, however, that the Influence of Emphasis, great as it is, is still subject to the Precision of written Language, and that if Orthography and Syntax do not accompany the Reader's Orthoepy and Emphasis, his Oratory will have no more Effect than the sounding Brass and the tinkling Cymbol.[88]

Rice thus reversed the relationship so insisted upon in Sheridan's work: rather than writing depending wholly on speech, speech, argued Rice, depended for its meaning on the 'Precision' of written language. By this 'Precision' Rice meant the grammatical order and clear articulation most fully displayed and preserved in writing. He did not disagree that prosody made an important contribution to the meaning of language, but this contribution was always *additional* to the sense displayed in writing: 'There is a general Meaning in every Sentence grammatically written or spoken, and which must always be considered antecedent to the particular Meaning given it by Emphasis.'[89]

A final argument made against Sheridan's teachings on elocution was that it was unnatural to intone most written language as if the reader were expounding deep-felt and personal sentiments. Most of what people read contains the thoughts and sentiments of others. And if, as Sheridan believed, writing is only a deficient imitation of speech, it seems contradictory to demand that reading be exactly like spontaneous utterance. As William Cockin contended in *The art of delivering written language* (1775), Sheridan confused 'two things so very different, as a *copy*, and *original*'.[90] Cockin did not mean to defend what Sheridan called 'reading tones' – the artificial sing-song manner often used by readers. He did argue, however, that the tones borrowed from speech should be 'more faintly characterised' in public reading. The orator should strive not for warmth of expression, but for 'ease and masterliness'.[91] This was the truly 'natural' way to pronounce written language, which was not well suited to expressing the passions, yet was able to address the understanding with precision and elegance. Cockin's appeal for dignity and restraint was widely shared by contemporaries. Samuel Johnson is reported even to have held down the arms of a person who was gesticulating vigorously while speaking.[92]

Behind this debate lay, in fact, certain points of agreement. Neither Sheridan nor his critics denied that written and spoken discourse were fundamentally different forms of discourse, at least in their present forms. The keener recognition of these differences is itself a signal feature of this whole debate: it suggests why few during this era had much enthusiasm for the seventeenth-century projects to form an ideal written language that could replace speech for the purposes of science and philosophy.[93] Even Sheridan's critics admitted that tone and gesture played an important part in language, and could not be dispensed with. But here a question quite naturally arises: might it not be possible to make writing more like speech by contriving a system to indicate intonation, gesture and other qualities exclusive to speech? We might briefly turn to some of the interesting graphic experiments that were inspired by this possibility.

EXPERIMENTS WITH NEW KINDS OF WRITING

Despite his general suspicion of written language, Sheridan did not entirely reject the possibility of forming a notation that indicated 'tones and cadences'. He nonetheless shared the pessimism of many previous reformers about weaning the public from their customary ways of writing. This was 'a speculative point', he grumbled, 'inasmuch as there is little likelihood that any change will be made in the art of writing'.[94] Other authors were even more sceptical. William Cockin said it was 'utopian' to try to reduce all the qualities of voice and gesture to some regular script, for there was an 'indefinite variety' of tones and other qualities affecting intonation.[95] Especially in the final two decades of the century, however, some members of the elocution movement showed greater optimism about the usefulness of written marks for intonation and gesture, at least for the use of 'those who philosophize on language'.[96] John Walker led what is sometimes called the 'mechanical' branch of the elocutionary movement. Against Sheridan's general message that the orator had to *feel* the expressed emotions – for insincere intonation is always noticeable – these teachers were more confident that appropriate tones of voice could be schematised and read off a score like music.[97] Walker did not deny that writing was inherently incapable of capturing the vast range of tones and pauses available to the speaker. But this limitation, he insisted, was no reason to give up all efforts to make writing a much better record of intonation than it currently was.[98]

The desire to make writing a more accurate reflection of tones, cadences, and pauses motivated some of the most interesting graphic experiments in history. Today, the most famous of these is a novel – Laurence Sterne's *Tristram Shandy* (1760–7). Tristram calls his writing 'but a different name for conversation',[99] and the various oddities in the typography of this novel were meant in part to duplicate intonation more completely than would be possible with ordinary writing. In the following dialogue with a fictional reader in the 1760 first volume, dashes of varying lengths signify pauses of differing length:

————How could you, Madam, be so inattentive in reading the last chapter? I told you in it, *That my mother was not a papist.*————Papist! You told me no such thing, Sir! Madam, I beg leave to repeat it over again, That I told you as plain, at least, as words, by direct inference, could tell you such a thing.————Then, Sir, I must have miss'd a page.—No, Madam,———you have not miss'd a word.————Then I was asleep, Sir.—My pride, Madam, cannot allow you that refuge.[100]

In this passage and throughout the early volumes of *Tristram Shandy*, dashes are used almost solely to supplement ordinary punctuation in order to indicate length of pauses. After volumes 5 and 6 (1762), however, Sterne more often used dashes *in place* of commas and other marks. Elsewhere, dashes, asterisks and other marks denote whispering, humming and various gestures. Sterne, who played the cello, was highly sensitive to the tonal properties of speech. In one amusing episode in volume 4, for example, 'Phutatorius' exclaims when a hot chestnut rolls from the table into his open breeches during a lively conversation:

Zounds! ————————————————————

————Z———— ds! cried *Phutatorius*, partly to himself – and yet high enough to be heard.

Such an exclamation might be mistaken for an objection to something said in the conversation, but Phutatorius's companions notice immediately that ''twas quite out of key' with the rest of their exchange. 'One or two who had very nice ears, and could distinguish the expression and mixture of the two tones as plainly as a *third* or a *fifth*, or any other chord in musick – were the most puzzled and perplexed with it.'[101] Here and elsewhere, Sterne's parallels between music and speech indicate that speech itself has a kind of melody. While Sterne's typography could hardly duplicate this melody with exactness, it was designed to keep us aware of this and other prosodic features that play an important role in the meaning of spoken language.

The deliberate irony of Sterne's typographical experiments will not, however, be lost on his admirers. In deploying his arsenal of dashes and asterisks to imitate the rhythm and tone of conversation, Sterne created the most visual and the most typographically obtrusive of English novels. We are never allowed to forget, in fact, that we are reading a book. Sterne's novel demonstrates why so few grammarians of his time felt a major reform of writing would be accepted, for even justifiable changes strike readers as odd and distracting.

A more scientific attempt to record intonation was presented by Joshua Steele in *An essay towards establishing the melody and measure of speech* (1775). In the words of a modern scholar of intonation, 'Steele's essay provided ... the first systematic transcriptional method for notating length, stress and pitch features.'[102] Steele's first intention, however, was not to furnish a new form of writing, but rather to refute the opinion of Lord Monboddo that 'the music of our language [is] ... nothing better than the music of a drum, in which we perceive no difference except that of louder and softer, according as the instrument is more or less forcibly struck'.[103] (Monboddo did agree that changes of tone occurred to indicate states of heightened passion.) Monboddo urged musicians to test his belief that there is no pitch change in English accents, and Steele obliged, duplicating speech sounds on a bass viol. By determining that English speakers do use pitch changes in ordinary speech (exclusive of states of passion), Steele challenged the assumption of Monboddo, Sheridan and others that the regular pronunciation of English was utterly toneless, marking the decline of language since the melodious speech of the Greeks.[104] He was not the first, however, to suspect tonal variation in English, for such variation was taken for granted in traditional ideas about prosody. The older view, though questioned by eighteenth-century scholars, has turned out to be correct: modern research, aided by electronic equipment, has confirmed the regular use of pitch change to create emphasis in English.[105]

Steele's prosodic transcription was thus contrived to make the case against Monboddo. He demonstrated pitch changes by recording them on the five-line staff of musical notation. In a significant insight into the special features of intonation, however, Steele used slanted marks, rather than the single notes of music, in order to indicate the tonal 'slides'. He conjectured that the Greek accents, which were similarly slanted, initially signified the same rise and fall of pitch. To these marks were added signs for duration, pauses, loudness and what he called 'poize', the cadence of 'heavy' and 'light' stresses which, in his view, differed from changes of loudness. Using this system, Steele transcribed the 'To be or not to be' speech in *Hamlet*, along with different ways of reading a speech by Demosthenes.[106] The great benefit of his notation, he predicted, was that it could be used to record the performances of great actors like Garrick, who took a personal interest in Steele's project.

But Steele's experiment, as the grammarians feared, attracted little more than academic interest. James Boswell would later regret that Steele had not recorded the speaking style of Samuel Johnson: 'His mode of speaking was indeed very impressive,' wrote Boswell of Johnson, 'and I wish it could be preserved as musick is written, according to the very ingenious method of Mr. Steele, who has shewn how the recitation of Mr. Garrick, and other eminent speakers, might be transmitted to posterity *in score*.'[107] There is some irony in thinking of Johnson as the subject for such transcription, for Johnson, who was almost deaf, shared little of the contemporary fascination with prosody and vocal sound. Boswell, on the contrary, was very much an author of his time in setting out to give the public a detailed record of a famous writer's conversation. Throughout *Life of Johnson*, we are meant not only to attend to Johnson's words, but to imagine how he said them: 'I cannot too frequently request of my readers, when they peruse my account of Johnson's conversation, to endeavour to keep in mind his deliberate and strong utterance.'[108] Many British poets of the late eighteenth century, as Murray Cohen has indicated, sought 'rhythms and tunes that will "vibrate" with their intended moods'.[109] We might think here of attempts to imitate the naturalness and spontaneiety of oral expression by Thomas Percy, Thomas Chatterton and Robbie Burns.

Experiments with making written language more like speech reflect important linguistic trends of the late eighteenth century. They demonstrate the extent to which the limitations of written language had become sharply apparent not only to many grammarians or elocutionists, but also to poets and novelists. This heightened awareness, it should be stressed, was occurring at a time when there were more books and more readers than ever before. In short, the growth of literacy and print culture did *not* lead in any clear or consistent way to the predominance of the visual over the aural in European intellectual culture. Just the opposite: despite the ascendancy of written language – even *because* its ascendancy had become so obvious – the late eighteenth century was a time when spoken language was valued more and understood better than in any previous era. Nor was this shift exclusive to Britain. It reflects an important and general trend in mid eighteenth-century thought that was also occurring, with special Gallic variations, on the other side of the English channel.

CHAPTER 6

Rousseau's Essai sur l'origine des langues *and its context*

Rousseau's attack on writing in *Essai sur l'origine des langues* is well known to readers from Jacques Derrida's lengthy 'deconstruction' of this text in *Of grammatology*. According to Derrida, the *Essai* articulates a hostility to writing that has been characteristic of Western philosophy since the time of Plato, who warned against the deceptions of the 'dead letter' in the *Phædrus*. He contends, further, that Rousseau's *Essai* belongs specifically to a time when the primacy of the *logos* or spoken word had been threatened by plans in the seventeenth century for a 'universal character', a writing that directly signified things or ideas, rather than speech. Like Hegel later on, Rousseau wished to reaffirm the privileged place of speech, foundation of truth and 'presence' in European metaphysics, by denigrating writing as a faded 'supplement' to the living voice.[1]

Derrida's portrayal of the 'universal character' as a mere intrusion into the traditional 'logocentrism' of Western philosophy is, however, highly questionable: as we have previously considered, those plans reflected the generally high status of graphic symbolism in the seventeenth century, a time when Plato was frequently censured for his supposed denunciation of writing. Scholars of the Renaissance had also regarded hieroglyphics and other non-alphabetical symbols as more 'spiritual' than speech and more suited to the expression of philosophical and religious truths. Nor is there much evidence that Rousseau was specifically concerned to refute schemes for a universal written language: his only reference to these projects was a brief allusion – in an unpublished fragment – to Leibniz's version of a philosophical notation, the 'general characteristic'.[2]

The evidence suggests, instead, that Rousseau had in mind the plans for orthographic reform that were being ardently championed by prominent members of the Académie Française. Rousseau did agree that written language should be adjusted to reflect, though imperfectly, the nature of speech. But he also felt that an exaggerated emphasis on the need to 'perfect' writing was harming language. In *Essai sur l'origine des langues*, he argued that writing was far too limited a medium ever to capture living speech in all its complexity. The effort by his contemporaries to make writing an exact copy of speech was causing them to neglect the special and inimitable powers of spoken language. More seriously, the modern obsession with writing and books was forcing the living tongue into the rigid mould of the dead letter.

So far from affirming the ancient view of writing as merely a copy of speech, therefore, Rousseau was among the first in France to make the case that writing and speech were, in important respects, independent and dissimilar forms of discourse. The inaccuracy of viewing writing as a 'depiction' of speech, even potentially, was pernicious to language and, more seriously, to the moral health of society. Here Rousseau's concerns intersected with those of Sheridan in Britain. Both were leaders in the study of intonation, which they felt had been greatly harmed by the dominance of the written word. And both blamed the reign of writing and books not only for the corruption of speech, but for undermining social order and morality.

ORTHOGRAPHIC REFORM IN FRANCE

As in England, the campaign to reform spelling began in the late Renaissance and seventeenth century, particularly among Humanists and rational-minded grammarians.[3] Fully to understand Rousseau's positions in the *Essai*, we need to return briefly to that previous era. Two distinct doctrines on orthography emerged from the seventeenth century. The first was the position of spelling reformers like Lartigaut, Blegny and Lesclache that 'écriture ét le portrait de la parole' (writing is the portrait of the spoken word), and should therefore be made to conform as closely as possible to pronunciation.[4] But this reasoning was opposed by the Port-Royal grammarians Arnauld and Lancelot in their 1660 *Grammaire générale and raisonnée*, the most influential grammar of the seventeenth century. These authors contended that superfluous or silent letters can be 'of some service in leading us to the knowledge of the thing signified by the words'.[5] For example, the silent ⟨p⟩ and ⟨t⟩ in the French ⟨champs⟩ and ⟨chant⟩ mark the derivation of these words from

the Latin ⟨campus⟩ and ⟨cantus⟩ respectively. The same principles were adopted by the Académie Française, whose spellings in
their 1694 *Dictionnaire* were governed by the criteria of etymology and
current usage rather than pronunciation.[6] In the 1709 *Traité de
la grammaire françoise* commissioned by the Académie, Régnier-
Desmarais argued that it was by no means a consistent rule that
'l'escriture doit se conformer à la prononciation' (writing must
conform to pronunciation). Like Samuel Johnson, he insisted that
pronunciation was too changeable to be made the basis for a consistent and permanent orthography. He also questioned the right
of individual authors to oppose the prevailing usage. If a person
needed permission from the prince to change the letters in his own
name, he remarked, what authority could he have to change the
letters in all the words of the language?[7]

Even the authority of the Académie Française, however, was
not enough to quell enthusiasm for radical orthographic reform,
which remained much higher in France than in England during
the eighteenth century. A large number of grammarians and other
authors – Girard, Buffier, Duclos, Du Marsais, Voltaire – adopted a
personal style of spelling, commonly dropping double consonants
and changing ⟨ph⟩ and ⟨th⟩ to ⟨f⟩ and ⟨t⟩ respectively. Hence
the spelling ⟨ortografe⟩ rather than ⟨orthographe⟩ was the recognised badge of a reform-minded author. Critics of major reform
argued that these innovators were turning written language into a
chaos of idiosyncratic styles. This was the view taken, for example, by
Nicolas Beauzée in his 1765 article 'Orthographe' in the *Encyclopédie*.
Besides supporting the usefulness of preserving traces of a word's
etymological root, Beauzée pointed out that writing, like speech, was
an arbitrary system, and depended entirely on uniform and consistent conventions. The most 'perfect' orthography was that which
remained closest to the conventions upon which all language relied.[8]
Voltaire responded to Beauzée's article in 1771, charging that
'l'orthographe de la plupart des livres français est ridicule' (the
orthography of most French books is ridiculous), and reaffirming
that 'l'écriture est la peinture de la voix: plus elle est ressemblante,
meilleure elle est' (writing is the depiction of the voice: the more
similar it is, the better it is).[9]

During the same period in Britain, as we have seen, enthusiasm for
making writing closer to speech had diminished considerably. Even
scholars who were generally dismayed by the perceived irrationalities

of English spelling, such as Abraham Tucker or Thomas Sheridan, were in fact conservative in their proposals for reform. Sheridan was more intent on re-invigorating speech than on changing orthography. In France, on the other hand, the campaign for orthographic reform gained in strength throughout the century. As authors like Voltaire and Duclos entered the Académie Française, the conservative *Dictionnaire* began to yield to the pressure for reform. Both the 1740 third and the 1762 fourth editions admitted important changes to make spelling a more accurate reflection of speech. The Académie increasingly abandoned its rule that etymology should have precedence over pronunciation in decisions about orthography. On the issue of orthography, therefore, British and French scholarship were developing in different ways. The British increasingly accepted that writing and speech would inevitably differ in many cases, whereas major French authors of the Enlightenment ceded few exceptions to the principle that writing should 'paint' speech as accurately as possible.

DUCLOS'S *REMARQUES* AND FRENCH STUDIES OF PROSODY

One work that urged orthographic reform is particularly worth closer consideration, as it both exemplifies conventional ideas about writing at that time, and was the immediate target of many of Rousseau's pronouncements about writing in *Essai sur l'origine des langues*. This was the *Remarques* appended to a 1754 edition of the Port-Royal *Grammaire générale and raisonnée* by Charles Pinot Duclos, Perpetual Secretary of the Académie Française. Duclos was highly critical of Arnauld and Lancelot's argument in the Port-Royal *Grammaire* that it is useful to preserve unpronounced letters indicating a word's etymology: they saw 'come [*sic*] un avantage ce qui est un véritable défaut; car enfin les caractèrs n'ont été inventés que pour représenter les sons' (as an advantage what is truly a fault; for after all [alphabetical] characters were invented to represent sounds).[10] Nor did Duclos agree that it was useless to challenge the orthography sanctioned by popular custom. The common people may rule over speech, he argued, but in issues concerning written language, 'les vrais législateurs sont les gens de lètres' (the true legislators are men of letters).[11] Learned bodies such as the Académie Française must lead the way in orthographic reform. Individual scholars must also set an example. Duclos himself eliminated almost all double consonants and other superfluous letters in his spelling. Aiming to make orthography more complete, he proposed the introduction of two new letters into French, the Greek gamma and lamba, as well as the use of new or more consistent values for many existing letters. Like other advocates of reform, Duclos was dismissive of the standard reply that a new orthography would render all past books useless. He pointed out that dramatic changes in French spelling over the centuries had not made old books indecipherable.[12]

Duclos's continued enthusiasm for extensive orthographic reform was based on his confidence that writing was capable of providing a far more accurate 'portrait' of speech than was presently the case. He showed little of the concern with the endless variations of pronunciation that led Samuel Johnson and other British authors to conclude that this was a vain ambition. Moreover, Duclos was generally undeterred by recent scholarship indicating that there was no point in attempting to duplicate the intonation of spoken French with written accents. We should briefly consider the study of prosody in French grammars, as this would be a central issue in Rousseau's response to the *Remarques*.

The understanding of French prosody in the eighteenth century had been heavily influenced by a single work, *Traité de la prosodie françoise* (1736) by the Abbé Pierre Joseph Thoulier d'Olivet, the only work recommended in the *Encyclopédie* articles 'Accent' and 'Prosodie'. It was Olivet who defined the three kinds of accent cited by almost all later writers on this subject – the 'accent prosodique', 'accent oratoire' and 'accent musical'. The 'prosodic accent' consisted of changes of 'ton' (tone or pitch) on particular syllables, and was regulated by the rules of pronunciation rather than by the individual speaker. 'Oratorical accent' referred to the tones of passion which, Olivet argued, seemed endlessly various, and could never be reduced to any formal science. 'Musical accent' referred specifically to the kind of intonation used in song: it was marked by much wider changes of tone than prosodic accent, and was more regular than the oratorical accent. Breaking significantly from the opinion of previous grammarians, Olivet contended that French actually did *not* possess any 'prosodic accent': he was among the first to point out what has since been recognised as a distinctive feature of French among the European languages – its lack of a regular pattern of stressed and unstressed syllables in individual words.[13] Instead,

Olivet argued, ordinary French intonation fell entirely into the category of 'oratorical accents', the pitch changes stimulated by the speaker's meaning and emotional state.[14]

Olivet's insights into the lack of a prosodic accent in French had important ramifications for orthography. The written accents of French, he contended, had almost nothing to do with actual changes of tone, though they sometimes indicated the difference between long and short vowels. In his view, the belief that French accents should mark actual changes of tone was misguided, because there was no regular pattern of pitch changes in individual French words.[15] Indeed, Olivet opposed almost all kinds of orthographic reform, advancing the unusual argument that current French spelling reflected speech more accurately than had been assumed, and had helped to stabilise pronunciation.[16]

But Olivet's claim that French lacked a prosodic accent was widely rejected, even by those who adopted his categorisation of accents. Duclos was typical of grammarians of his time in continuing to assume both that French had a prosodic accent, and that this regular pattern of intonation was characterised by changes of pitch, rather than by changes of duration or loudness. Duclos was thus far more sanguine than Olivet about the possibility of marking French intonation with accents. He did agree that *oratorical* accents seemed almost endlessly various: 'nous marquons dans l'écriture l'intéro-gation et la surprise,' he observed, 'mais combien avons-nous de mouvemens de l'âme, et par conséquent d'inflexions oratoires, qui n'ont point de signes écrits, et que l'intelligence et le sentiment peuvent seuls faire saisir!' (We mark interrogation and surprise in writing; but how many movements of the soul do we have, and consequently how many oratorical inflections, which have no written signs, and which intelligence and sentiment alone can seize!).[17] In order to mark *prosodic* accent more accurately, however, 'il ne seroit pas même nécessaire d'imaginer de nouvaus [*sic*] signes' (it would not even be necessary to imagine new signs).[18] The old accent marks merely had to be used more efficiently.

This more accurate use of written accents would restore writing to the kind of perfection that it had achieved under the Greeks. Like their British counterparts, French grammarians held up ancient Greek as the great model of a beautifully musical language, honed by the study of eloquence. Such was the idealised image of Greek intonation set forth by a prominent scholar of language, César

Chesneau Du Marsais, in his article 'Accent' in the *Encyclopédie*. According to Du Marsais, moreover, the Greeks achieved the same refinement in their written language, particularly in the notation of musical accents. He rejected the view – advanced by the Port-Royal authors – that the Greeks introduced accents only very late, possibly not until the arrival of the Romans:

… j'ai bien de la peine à croire que lorsqu'une langue a eu acquis un certain degré de perfection, lorsqu'elle a eu des Orateurs & des Poëtes … j'ai, dis-je, bien de la peine à me persuader qu'alors les copistes habiles n'aient pas fait tout ce qu'il falloit pour peindre la parole avec toute l'exactitude dont ils étoient capables … & qu'ils ne se soient pas servis de quelques signes pour indiquer la bonne prononciation.[19]

(… I have trouble believing that when a language has acquired a certain degree of perfection, when it has had orators and poets … I can hardly persuade myself, I say, that able copyists have then not done all that they could to represent speech with all the exactitude they were capable of … and that they have not made use of certain signs to indicate good pronunciation.)

Du Marsais thus thought that the development of a more accurate and elaborate writing was part of the general perfection of language in a highly advanced nation. The French, like the Greeks, could achieve a far more complete and exact notation of both speech sounds and accents, with the leadership of men of letters. He believed that the Athenians themselves must have had some particularly effective counterpart to the Académie Française.[20]

It would be wrong to conclude, however, that the problems of intonation really played a major part in French grammatical writing of the mid eighteenth century. Olivet's *Traité* remained virtually unrivalled as the standard work on this subject. Duclos only touched briefly on these subjects in his *Remarques*, and he showed little sign of having thought very deeply about the nature of French prosody. Moreover, when Duclos called for the revitalisation of French eloquence, his major concern was not, like Sheridan's, that language had become too dispassionate and monotone as the result of a bookish culture. Rather, he was most concerned that public oratory had become indistinct and inarticulate. A sloppy conversational style of speech, he claimed, was corrupting 'le discours soutenu' (the elevated style) of the tribune, bar and stage.

As described in French grammars and works on elocution of this time, 'le discours soutenu' was typified by the distinct articulation of many letters normally elided in conversation. Hence, as Pierre

Restaut observed in his *Principes généraux et raisonnés de la grammaire françoise* (1732), diphthongs tended to be pronounced as two letters: 'musicien' was pronounced 'mu-si-ci-en,' and 'condition' pronounced 'con-di-ti-on'. Final consonants were distinctly articulated before vowels.[21] Duclos claimed that the degeneration of this elevated style would have grave consequences not only for the beauty of language, but also for the political health of society. Only such a carefully pronounced language, he argued, could be clearly heard by a large assembly:

Une prononciation soutenue et une prosodie fixe et distincte doivent se conserver particulièrement chés des peuples qui sont obligés de traiter publiquement des matières intéressantes pour tous les auditeurs, parce que, toutes choses égales d'ailleurs, un orateur dont la prononciation est ferme et variée, doit être entendu de plus loin qu'un autre qui n'auroit pas les mêmes avantages dans sa langue, quoiqu'il parlât d'un ton aussi élevé.[22]

(It is particularly necessary to preserve an elevated pronunciation and fixed and distinct prosody among peoples obliged to give public airing to matters of interest to all auditors, for, all else being equal, an orator with a firm and varied pronunciation must be heard from further away than another without these advantages, even if he spoke as loud.)

It was in this way that the regulation of oratory and pronunciation was of greater importance to a nation than most suspected. Duclos concluded this section of his *Remarques* by observing that it would be 'un examen assés filosofique' (quite a philosophical inquiry) to determine how the interests and morals of a people influenced their language.[23]

There is an irony in Duclos's advocacy of 'le discours soutenu' which was not lost on Rousseau. On the one hand, Duclos assailed the 'vicious' orthography of French; on the other hand, he wished to retain a style of pronunciation that remained much closer to written rather than to spoken French. The French ideal of elevated speech generally conformed with Samuel Johnson's precept that pronunciation should follow orthography, rather than the other way around. Indeed, as the English grammarian John Rice remarked, the formal pronunciation in French was so different from common speech that it could hardly be understood by the illiterate.[24] It was in this way that conventional strictures concerning the deficiency of writing could co-exist with the view that writing should be the model of speech. Even in the same work, writing could be both decried and held up as the highest standard of language, a paradox that had characterised much grammatical commentary since the seventeenth century.

ROUSSEAU'S VIEWS ON ORTHOGRAPHIC REFORM

Rousseau's interest in the issues raised by orthographic reform is revealed most explicitly in an unpublished fragment on 'Prononciation'. This is the text – really a series of quickly sketched thoughts – that Derrida cites as evidence of Rousseau's hostility to the seventeenth-century projects for a universal writing. Rousseau particularly objected to Leibniz's philosophical character as an 'algébre' that was 'probablement... plus comode à un Métaphysicien qu'à un Artisan' (probably more convenient for a Metaphysician than an Artisan). Besides questioning the usefulness of this character to 'la vie civile', Rousseau insisted that as 'les langues sont faites pour être parlées, l'écriture ne sert que de supplément à la parole' (languages are made to be spoken, writing serves only as the supplement of the spoken word).[25]

Rousseau's scepticism with projects for a universal written language was common in his time. He was echoing the conviction of many contemporary philosophers and grammarians that no form of writing could adequately replace speech. In 1759, for example, the distinguished German scholar Johann David Michaëlis was honoured by the Berlin Academy for an essay which in the final section dismissed hopes for a universal written character as 'built on a slender foundation'. Michaëlis's reasoning was, in part, that spoken words possess a 'natural' affinity with ideas which is lacked by written characters.[26] It is certainly an exaggeration, however, to suggest that Rousseau's scepticism with the Leibnizian characteristic reflects a general determination in eighteenth-century intellectual culture to impugn or suppress all kinds of non-alphabetical writing. We might recall le Chevalier du Jaucourt's assertion in the *Encyclopédie* that hieroglyphical script is 'le moyen le plus propre à faire connoître la pensée' (the most proper means of making thought known).[27] And nearer the end of the century, there was even an important revival of plans for a 'universal character' encouraged by the French literary establishment. The most elaborate of these projects, Joseph de Maimieux's *Pasigraphie* (1797), proposed a form of ideographic writing designed on philosophical principles. Maimieux cited Leibniz among his precursors.[28]

Rousseau's rejection of the Leibnizian 'characteristic' is, moreover, less important than other issues raised by the fragment on 'Prononciation'. For the main subject in this fragment was the contemporary study of spelling and pronunciation. In a general way, Rousseau was supportive of the cause of making orthography more like speech, complaining that 'la prononciation qui devroit toujours régler l'orthographe est souvent réduite à la consulter' (the pronunciation that should rule over orthography is often reduced to consulting it).[29] While Rousseau was well aware that pronunciation changed more quickly than orthography, this was all the more reason, in his view, to ensure that spelling closely followed speech. Otherwise spoken and written language would become so different as to constitute different dialects, as he said had occurred with Italian and Latin.[30]

Rousseau's support for orthographic reform was, however, far from whole-hearted, as evidenced by his own conventional spelling. Rousseau worried in particular that grammarians were spending too much time correcting writing, and not enough time improving pronunciation. 'Plus l'art d'écrire se perfectionne,' he observed, 'plus celui de parler est négligé' (The more the art of writing is perfected, the more that of speaking is neglected).[31] He lamented that the quality of speech seemed to decline in direct proportion as 'lettres' became dominant. Rousseau was thus preoccupied with the damaging effects of an increasingly literate culture on speech and eloquence, a concern very similar to that of Sheridan in his 1756 *British education*. This affinity seems due entirely to the similar intellectual and social conditions surrounding both authors. Rousseau never mentioned Sheridan. Sheridan, in turn, could not have seen either the fragment on 'Prononciation' or *Essai sur l'origine des langues*, which remained unpublished until after Rousseau's death.

The fragment on 'Prononciation' and the *Essai sur l'origine des langues* coincide in decrying the evil effects of literacy on speech. Nevertheless, the latter work takes a different tack on this issue. In the *Essai*, Rousseau expresses serious reservations with the very rationale of orthographic reform, particularly as advanced by Duclos in his *Remarques*, which is cited twice. Duclos's arguments seem to be on Rousseau's mind throughout chapters 5 and 7 on writing and prosody – a fact that suggests that this portion of the *Essai* was written shortly after the 1754 *Remarques*.[32] A long-time friend of the Perpetual Secretary, Rousseau had helped with Duclos's edition of the Port-Royal *Grammaire*.[33] His point against Duclos, and against the whole literary establishment of that time, was that it was misguided to believe that alphabetical writing could ever be made an accurate copy of speech. Indeed, paradoxically, the drive to make writing a copy of speech was really having the effect of making speech more like writing. In their preoccupation with the perfection of written language, grammarians were tailoring speech to a graphic medium that was inherently too rigid and jejune ever to do justice to the innumerable variations of a living tongue.

One best understood written language, according to Rousseau, as a different *kind* of discourse than speech – one that was much less rich and expressive. The essential difference between written and spoken discourse is the main point of Rousseau's comparison of different kinds of script in chapter 5, 'De l'écriture'. 'The original method of writing,' he began, 'is not to depict sounds but the objects themselves.' This is the method exemplified by the Mexican pictographs and the ancient Egyptian hieroglyphics. The Chinese method of writing exemplifies a later development when people began to 'represent words and propositions by conventional characters'.[34] Rousseau took an unusual view of Chinese writing for his time. Anticipating the opinion of some modern scholars like I. C. Gelb, he saw Chinese characters as logograms, not ideograms: they referred primarily to spoken words rather than objects or ideas.[35] Indeed, only the Chinese method could be truly said to 'depict (*peindre*) sounds and to speak to the eyes'. It was this *non-alphabetic* form of writing, in his view, that could truly be said to represent spoken language. Alphabetical writing, on the other hand, breaks up speech into 'a number of elementary parts such as vowels and consonants'. 'To do this is not exactly to depict speech,' he claimed, 'but to analyze it.'[36]

Why did Rousseau wish to draw this distinction between the depiction and the analysis of speech? His main point was that humans had *not* invented alphabetical writing in order to 'paint' speech, or to preserve speech sounds. Writing had evolved quite separately from speech to serve quite different functions. 'The art of writing does not in any way depend on that of speaking,' he asserted: 'It depends on needs of a different nature.'[37] He conjectured that the first to develop alphabetical writing were commercial people who needed a common script for trade with other nations. This argument had been fairly conventional since the seventeenth century. Sir Isaac

Newton had proposed that merchants were the first to invent letters for use in trade,[38] an argument re-echoed in Rousseau's time by Voltaire, among others. But Rousseau had quite novel reasons for tracing alphabetical writing to this commercial origin. For Voltaire, the commercial beginnings of the alphabet revealed its basis in a more enlightened, open and dynamic culture, free from the mysterious priest-craft and hierarchy of the Egyptians.[39] For Rousseau, on the contrary, writing was tainted by its historical roots in self-interest and money. Even more important, he indicated that the traders had not contrived letters to provide an accurate portrayal of speech. Their goals were purely practical. They aimed only to give a rough idea of basic speech sounds in order to write quite different tongues in an internationally comprehensible alphabet.

Yet here originated the essentially false understanding of speech that prevailed among contemporary grammarians. For, in fact, there is no common stock of identical speech sounds used by all different languages. 'There is no absolutely fixed number of letters or elements of speech; some have more, some fewer, depending on the language and on the various modifications accorded to vowels and consonants'.[40] This argument was not entirely new to Rousseau in the French tradition. In a work referred to in chapter 4 of the *Essai, La rhétorique, ou l'art de parler* (1670), Bernard Lamy had made a similar observation:

> ... les organes de la parole peuvent diversifier la voix en tant de manieres differentes, que si on marquoit ces manieres par autant de caracteres particuliers, on feroit des alphabets qui auroient une infinité de differentes lettres. On le voit par experience, chaque nation a des manieres si particulieres de prononcer certaines lettres, que s'il leur falloit donner un signe propre, il faudroit leur en donner un tout different de ceux qui sont ordinaires.[41]

> (... the organs of speech are able to diversify the voice in so many different ways that if one marked these ways by as many particular characters, one would make alphabets which had an infinity of different letters. One sees by experience that each nation has such particular ways of pronouncing certain letters that, if it were necessary to give each a proper sign, it would be necessary to give a totally different [sign] from the current one.)

Lamy knew of the efforts of English grammarians such as William Holder to invent a 'natural alphabet' that would refer to the vocal elements, as revealed by the position of the speech organs. While admiring this work, his view was that such an alphabet could never truly be 'natural' or applicable to all languages. Each nation based its alphabet not on a set of sounds common to all languages, but on those sounds which were most noticeable and important in its particular tongue. 'Habituated' to pronouncing the sounds of their language in a peculiar way, each people gives appropriately different values to all their written letters:

La prononciation se peut diversifier comme nous venons de le dire. Lors que cette diversité est notable, on est obligé de la marquer par un signe particulier, c'est à dire, par une lettre ou caractere particulier.[42]

(Pronunciation can be diversified as we have just said. When this diversity is notable, one is obliged to mark it by a particular sign, that is to say, by a particular letter or character.)

In chapter 5 of the *Essai*, Rousseau also pointed out that different nations in Europe had adopted the same written marks to designate differing sounds. Recalling an argument that we have previously seen in Wilkins's *Essay towards a real character*, he remarked that sounds denoted by letters are not discrete units, as writing suggests, but rather points along a continuous modulation of sound:

Depending on the refinement of the organs of speech and hearing, a greater or smaller number of these modifications will be discovered between the acute *a* and the grave *o*, between the open *i* and the open *e*, etc. Anyone can experience this by moving from one vowel to the next in a continuous, modulated voice; for to the extent that habit has made one more or less sensitive to them, one can single out a greater or lesser number of these nuances and mark each with its own distinctive character, and this habituation depends on the kinds of vocalizations (*voix*) common in the language to which the organ of speech or hearing imperceptibly conforms. Much the same can be said about articulated letters, or consonants.[43]

Rousseau agreed with Lamy that alphabetical letters do not correspond with discrete and unchanging units of sound. Rather, letters designate those sounds that speakers of a language have become accustomed to hearing amidst the unbounded 'nuances' of the human voice. Writing could be called an 'analysis' of speech, as he previously indicated, but it could never be said to 'paint' speech, in all its unbounded complexity. Invented by men of business, and not by grammarians or some linguistic genius, writing was originally meant to fulfil a merely practical end. The first alphabets, like the Phoenician, utilised an exceedingly rough analysis of speech sounds to serve the needs at hand. Only in modern times had grammarians become obsessed with the mistaken conception of writing as a potentially exact image of speech meant originally to 'crystallise' and preserve the component sounds of language.

Jacques Derrida and other scholars have portrayed Rousseau as essentially confirming Aristotle's dictum, at the opening of *De interpretatione*, that 'spoken words are the symbols of mental experience and written words are the symbols of spoken words'.[44] As I have argued, however, Rousseau was in fact drawing away from this conception of the relationship between writing and speech. In *Essai sur l'origine des langues*, he pointed consistently to the ways in which writing fell well short of being a complete and accurate representation of speech. Alphabetical writing, he argued, is not even meant to be a complete 'phonetic' transcription of speech. It only indicates in a general way those sounds that are habitually noticed and imitated in a given language.

This position was still unusual in France. Yet Rousseau was clearly on the leading edge of linguistic thought in insisting on the essential independence of speech and alphabetical writing. J. G. Herder's renowned treatise on language, *Abhandlung über den Ursprung der Sprache* (1772), contains much the same contention that speech sounds are far too varied ever to be reduced to a complete and accurate alphabet. 'There is no language whose living tones can be totally reduced to letters, let alone to twenty,' wrote Herder. Like Rousseau, Herder argued that 'the idiosyncrasies of orthography' could not be eliminated by attempting to make writing an exact copy of speech. Indeed, it was a sign of a truly 'living' language that it was too multifarious and changing ever to be fully captured in letters: 'The more alive a language is – the less one has thought of reducing it to letters, the more spontaneously it rises to the full unsorted sounds of nature – the less, too, is it writable, the less writable in twenty letters.'[45] Herder and Rousseau were of one mind in rejecting the belief that writing could ever adequately perform its supposed task of 'painting' speech in all its complexity. For Herder, however, this passing observation justified his decision to ignore writing as irrelevant to his study of the natural evolution of language and its relationship with thought. Contrary to what many contemporaries assumed, the invention of letters was by no means an act of brilliant insight beyond the power of humans, unassisted by God. For Rousseau, on the other hand, writing had exercised a significant and disastrous influence on the development of language. It had created the false image of speech as naturally consisting of distinct articulations. And as writing came to dominate over speech in literate cultures, it had ruptured the fluid intonations that were the true source of its expressive power.

WRITING AND PROSODY IN THE *ESSAI*

Rousseau had a second major reason for denying that alphabetical writing could accurately be called a 'depiction' of speech. This concerned the issues of 'tone' and 'accent' treated at length in chapter 7 of the *Essai*, 'De la prosodie moderne'. Derrida has claimed that this chapter was largely 'inspired' by Duclos: 'the borrowings are declared, massive, determining'.[46] We should keep in mind, however, that Rousseau was a composer and musicologist: he had a keen, personal interest in vocal sound, much stronger than that of the grammarian and lexicographer Duclos. In his article 'Accent' in the *Dictionnaire de musique* (1758), for example, Rousseau presented an analysis of prosody which, while it owes something to Olivet's categorisations, shows that Rousseau had thought long and independently on this subject. He distinguished between 'l'accent pathétique oratoire' and 'l'accent grammatical', the latter corresponding to Olivet's 'l'accent prosodique'. But he also added what he called a 'l'accent logique ou rationnel' – a change of tone that indicated the logical connection between terms rather than some emotional state.[47]

Unlike Duclos or Du Marsais, moreover, Rousseau agreed with Olivet that French lacked a 'prosodic' or 'grammatical' accent, a view that he stated with his wonted bluntness: 'we believe that we have accents in our language, although we have none whatsoever. Our supposed accents are nothing but vowels or signs of quantity.'[48] The phrasing of this statement is deceptively sweeping: later, Rousseau made clear that he was referring here only to the 'grammatical' (i.e. Olivet's 'prosodic') accent and not to the 'oratorical' accent. In short, he denied that French words are marked by a regular pattern of tone changes on particular syllables. Expecting that many grammarians would 'tax me with paradoxes' for taking this position, he challenged them to duplicate the sound of French words on a musical instrument. While it might be discovered that French words varied in quantity (duration), this experiment would reveal no changes of tone.[49]

Rousseau seemed anxious to enlist his friend Duclos as an ally on this issue. He inferred, from a passage on Greek prosody in the *Remarques*, that the Perpetual Secretary also denied the existence of a 'musical' accent in French, though he accepted the existence of 'the prosodic and the vocal accents'.[50] In fact, Duclos defined the very word 'accent' as a change of 'tone'. He meant only to show that the accents of French were less marked, and hence less 'musical', than in the ancient languages.[51] Most important, Duclos was enthusiastic about reforming the written accents of French: 'le moyen de marquer exactement la prosodie seroit d'abord d'en déterminer les signes et d'en fixer l'usage, sans jamais en faire d'emplois inutiles' (the means of marking prosody more exactly would be first to determine its signs and to fix their use, without ever employing them uselessly).[52] Rousseau, on the contrary, asserted that 'it is an error to believe that written accents can replace vocal accents'.[53] French *had* no 'settled musical accent' that could be marked. And its present system of written accents, whatever the 'grammarians' might believe, had absolutely nothing to do with changes of tone.

According to Rousseau, the use of written accents could by no means be called a 'perfection' even in languages, like ancient Greek, that had a regular 'musical accent'. This was a position that he took in direct opposition to Du Marsais, whose article on 'Accent' for the *Encyclopédie* is cited in a long note. 'Written accents', replied Rousseau, are 'invented only once vocal accent is lost'. Against Du Marsais, he went on to reaffirm the position of the Port-Royal authors that Greek scribes used accents only for the guidance of the Romans who came to Athens. The Greeks themselves 'had no need of them'.[54] So far from being a perfection of the Greek language in its heyday, then, the accents were meant only for foreigners. And in other languages, such as Hebrew, additional marks were added only when the spoken language started to be forgotten and to degenerate as the result of mixture with other peoples.[55]

In *Essai sur l'origine des langues*, therefore, Rousseau was consistently sceptical with the preoccupation of his learned contemporaries with the improvement of written language. Writing could not possibly duplicate the full range of speech sounds, with all their innumerable 'nuances'. Nor was it of any use in marking accents. There is evidence that Rousseau's ideas about orthographic reform were not fully settled: in the fragment on 'Prononciation', probably a slightly later work, he seemed warmer to the idea that writing should closely duplicate speech. In both the fragment and the *Essai*, however, Rousseau's central criticism was that too much emphasis on the quality of written language had damaged the expressive power of speech.

That language had become less eloquent and musical since the Greeks was a conventional point of view in the mid eighteenth century. On this point, indeed, Rousseau agreed with Du Marsais, who said that ancient Greek pronunciation was 'plus soutenue & plus chantante' (more elevated and song-like). But Rousseau had his own explanation for this phenomenon. Most scholars of his time ascribed the beauties of Greek pronunciation to the diligent study and cultivation of eloquence in ancient Athens. In Rousseau's opinion, on the contrary, the musicality of Greek was due not to art but rather to *nature*. In response to what he perceived as the elitism of French men of letters, with their determination to lead the reform of language and writing, Rousseau quipped that 'in order to cause a language to grow rapidly frigid and monotonous one need only establish academies among the people who speak it'.[56] If 'we are always astounded by the prodigious effects of eloquence, poetry, and music among the Greeks', he wrote later, it is because 'we no longer experience anything like them'. Our ideas of language and melody have so completely changed that no amount of study and training could ever recover the energy and beauty of the ancient tongues.[57]

The beauty of Greek music and eloquence thus resulted from their closeness to the original state of language, before the rise of philosophy and 'sophistry', when people still spoke naturally in a strongly intoned and impassioned tongue.[58] Writing and the literate culture it promoted, including the grammarians and the encyclopedists, had been largely responsible for robbing language of the expressive power it once possessed.

HOW WRITING HAS ALTERED SPEECH

The destructive effect of writing on language is the subject of an important statement at the end of chapter 5: 'Writing, which might be expected to fix language, is precisely what alters it; it changes not its words but its genius; it substitutes precision for expressiveness. One conveys one's sentiments in speaking, and one's ideas in writing.' This is much the same distinction that would be drawn by Thomas

Sheridan in Britain: writing, argued Sheridan, is adequate for reason, but only the tones of speech could convey the passions. Rousseau's explanation for this difference between writing and speech was, however, rather different from Sheridan's. He pointed out that the writer is 'constrained to be clear', for he lacks the resources of tone that can determine the meaning of words exactly as wished. The writer must also use more words to get his meaning across: 'The means to compensate for this feature of spoken language enlarge and stretch written language, and as they pass from books into discourse, they enervate speech itself.' Under the influence of writing, speech not only relies less on accents, becoming monotone and dispassionate, but also more prolix and 'sluggish' (*traintante*). Unlike Sheridan, therefore, who thought mostly of the effect of literacy on pronunciation, Rousseau pointed to how writing changes the very structure of language. As so often in his work, he rivetted on a paradox: writers must strive to be especially clear because written language lacks the ready means to be exact and clear that are available to the speaker.[59]

According to some previous philosophers, such as Condillac, the natural development of language had been towards greater clarity, though at the expense of the greater expressiveness and harmony of primitive speech.[60] This is much like the pattern described by Rousseau. But whereas Condillac had seen both loss and gain in this process, Rousseau saw mostly loss. Language, he said, is now able to convey ideas, but it cannot move the feelings or 'persuade'. This was the complaint being made in Britain by Sheridan and the elocutionists. But Sheridan saw hope for a more passionate eloquence, freed from the deadening spell of writing by the rejuvenation of oratory. Rousseau indicated in the *Essai* that melodic speech had been sickened beyond recovery: 'Popular languages have become as thoroughly useless as has eloquence.' In Rousseau's view, the enfeeblement of eloquence reflected the inherent violence of modern society, its use of 'force' rather than genuine appeals to the natural sentiments of humanity.[61]

Once again, it was Duclos who came into Rousseau's immediate line of fire. Duclos had urged that it was essential to sustain a high level of eloquence in a nation where large groups of people were consulted on matters of public interest. For this reason, the lazy intonation of normal speech could not be allowed to infect the elevated style of the tribune, where words are clearly and distinctly articulated in order to be easily heard by a crowd. Rousseau ended the last chapter of the *Essai* by citing, with some irony, Duclos's musings on how 'les intérêts d'un peuple influent sur sa langue' (the interests of a people influence its language).[62] In Rousseau's view, there seemed to be little need for public eloquence in a nation where 'public force replaces persuasion'. He observed that the demands of a government could be conveyed just as effectively by 'posters on street corners' as by live oratory. He even denied Duclos's view that distinctly articulated speech, 'le discours soutenu', could be heard more easily in large crowds than the natural tones of conversation. 'Among the ancients it was easy to be heard of the people in a public square,' he asserted, evidently thinking of the melodious eloquence of the Greeks. But 'nowadays, an academician who reads a paper at a public session can hardly be heard at the back of the hall'.[63]

Jean Starobinski has noted a significant paradox in this final attack on modern eloquence. Rousseau blamed writing for flattening speech into an inexpressive monotone no longer able to reach a large audience. Yet Rousseau himself was using writing, re-energised in his own passionate and vigorous style, to broadcast his critique of modern language and morals: 'Il désigne, par l'écriture qui fut décriée dans l'*Essai* comme l'ennemie de l'énergie du langage, une voie d'accès vers un nouveau pouvoir politique' (he sets out a route to a new political power with the writing which was decried in the *Essay* as inimical to the energy of language).[64] Rousseau was certainly conscious of the irony of using writing to denounce writing, as it had been brought defiantly to his attention by contemporary opponents. When Rousseau burst into literary notoriety with his 1750 *Discours sur les sciences et les arts*, the work that condemned the 'scourge of letters' for corrupting modern society, he was derided for attacking learning with learning, books with a book.[65] Rousseau was undeterred. As Starobinski notes, the condition of society demanded that one use evil as the means to combatting evil itself.

There are indeed important links between the first *Discours* and Rousseau's attack on writing in the *Essai sur l'origine des langues*. Both works broke with the established view that writing and literacy, with all the arts that they had fostered, were an enormous boon to the moral and physical welfare of civilised people. In questioning this belief, suggesting instead that writing had undermined the health of both language and society, Rousseau was challenging one of the cherished beliefs of the Enlightenment and one of the pillars of the

European scholarly establishment. He summarised his opponents' furious reactions to the first *Discours*: 'How can one possibly trust shocking Writers who dare to praise barbarians unable to read or write!'[66] Yet the audacious Jean-Jacques was doing just that, adding his voice to a historic debate concerning the virtues and evils of the literate culture now established in Europe.

ROUSSEAU AND THE SCOURGE OF 'LETTERS'

As I have argued, Rousseau's disparagement of writing in the *Essai* was directed specifically against linguistic doctrines championed within the Académie Française. Against Duclos, Du Marsais and the 'academicians', he denied that writing could be made an accurate copy of speech. The very preoccupation with this cause of perfecting orthography, he argued, had led his contemporaries to neglect the cultivation of the natural powers of speech. They thought too much about how language was *written* rather than spoken. But this was certainly more than just a linguistic issue for Rousseau. Jean Starobinski has traced the philosophical and psychological roots of Rousseau's outbursts against writing: Rousseau disliked all kinds of 'supplementation' and all instituted signs – particularly written signs, which he considered further removed from the natural origin of speech and from gesture and facial expression, the natural language of the body.[67] This rejection of writing was not without complicated exceptions. Distrustful of his ability to make his true nature known in speech, he turned to writing in the *Confessions* to reveal himself as completely as possible while also, paradoxically, hiding himself from the world. Writing permitted him to order his thoughts and recover his memories in a way impossible in speech.[68] Still, as Starobinski shows, Rousseau's writing style exudes nostalgia for the primitive, 'sung-speech' idealised in the *Essai sur l'origine des langues*. Only that lost idiom achieved Rousseau's ideal of total 'transparency'.[69]

Rousseau's deprecation of writing is closely connected as well with his general challenge to the belief that 'letters' – the arts and sciences made possible by the invention of writing – had made Europeans happier and wiser than all other peoples of the world. In the first *Discours*, books are indicted for undermining religion and patriotism, for engendering artificial desires, and, above all, for distracting people from the 'principles engraved in all hearts'.[70] Instead of attending to the voice of conscience, even the vulgar idly debated abstract theories of right and wrong. The same bad effects of written language are condemned in Rousseau's educational treatise *Émile*. 'I hate books,' he asserts there. 'They only teach one to talk about what one does not know.'[71] A major principle of this treatise is that the child should be taught through experience, 'the book of nature', rather than with the books of philosophers and moralists.[72] Convinced that uncorrupted 'nature' is the true well-spring of wisdom, Rousseau drew a provocative contrast between the modern literati and the unlettered wisdom of 'savage' peoples. 'There are certainly more errors in the Academies of Science,' he declared, 'than in a whole nation of Hurons.'[73]

No author of the age raised such a storm with such outrageous affronts to the lettered establishment. But Rousseau was not alone in questioning the virtues of literate society, or in indicating that 'the noble savage' was all the wiser and happier for lacking alphabetical writing. This condition of noble illiteracy was, for example, forcefully depicted early in the century by the Baron de Lahontan in his accounts of his travels to North America. An army officer serving in eastern Canada between 1683 and 1693, Lahontan recalled the Iroquois people of this region not as brutes or barbarians, but as 'Natural Philosophers' living in happiness and virtue, endowed with 'a perfect Mechanism' of 'Laws, Judges, and Priests'.[74] Anticipating Rousseau's vision of primitive innocence half a century later, Lahontan suggested that the people of North America had actually benefited from their lack of writing and all the arts and sciences. This case against 'letters' is made in an obviously fictionalised dialogue, published in 1704, with a Huron chief named 'Adario'. Adario is visiting France, and is profoundly unimpressed, despite the best efforts of the Baron's fatuous and boastful narrator to persuade him of the glories of European life. 'I would give a hundred Beaver Skins that you could Read and Write like a *Frenchman*,' declares this narrator. 'Had you that Qualification, you would not so shamefully contemn the happy Condition of the *Europeans*.'[75] But Adario refuses to admit that his nation would benefit from literacy. Citing the unhappiness and corruption caused by law-suits, *billets doux* and immoral books, he argues that the French have suffered rather than gained from knowing letters:

Every Day gives us fresh Instances of an infinity of Disputes among the *Coureurs de Bois* upon the account of *Writings*, which tend to nothing but Litigiousness and Law Suits. One bit of Paper is enough to ruin a whole

Family. With a slip of a Letter a Woman betrays her Husband, and concerts ways to have her turn serv'd; a Mother sells her Daughter, and a Forger of Writings cheats whom he pleases. In your Books which are publish'd every Day, you write Lies and impertinent Stories.[76]

Nor would the simple and virtuous life of the Hurons be made better or easier by the possession of letters. They do not need the lettered arts of geography, astronomy and navigation, for they move about their territory with a sureness that astonishes even the Europeans. Since the Hurons have 'a Community of Goods', they have no need for the apparatus of contracts, property laws and law-suits. And without letters, they perform all their ceremonies of war and diplomacy, treaties and pledges.[77] Lahontan was among the first travellers to describe 'wampum', ceremonial belts of coloured shells, used by the native peoples in place of formal contracts and treaties.[78]

Nor had the language of the 'noble savage' suffered through the lack of writing. Eighteenth-century accounts of the New World abounded with praise for the impassioned natural eloquence of native peoples. Their oratory, a central feature of tribal assemblies, even reminded Europeans of the oratory of the Greeks and Romans. Joseph François Lafitau, a Jesuit who lived with the Iroquois between 1712 and 1718, observed that the eloquence of native orators did not 'consist of long harangues, composed on the model of Demosthenes or Cicero. The Iroquois, like the Lacedaemonians, wish a quick and concise discourse. Their style is, however, full of figures of speech and quite metaphorical; it is varied according to the different nature of business.'[79] According to some authors, such as the Abbé Raynal in *Histoire philosophique et politique des établissemens et du commerce des Européens dans les deux Indes* (1770), even the ordinary language of native Americans was bold and figurative in the style of the epic: 'Their metaphors were bolder and more familiar to them in common conversation, than they are even in epic poetry in the European languages. Their speeches in public assemblies, especially, were full of images, energy, and pathos. No Greek or Roman orator ever spoke, perhaps, with more strength and sublimity than one of their chiefs.'[80] These accounts bolstered the opinion that society had thrived when letters were scarce, as notably in the golden years of Grecian eloquence. It was, significantly, in this context that historians began to consider seriously the possibility that the original epic was indeed the product of a pre-literate culture, as in North America. Rousseau himself proposed in his *Essai* that Homer was illiterate.[81]

And the same case was made convincingly by the Englishman Robert Wood and the German F. A. Wolf before the end of the century.[82]

Rousseau's case against writing thus drew from a number of intellectual currents, all of which had been gaining in force since the beginning of the century. Scholars of language were underlining the importance of intonation, gesture and other features of oral communication that could not be fully duplicated in writing. 'The Age of Sensibility', with its preference for passion over reason, 'nature' over art, offered a fertile context for studies of the 'natural signs' of passion. Increased knowledge of the New World dispelled the image of pre-literate peoples as utterly lawless barbarians. It is distorting to abstract Rousseau's statements against writing from this intellectual context. Contrary to what Derrida claims, Rousseau was not rehearsing a 'logocentric gesture' re-enacted at all times in Western history since Plato, but was militating *against* the belief that writing was a mark of European greatness, the *via magna* to civilisation and enlightenment – a doctrine that held virtually unquestioned authority a century before.

Even in Rousseau's time, furthermore, not every one was prepared to denigrate writing as a corrupting innovation of modern civilisation. The exalted reputation of writing, rich loam of enlightened culture, was widely re-affirmed in the same era, as by Antoine Yves Goguet in *L'origine des lois, des arts et des sciences* (1758). Here is a work without a shadow of sympathy for Rousseau's celebration of oral societies. Give those barbarians an alphabet, Goguet asserted, and they would become as advanced and wise as Europeans: 'If there are still some nations of savages to be seen in both continents, who by their ignorance, fierceness, and barbarity, are a disgrace to human nature, it is owing to their ignorance of the art of writing.' The introduction of writing into these barbaric nations was therefore the key to civilising them: 'Let this art be introduced amongst these ferocious people, let them once apply to the cultivation of letters, they will instantly be humanised.'[83] Goguet's opinions were entirely congenial to a large segment of the Enlightenment intelligentsia, who persisted in expounding the equation between alphabetical literacy and all the moral and intellectual virtues of modern civilisation. It is best to think of the late eighteenth century as a time of intense division and disagreement concerning the merits of written language. Opinions on this issue had become sharply polarised, a stolid reverence for the written word challenged by a new wave of radical scepticism concerning both literacy and the institutions that it fostered.

This polarisation was, however, more characteristic of the late eighteenth century than of the period that immediately followed. In contrast with their more combative predecessors, poets and philosophers of the Romantic period sought to reconcile the virtues of writing and speech, literacy and orality, civilisation and nature. In this effort to summarise and resolve the debate that had gone before, the Romantics represent the culmination of the intellectual process that we have traced from the seventeenth century.

CHAPTER 7

The new mediation: perceptions of writing in the Romantic era

In the early nineteenth century, condemnations of the 'dead letter' and laments for a lost age of orality became less frequent, replaced by a greater willingness to accept the presence of written language in modern culture, and to utilise its special powers and benefits. Thus to portray the Romantics as defenders of writing may surprise some readers. Were not the Romantics deeply unsettled by the innovations and artificiality of modern civilisation? Are not spontaneity, naturalness and passion, the much vaunted powers of living speech, linguistic ideals championed by Romantic poets against the formal and rational principles of the Age of Reason? Yet spontaneity and passion were qualities that the Romantics believed could be achieved in writing as well as speech. They wished not to reject, but above all to re-invigorate written expression. They sought to combine the permanence and universality of written discourse with the immediacy and individuality typical of the living voice.

Romantic authors were thus less inclined to adopt the extreme positions for or against writing that had become so marked in late eighteenth-century philosophy and linguistics. But there remained considerable variation within the range of Romantic thought. The legacy of the old conflicts can be discerned, for example, in the famous exchange between Wordsworth and Coleridge on poetic diction. Wordsworth's defence of spontaneous and passionate diction in the Preface to *Lyrical ballads* recalls the linguistic ideas of Sheridan or Rousseau. Central to Coleridge's critique of Wordsworth, on the other hand, was a strong conviction in the linguistic and social benefits of writing and literacy. Yet behind this dispute lay a more essential agreement concerning the possibility of making written poetry the vigorous medium of the human soul. Nor was this optimism concerning the potential of writing restricted to poets and critics. Philosophers of the same era, such as Degérando and Hegel, praised written language as conducive to the self-conscious habits of mind appropriate to the highest states of spiritual enlightenment. G. W. F. Hegel particularly stands out as a thinker keenly attuned to the momentous developments in the history of writing in his own day. The great theorist of dialectic, Hegel formulated most succinctly the goal of harmonising the powers of writing and speech, and of exploiting both the civilising effects of literacy and the energies of living speech.

SPEECH, ORALITY AND LITERACY IN WORDSWORTH'S CRITICISM AND POETRY

The true poet, wrote Wordsworth in his 1800 Preface to *Lyrical ballads*, is 'a man speaking to men'.[1] It is this tendency to describe poetry as the immediate, oral expression of the author's deepest sentiments that seems most memorable about Wordsworth's literary criticism. Wordsworth sought a 'natural' language expressive of the poet's inner being, 'liveliest thoughts in lively words / As native passion dictates'.[2] He was critical of poets who relied too much on stock phrases culled from literary tradition, and of 'languages that want the living voice / To carry meaning to the natural heart'.[3] As James K. Chandler has pointed out, Wordsworth's poetry often celebrates the rustic wisdom passed down through 'oral record, and the silent heart',[4] the tradition of communal story-telling that Wordsworth revered for its closeness to basic human concerns.[5]

Can we agree, however, that Wordsworth's ideal of poetic language is 'primitivistic',[6] and that his poetic ideas are characterised by a 'deprecation of writing in favour of speech'?[7] This assumption is complicated by Wordsworth's preoccupation with the written text of his poems. A meticulous reviser of his works, Wordsworth also stressed the need for 'minute' textual criticism to the training of the poet.[8] Despite his definition of the poet as 'a man speaking to men', he generally described his poems as written compositions. The subject of the Preface to *Lyrical ballads* is professedly 'the act of *writing* in verse' (my italics).[9] Consider, for example, his famous observation that the overflow of powerful feelings in the best poetry 'takes its origin from emotion recollected in tranquillity'.[10] In this and other statements, he was distinguishing between the kind of feelings ignited by 'real events', and the feelings 'conjured' in the poet's mind 'without external excitement'. A primary difference between the poet and other people, he remarked, was that 'he has added a disposition to be affected more than other men by absent things as if they were present'.[11] Wordsworth was imagining the poet specifically as a writer, composing in privacy and tranquillity, and wilfully producing feelings in himself that only approximated those experienced by ordinary people speaking in response to immediate stimuli.

Thus the 'spontaneity' that Wordsworth praised as the ideal of poetic diction should not be confused with the impassioned immediacy of the actual speaking voice. It is particularly significant that Wordsworth said almost nothing about intonation and gesture or those other features of speech so highly praised by authors of the eighteenth century. It is true that he encouraged 'an animated and impassioned recitation' of his poems.[12] But he also mocked an affected oralism: even the *Iliad*, he remarked, 'would gain little in our estimation from being chanted'.[13] Wordsworth not only accepted the impact of literate culture on his own consciousness, but often suggested that this influence had been beneficial to his development as a poet. In book 8 of *The Prelude*, he recalled how the avid reading of his youth helped to cultivate his mature outlook on the world. Books implanted his 'wilful fancy',[14] the power to populate the natural landscape with the beings of myth and legend. Reading also deepened and enriched the young Wordsworth's perceptions of the world, giving him a sense of the connection between present sensations and 'old usages, and local privileges', the 'colouring of other times'.[15] Most important, he valued books, 'dearest Helpers',[16] for giving him a sensitivity to human concerns, and lending a new beauty even to the city, which had initially struck him only as tawdry and unnatural.[17]

Unlike Rousseau, therefore, Wordsworth did not declaim against the evils of literate culture, or wax nostalgic for a purer, more eloquent time of orality. To reject books, he asserted, 'were to lack / All sense'.[18] Wordsworth's criticism was, instead, concerned with the ways in which the written language of poetry could be rehabilitated from the affectation and conventionality into which it had fallen, and given the liveliness and sincerity of the 'real language of men'. His goal, we might well say, was to combine the qualities of speech with those of writing – immediacy with permanence, personal expression with an audience unlimited by time and place.

This ideal is exemplified by Wordsworth's peculiar interest in cultivating a form of verse previously dismissed as having little artistic value – the inscription. The poem that opens *Lyrical ballads*, 'Lines left on a seat in a yew-tree', derives from this genre of verse inscribed on objects in the natural world, be it a tree, a seat, or a gravestone. The lines directly address the reader in a personal tone – 'Nay! Traveller! rest' – but also form a permanent part of the landscape to which the lines draw attention: 'This lonely Yew-tree stands / Far from all human dwelling: what if here / No sparkling rivulet spread the verdant herb?'[19] Wordsworth would write many more of the same kind of poem over the remainder of his career. What he valued in the inscription was its capacity to bridge the gap between fixity and immediacy, lapidary permanence and impassioned effusion. Indeed, it was much the same paradoxical combination of virtues that Wordsworth sought generally in lyric poetry, a form that he did much to create in its modern form. As Geoffrey Hartman has argued in an essay on Wordsworth's inscriptions, 'the modern lyric attempts the impossible': it is 'a monument to spontaneity, a poem that co-incides with the act and passion of its utterance'. In his effort to achieve this combination, Wordsworth frequently dramatised the very act of writing. In 'Lines left upon a seat', and even in major poems such as 'Tintern Abbey', we seem to witness the poem being composed before our eyes, a pretext that gives the fixed printed text an unprecedented liveliness and directness.[20]

Wordsworth's interest in the inscription helps to explain his lengthy ruminations on gravestone verse in his three 'Essays upon epitaphs', the first of which appeared in 1810 in Coleridge's journal *The Friend*. Wordsworth considered epitaphs an important form of popular poetry exclusive to literate cultures: they were an improvement on the 'rude stones' used to memorialise the dead in 'savage tribes unacquainted with letters'.[21] He had very clear opinions on the kind of subject matter suitable to these inscriptions. Given their public and permanent nature, they could not express merely personal or passing feelings, as might be suitable in an elegiac speech. The very fixity of engraved letters, he contended, made fleeting expostulations unsuitable to epitaphs:

The very form and substance of the monument which has received the inscription, and the appearance of the letters testifying with what a slow and laborious hand they might have been engraven, might seem to reproach the author who had given way upon this occasion to transports of mind, or to quick turns of conflicting passion; though the same might constitute the life and beauty of a funeral oration or elegiac poem.[22]

Whereas passing sentiments were inappropriate, 'commonplace' expressions possessed a durability commensurate with engraved stone. Wordsworth thought of conventional locutions as more appropriate to written rather than oral expression, for they expressed general and lasting truths to people at all times. 'In a permanent Inscription', he wrote, 'things only should be admitted that have an enduring place in the mind.'[23]

On the other hand, Wordsworth disliked inscriptions that seemed artificial and insincere. Commonplaces in epitaphs had to be 'uttered', as he put it, 'in such connection as shall make it felt that they are not adopted – not spoken by rote, but perceived in their whole compass with the freshness and clearness of an original intuition'.[24] This concern to express durable human truths in a way that seemed spontaneous and genuinely felt was consistent with Wordsworth's more general poetic values. Complaining of 'the artifices which have overrun our writings in metre since the days of Dryden and Pope',[25] he argued that too much modern poetry seemed obviously contrived, and to have no connection with the poet's real feelings. But the best epitaphs, like much of the best poetry of any kind, gave 'universally received truths a pathos and spirit which shall re-admit them into the soul like revelations of the moment'.[26] They captured, in a stable and written form, the force and immediacy of feelings 'instinctively ejaculated'.[27]

The poetic virtues outlined in the 'Essays upon epitaphs' reflect Wordsworth's project to combine the powers of writing and the living voice – to address a theoretically unlimited audience in a form that retained the directness and sincerity of speech. The capacity of print to preserve the name and genius of a poet was integral to Wordsworth's understanding of literary art. Aiming to protect the lasting fame of authors, he campaigned diligently, even obsessively, for the extension of copyright protection of an author's works.[28] This preoccupation with the printed text of poetry clearly differentiates his aesthetic outlook from that of Sheridan and the elocutionists. Those theorists valued only the immediate performance. While Wordsworth shared the elocutionists' dislike of artificial language, he also prized the advantages of fixity and universality offered by books, literacy and writing. Unlike his predecessors, he wished not to depreciate writing in favour of speech, but rather to give written expression new energy and greater relevance to human concerns. This objective was widely shared by Wordsworth's contemporaries in the Romantic movement such as Coleridge, who differed from his friend largely in more explicitly and forcefully rejecting the debasement of writing and the nostalgia for an uncorrupted orality.

COLERIDGE'S DEFENCE OF LITERACY

'Civilization, and the conditions under which a people have become progressive and historical, commences with an alphabet, or with some equivalent discovery imperfectly answering the same purpose'.[29] These are the words not of a seventeenth-century explorer or of Samuel Johnson, but of Coleridge in his *Logic*. If Wordsworth tended to highlight the need to make written poetry more like speech, Coleridge's emphasis was just the opposite: he was a strong and consistent advocate of the virtues of writing as a medium of poetic expression and of the benefits of literacy on language and culture. Many before had praised the benefits of literacy. In Coleridge's work, however, we find a new vindication of written language constructed on central principles of Romantic philosophy and linguistics.

In his *Notebooks*, in an entry of 10 March 1818, Coleridge described 'the *steps*, of which the instances are still presented to us in the lower degrees of civilisation – gesticulation and rosaries or Wampum, in the lowest – picture Language – Hieroglyphics – and finally, Alphabetic'. This was the evolution of writing described by Warburton in *The divine legation of Moses*. But Coleridge found an added philosophical significance in this process: it represented, he argued, 'the *translation*, as it were, of Man into Nature'.[30] Contrary to the usual assumption, therefore, Coleridge suggested that the development of writing had brought humans *closer* to 'Nature', rather than further away.

How could this be? In the same notebook entry, Coleridge argued that 'Nature', meaning the external world, was apprehended by the human mind largely by means of the eye. It was the eye that established the memory of things far better than did sound or any of the other senses. Writing thus translated 'man into Nature' by making thoughts visible. More important, however, writing and later civilised arts '[elevate] the Mind by making its feelings the Objects of its reflection'. Writing was, for this reason, 'purely *human*'. The mere expression of 'Passion by the sounds which the Passion itself necessitates' could be accomplished by animals as well as humans. But the act of self-reflection, as facilitated by 'the use of the visible in place of the Audible', was the exclusive and typical prerogative of human nature.[31]

Through the 'steps' that led to the use of alphabetical writing, therefore, humans evolved *towards* – not away from – the realisation of what was most fundamental to their own being. This process is cognate with Coleridge's famous distinction between the 'primary' and the 'secondary' Imagination in chapter 13 of *Biographia literaria*. The 'primary Imagination' is the power by which, in imitation of the divine 'I AM', the human spirit first creates its own identity by distinguishing the thinking self from outward 'Nature'. But this primary act is unconscious, whereas the 'secondary Imagination' is a *conscious* re-enactment of the same self-creating fiat: 'the secondary I consider as an echo of the former, co-existing with the conscious will, yet still as identical with the primary in the kind of its agency, and differing only in degree, and in the mode of its operation'. The secondary Imagination corresponds with the activity of the artist, who wilfully creates an outward world in order to reflect his own being.[32] The same reasoning led Coleridge, in his *Notebooks*, to assert that 'the primary Art is *Writing*'.[33] As the first 'art', writing corresponds with the secondary Imagination. It marks the beginning of the human capacity to reflect rationally on the activities of the human mind that were previously performed unconsciously. As he illustrated in the *Logic*, every school child is able to think abstractly. Only when the child learns 'an alphabet and an accidence', however, does it become conscious of its capacity for abstract thought and thereby achieve the full and unique potential of human intelligence.[34]

These considerations were central to Coleridge's criticism in *Biographia literaria* of Wordsworth's poetics. By 'humble and rustic' people, Coleridge inferred, Wordsworth meant people who had received little education, and who spoke a direct, 'natural' language unchanged by books and literate forms of expression. Was this kind of language likely to be appropriate for the expression of poetic thoughts? That not even Wordsworth really believed this was indicated, in Coleridge's view, by his acknowledgement that he had purified rustic speech of 'all lasting and rational causes of dislike or disgust'.[35] If, as Coleridge assumed, Wordsworth meant that he had purified rustic speech of all 'provincialism and grossness', making it 'consistent with the rules of grammar', he had corrected poetic language according to rules known only through education.[36]

Rustic people, removed from the direct influence of literate society, would also lack the habits of self-reflection that Coleridge believed was the 'primary' and distinctive activity of human intelligence. 'The best part of human language, properly so called', argued Coleridge in an important passage, 'is derived from reflection on the acts of the mind itself.' Such language was found only among the educated: 'it is formed by a voluntary appropriation of fixed symbols to internal acts, to processes and results of imagination, the greater part of which have no place in the consciousness of uneducated man'.[37] This willed language of self-reflection, the 'voluntary appropriation of fixed symbols to internal acts', was contrasted by Coleridge with the involuntary language of passion. He was highly sceptical of the belief that passion, understood in the narrow sense of affections such as 'joy, grief, or anger', was the source of poetic language: 'the property of passion is not to *create*, but to set in increased activity'. Excited passions were indeed more likely to induce 'unmeaning repetitions, habitual phrases and other blank counters' than the kind of stirring eloquence imagined by the elocutionists, whose ideas and practice Coleridge excoriated in a long note. He drew a link between Wordsworth's poetic principles and the error of teachers who 'torment' school children with 'the necessity of reading as they would talk'.[38] Coleridge did agree with Wordsworth that the '*apparent* tautologies of intense and turbulent feeling' could be imitated with success.[39] But he differed from Wordsworth in giving first place to the willed, self-conscious language of the *literate* classes.

It is quite arguable that Coleridge was misrepresenting Wordsworth's meaning in the Preface to *Lyrical ballads*, and that their differences were less significant than he made them appear.[40] There is ample evidence that Wordsworth did not mean to exalt mere passionate expostulations when he set out his ideal of 'the real language of men'. As we have noted, he was not undiscerning of the beneficial influence of literate culture on the poet and on language generally. It is significant, nonetheless, that Coleridge was critical of precisely those parts of Wordsworth's theory that seemed to recall the oralism of late eighteenth-century philosophy and poetics. Nor was Coleridge peculiar in this respect. Both in rejecting the veneration for speech and oral culture, and in defending the importance of writing as a stimulus to the highest human faculties, Coleridge was echoing the views of many critics and philosophers of the Romantic period.

PRAISE FOR WRITING IN THE ROMANTIC ERA

Like Coleridge, Joseph Marie Degérando and William Hazlitt gave a prominent status to writing in their discussions of language, and even indicated that writing was superior to speech for certain purposes. But these authors did not praise writing for exactly the same reasons. Degérando demonstrates the persistence of certain ideas about language and the mind that were fundamentally unchanged since the eighteenth century, though they had been greatly elaborated and refined. Hazlitt, on the contrary, was representative of the new wave of ideas. A major theorist of Romanticism, he demonstrates how an interest in the special properties of writing could support this movement's characteristic values of individuality and originality.

'De tous les systèmes de langage institué', wrote Joseph Marie Degérando in Des signes (1800), 'l'écriture est sans comparaison le plus philosophique, le plus propre à développer en nous les facultés méditatives' (Of all the systems of instituted language, writing is without comparison the most philosophical, the most proper to develop our meditative faculties).[41] Like Coleridge later on, Degérando valued writing because it 'fournit de précieux secours à la faculté de réflexion' (furnishes precious help to the faculty of reflection).[42] Beyond these basic similarities, however, Degérando and Coleridge held very different philosophies of mind and language. Whereas Coleridge was strongly influenced by German transcendental philosophy, Degérando was an important exponent of idéologie, the French empirical philosophy most fully delineated in Antoine Destutt de Tracy's Élémens d'idéologie (1804–15), and derived from the associationist psychology of Condillac. Like Condillac, Degérando believed that the senses were the sole source of all human knowledge: he paid no attention to Kantian demonstrations of the a priori principles of reason or to the German metaphysics that Kant inspired. Also in keeping with Condillac's philosophy, Degérando believed that language played a fundamental role in ordering the sensations. Until humans had use of linguistic signs, they could exert no control over the impressions that flooded into the mind through the senses.

Signs, and particularly *written* signs, 'decompose' our sensations into units, and allow us to direct our thoughts wilfully, free from merely random associations between one sensation and another.

In Degérando's opinion, writing was superior to speech in allowing us to review our words and ideas again and again, sharpening our recognition of their differences and connections, reinforcing the memory and strengthening our control over language:

En arrêtant mes regards sur le papier, je vois simultanément une ligne, une phrase, j'apperçois même les rapports de plusieurs phrases; je saisis quelquefois l'ensemble d'une page entière. Mais je ne puis écouter à-la-fois deux ou plusieurs mots; il me faut les admettre seulement les uns à la suite des autres.

(In scanning the page, I see simultaneously a line, a sentence, I even perceive the relations between several sentences; I sometimes seize the complete sense of the whole page. But when I can only hear two or more words at once, I must consider only one word after another.)[43]

We have seen that previous authors, like Johnson and Priestley, had remarked similarly on the importance of writing in enabling us to reflect on language and by this means to improve and stabilise it. In tracts on education, authors placed a new importance on writing as a mental discipline that, as Mary Wollstonecraft observed in her 1787 defence of female literacy, 'teaches a person to arrange their thoughts, and to digest them'.[44] Degérando thus reflects a growing awareness of how written language influences the mind. Closely anticipating modern theorists of literacy, he argued that philosophers and all educated people reason as they do because they have use of writing.[45]

While both Degérando and Coleridge valued writing as a foundation of philosophical enlightenment, however, they were motivated by very different theories of language and knowledge. For Degérando, written language facilitated the act of reducing sense impressions to order and control; for Coleridge, writing evinced the 'spirit's' entirely free act of self-consciousness, the 'translation' of immaterial intelligence into material 'Nature'. The differences between these authors are revealed by their contrasting attitudes towards the role of writing in poetry. Degérando followed the increasingly hackneyed distinction of mid eighteenth-century linguistics and poetics: writing was the most 'philosophical' language, but speech, being closer to music, addressed the 'soul', and was thus better adapted to poetry and to the expression of passion.[46] But Coleridge did not abide by this old distinction. Coleridge thought of writing as the appropriate medium for poetic expression, for poetry, in his view, was an emanation of the *spirit* and not merely a primitive and spontaneous reflex to heightened passions.

On the role of the passions in poetry, therefore, the characteristically 'Romantic' conception of poetic language was fundamentally different from the so-called 'pre-Romantic' attitude of the late eighteenth century. Although it is true that Wordsworth owed a great deal to the pre-Romantic conception of poetry as the effusion of 'feeling', he thought of great poetry as the product of written composition, the poet's sentiments softened and deepened by memory and the distance of time. 'High' Romantics like Coleridge were even less sympathetic to the eighteenth-century ideal of immediate and impassioned utterance. When Coleridge, Hazlitt and Hegel referred to the spontaneous effusions of 'feeling', they did not mean impassioned cries or 'sung speech' induced automatically by sense impressions, but rather the expression of the most refined faculties of the mind. 'Impassioned poetry', wrote Hazlitt, 'is an emanation of the moral and intellectual part of our nature, as well as of the sensitive.'[47] And it was very much for this reason that they shared little of the hostility to writing and literacy expressed by Rousseau or Sheridan.

With Hazlitt, we must attend to another important change in the way authors of his time were thinking about visual language. Most strikingly, Hazlitt recognised that *print* was an inherently different medium from writing, and that the press had exerted a special influence on society that could never have been exerted by the pen alone. In the seventeenth century, authors conventionally pointed to alphabetical writing as the peculiar mark of a 'civilised' people; in the late eighteenth century, however, many authors were more inclined to portray printing as the primary basis for modern 'progress'. As a future prime minister, William Lamb, Viscount Melbourne, asserted in a 1798 speech at Cambridge, 'before this discovery [of printing], the improvement of mankind could not be termed progressive; it was confined in its operation, and liable to long and frequent interruption'.[48] Hazlitt, a political radical, saw a vivid demonstration of the power of the press in the events of the French Revolution. As he asserted dramatically in the *Life of Napoleon* (1828), 'the French Revolution might be described as a remote but inevitable result of the invention of the art of printing'.[49] He strongly anticipated the views of modern historians like Robert Darnton in stressing the importance of the press in widely disseminating the radical ideas that led to the toppling of the monarchy.[50] His essay 'The influence of books' is a remarkably modern and astute discussion of how the printing press has promoted new political movements, fashions and life-styles, particularly by making new ideas widely available to the public.[51]

The special virtues of writing and print as media of literary expression are the subject of Hazlitt's 1826 essay 'The difference between writing and speaking'. Hazlitt expressed a decided preference for writing over speech because, in his view, it promoted the quintessentially Romantic values of originality and individuality. Unlike the speaker, he observed, 'the writer must be original, or he is nothing'.[52] The writer could not rely on the various tricks available to the public orator to cover up a dearth of original thought. The orator could please 'a gaping multitude' with 'a set of cant-phrases, arranged in sounding sentences, and pronounced "with good emphasis and discretion"'.[53] Hazlitt echoed a criticism often made of Thomas Sheridan's elocutionary teachings – that a preoccupation with stirring delivery encouraged vulgar exhibitionism. The speaker could gesticulate, swagger and roar to impress the audience. But the writer, composing at a desk, was removed from much of this temptation to play to the gallery: 'Nature is his mistress, truth his idol'.[54] The writer was far more likely than the speaker to aim at nothing but the expression of truth in a language selected with the greatest care and sensitivity.

Hazlitt's image of the writer, communing with his soul in the privacy and gloom of his study, is a typically 'Romantic' image. It corresponds with the emerging cult of the isolated poetic genius, and with Hazlitt's definition of poetry elsewhere as 'the universal language which the heart holds with nature and *itself*' (my emphasis).[55] Here, then, was a vindication of the special powers of writing for artistic expression – a vindication based on values of individual expression and self-reflection. But Hazlitt's goal was not to condemn speech, or to argue that visual language could replace speech for all purposes. At many points in his literary criticism, Hazlitt revealed the continuing legacy of late eighteenth-century theories of language, with their characteristic emphasis on the 'melody' of spoken language and on the 'natural' expression of the affections. Rousseau or Sheridan would have applauded his statement that there is 'a near connection between music and deep-rooted passion', or that poetry begins when 'articulation passes into intonation'.[56] But this interest in the expressive power of melody or intonation was combined, in Hazlitt's case, with a heightened value for the contribution of writing to the creative process: reduced in writing to a barely audible murmur, he argued, the music of poetry was more suitable to the 'brooding' emotions linked with the moral faculties and typical of the best art. Writing tempered and restrained the passionate music of language.[57] As he observed in another essay, 'Authors, as they write, may be said to "hear a sound so fine, there's nothing lives 'twixt it and silence"'.[58]

Music on the threshold of silence: this image of a poetic language somewhere *between* writing and speech is the linking thread between the authors that we have considered. The differences between these authors are, indeed, largely differences of emphasis. Wordsworth was more anxious than Coleridge or Hazlitt to underline the necessity of naturalness, directness and passion in an age increasingly dominated by print. But all agreed on the need for a powerful new language for the modern age, both immediate and lasting, 'spoken' and 'written'. Even Coleridge, though a strong defender of the benefits of writing and books, described the ideal 'natural language' as a Golden Mean between writing and common speech, 'neither bookish, nor vulgar, neither redolent of the lamp, or [*sic*] of the kennel'.[59] Despite his criticism of Wordsworth's theories on poetic diction, he greatly admired his friend's poetic practice, and agreed on the need to re-inject vigour and passion into written language.

The ideal combination of writing and speech was, moreover, possible only in *alphabetic writing*. We will recall Coleridge's dismissal of hieroglyphics as merely an early, primitive step towards the alphabet. And a similar indifference to non-alphabetical scripts was characteristic of all the authors that we have mentioned. They pointed, instead, to what Degérando called the 'effets très-heureux qui résultent pour nous de l'association que nous avons établi entre les signes de la parole et ceux de l'écriture' (very happy effects of the association that we have established between the signs of speech and those of writing).[60] Other authors of the same period dwelled on the great inferiority of hieroglyphics to alphabetical writing. According to Antoine Destutt de Tracy, the leading philosopher of *idéologie*, hieroglyphics were 'une véritable langue morte' (a truly dead language).[61] He claimed that hieroglyphics could not possibly increase knowledge, for they could preserve only what was previously known. Where this kind of writing was used, therefore, the mass of the people were utterly ignorant, and laboured under the tyranny of a small elite class of educated people.[62] Such was allegedly the situation in China, whose writing was still confused by Destutt de Tracy and others of his time with 'hieroglyphics'.[63]

Destutt de Tracy insisted strongly on the superiority of speech to all other forms of communication. Articulate sound was humanity's 'natural' medium of language and thought. But a large part of the superiority of articulate sounds to any other kind of communication, such as gestures or inarticulate cries, was precisely that speech could be *written down*: 'les sons ... ont encore une propriété très-précieuse, c'est de pouvoir devenir des signes permanens' (sounds ... have again a very precious property, the power to become permanent signs). Admittedly, gestures or cries could be recorded by means of some kind of notation. But this was really a 'translation' from one medium into another: only speech could be directly represented in a written form that remained firmly attached to its source: 'Tous les signes quelconques, peuvent bien être traduits, mais nuls, excepté les sons, ne peuvent être écrits' (all signs whatsoever can be well translated, but none, except sounds, can be written).[64] Clearly, Destutt de Tracy's main concern was not that writing menaced the purity of speech, and must always remain subservient to the living voice. His point was rather that alphabetical writing fulfilled the destiny of speech. It allowed language to achieve roles that were beyond the powers of speech alone. It refined language, improved the powers of reason, and laid the foundations of an equitable, democratic and civilised culture.

Only in literate cultures, in short, were writing and speech inter-dependent and mutually beneficial. While speech gave writing 'life', writing gave speech precision and range. This harmonious inter-action of writing and speech was a salient theme in the linguistic thought of the most comprehensive and magisterial mind of the early nineteenth century, G. W. F. Hegel.

HEGEL AND THE BENEFITS OF ALPHABETICAL WRITING

Hegel's dominance as an intellectual figure of the Romantic period is due in large part to his capacity to embrace so much of the history of Western thought, and to trace, in convincing fashion, the progress of human arts towards the successful expression of Spirit in the material world. In the history of writing, this progress was towards the invention of alphabetical writing. In dismissing earlier forms of writing, such as hieroglyphics and Chinese characters, as inadequate precursors to the alphabet, Hegel basically re-echoed the opinion of scholars since Warburton. But Hegel was also a distinctively nineteenth-century author in his sharp awareness of the significant and, in his view, beneficial influence of writing on speech, culture and ways of thinking.

Almost all of Hegel's discussions of writing were composed during the final decade before his death in 1831. This was the period when Young and Champollion changed the course of grammatology by determining the true nature of the ancient hieroglyphics. These ancient characters were not mystical symbols, they showed, but a real form of writing that combined ideographic, phonographic and determinative signs. Unlike many others living in the 1820s, Hegel adjusted to this revelation – though incompletely. He still tended to refer to hieroglyphics as if they were some sort of symbolic art form, rather than an actual form of written communication.[65] More seriously, he still used the term 'hieroglyphic' as a virtual synonym for 'ideograph'. Like Destutt de Tracy, he repeated the old mistake of calling Chinese characters 'hieroglyphs'.[66] But this error reflects the endurance of old habits in the early years of a new era. In other respects, Hegel was up to date with modern research, as in his total rejection of the belief that hieroglyphics contained religious or philosophical wisdom. If hieroglyphics seemed mysterious, he asserted, it was merely because the ancient scribes lacked the means of clear expression.[67] Moreover, despite his terminology, he *was* acquainted with the very recent discovery that 'a great part of hieroglyphics are phonetic, that is, express sounds'.[68] Hieroglyphics were not entirely ideographic. Nor indeed were alphabetical systems entirely phonographic, for they contained numerous marks such as punctuation, numbers and other indicators that did not denote sounds. Hegel's commentary thus reflects a historic change in the understanding of writing. The division between ideographic and alphabetical writing, so central to discussions of writing from the Renaissance to the nineteenth century, was breaking down, giving way to a more subtle understanding of the complex nature of all writing systems.

Hegel was nonetheless convinced that largely alphabetical systems represented the last and most successful stage in the evolution of visual language. His reasons for this conclusion, set forth in substantial additions to the 1827 edition of the *Encyclopädie der philosophishen Wissenschaften*, exemplify significant trends in the linguistic thought of the Romantic period. Early hieroglyphical forms of writing were inadequate, he contended, because they were so inflexible to changing ideas and circumstances, new discoveries and progress in all fields of human knowledge:

a comprehensive and fixed hieroglyphic language is ... out of the question, for although general sensuous objects certainly admit of permanent signs, in the case of signs for what is spiritual, progress in the formulation of thought gives rise to the progressive logical development of changing views concerning their inner relationships and so of their nature, and so to the setting in of another hieroglyphic determination.[69]

This statement was aimed primarily at Leibniz, whose philosophical writing, denoting ideas rather than sounds, seemed 'hieroglyphical' to Hegel. His objections were nonetheless pertinent to the entire universal writing tradition of the seventeenth century. Wilkins, Dalgarno, Lodwick and others of that time had aspired, above all, to create a fixed nomenclature that would accurately mirror the equally stable categories of objects and ideas. For Hegel, such an aspiration was contrary to the progressive nature of history, the principle at the foundation of his philosophical edifice. Only speech and alphabetical writing, he reasoned, could be adapted endlessly and easily to the need for new words and expressions.

Hegel shared little of the anxiety of eighteenth-century lexicographers, such as Samuel Johnson, with the need to reduce language to an immovable written standard. He believed that linguistic change was a positive force, a view widely shared by scholars of his time. Coleridge, himself a rich mint of new coinages, often praised the 'organic' nature of language, its cell-like capacity for mutation and growth.[70] Wilhelm von Humboldt stated famously that language 'is no product (*Ergon*) but an activity (*Energia*)' constantly responding to new human needs and development. By freezing this activity at any moment, therefore, writing was always 'an incomplete, mummy-like preservation' of 'living utterance'.[71] But Hegel also recognised important advantages in the institution of a fixed standard of speech sounds. In languages such as Chinese that lacked an alphabet, speakers pronounced their letters indistinctly, he claimed, rendering speech vague and ambivalent. The reliance of the Chinese on vocal tones revealed their failure to achieve the 'determinateness and purity of articulation' characteristic of languages with alphabetical script.[72] Only through the practices of reading and writing does a language become 'cultured'[73] or, as he said elsewhere, 'matured to distinctness'.[74]

In an essay on Hegel's semiotics, and particularly this section of the *Encyclopädie*, Jacques Derrida refers to this philosopher's apprehension of the 'nefarious' influence of writing on speech ('l'influence néfaste de l'écriture sur le langage parlé').[75] It is difficult to see how this description is justified. In contrast with Rousseau, for example, Hegel believed that writing had beneficially influenced language by inducing the sharper articulation of speech and by removing the traces of indistinctness typical of speech before the invention of an alphabet. He placed virtually no importance on intonation or the 'music' of speech as necessary features of communication. This was true even of poetic language, which he believed could be spoken or read without difference of power: poetry derived its effect from its content, not from its sound.[76] In this respect, indeed, Hegel differed from other scholars of poetry in his day who continued to stress the connection between 'music and deep-rooted passion', to cite Hazlitt again. But Hegel was perfectly in accord with Coleridge, Degérando, Hazlitt and others in lauding the enlightenment of literate culture and in pointing to the salutary influence of writing on speech and culture. 'It... follows from what has been said', he concluded, 'that learning to read and write an alphabetical script is to be regarded as an infinitely rewarding means of education.' Writing not only improved speech; it also cultivated the mind, for it facilitated the kind of self-reflective habits that Coleridge had found so crucial to the fulfilment of human potential: 'it leads spirit from what is sensuously concrete into awareness of the more formal nature of the spoken word and its abstract elements, and does what is essential in order to establish and purify the basis of inwardness within the subject'.[77]

Hegel never questioned the primacy of speech as the basis of human communication. 'The spoken language is primary, the main thing being that what is spoken, the word, the tone, should be designated.'[78] But this view was accompanied by no hostility to writing, or anxiety that writing threatened to intrude between the mind and the spoken word. Hegel even pointed out that alphabetical writing itself became a kind of 'hieroglyphics' for skilled readers, who refer directly to the meaning without thinking of speech sounds: 'For us... it becomes a hieroglyphic script, and in using it we do not need to have the mediation of the tones consciously before us, whereas people who are less in the habit of reading will do it aloud in order to catch the meaning in the sound.'[79] Hegel thus admitted the possibility of an immediate link between the grapheme and the mind, especially among the most learned. So far from rehearsing some 'logocentric gesture' played out from Plato to his own day, he closely associated literacy with a self-reflective, philosophical and civilised state of mind. His statements reflect attitudes shared by many contemporaries who had become sceptical of simplistic rejections of writing and who pointed instead to the positive influence of written language on modern speech and culture.

Conclusions: a continuing legacy of debate

I have argued that perceptions of writing in the Romantic era are typified by the effort to mediate the dialectic of opinions for and against writing since the Renaissance. Writing, as we have seen, held an eminent position in the philosophical and linguistic thought of the late Renaissance and seventeenth century. Praised as the greatest of human inventions, writing seemed to many to be superior to speech in its capacity to meet the needs of human communication. This confidence in written language was, however, widely challenged in the eighteenth century by authors who insisted on the special and inimitable powers of the living voice, and who were generally disenchanted with the impact of literacy and books on modern speech and culture. In the Romantic Age, however, there was a reassertion of the value of writing and literacy as means of improving speech and even the mind itself. This is not to claim that the Romantic Age marks a return to the attitudes of the seventeenth century. There was some revived interest in 'pasigraphy' or a new ideographic script, especially in France.[1] But authors of the early nineteenth century were not generally inclined to decry the inaccuracy and mutability of 'vulgar' speech, or to question the primacy of speech as the richest and most accurate medium of expression.

It is commonly said that we remain the heirs of Romantic ideologies and agonies.[2] To what extent, then, have we inherited Romantic ideas about the nature of writing? It should be made clear, first, that the general understanding of the origin and history of writing initially inspired by Warburton, and then confirmed by Young and Champollion, has not changed substantially since the nineteenth century, though archaeological research has contributed a vast wealth of new detail. Research has confirmed that, while phonographic symbols exist even in the earliest forms of writing (excluding pictographs), the alphabet emerged from a long and difficult process culminating in the Greek addition of vowels to Semitic syllabaries. In the scholarship of the twentieth century, there is, however, evidence of a renewed debate about the benefits of that great and continuing legacy of Greek culture, alphabetical literacy. Evidently, Romantic efforts at mediating this conflict, ignited in the Enlightenment, have not succeeded entirely, for modern scholars tend either to extol the virtues of writing or to lament its corrupting effects on modern culture.

The terms of this opposition have not changed greatly since the days of Sheridan, Rousseau and Johnson. On the one hand, modern scholars still portray writing as the primary badge of the 'civilised' world. In the words of the noted decipherer and historian of ancient writing, I. C. Gelb, 'as language distinguishes man from animal, so writing distinguishes civilised man from barbarian'.[3] And within literate communities, the capacity to write and to read is still considered the necessary attribute of 'an intelligent and cultured person'.[4] There remains in much modern scholarship an implicit but intense pride in the Western accomplishment of alphabetical writing, and the feeling that non-alphabetical scripts reflect the failure of the Chinese and other peoples to arrive at a similarly happy destiny.[5] One phalanx of scholars interested in 'print culture', headed by Elizabeth L. Eisenstein, has traced virtually all the intellectual accomplishments of post-Renaissance Europe to Gutenberg's invention and the consequent proliferation of written language.[6]

Yet nostalgia for the innocence and creative fecundity of pre-literate societies has survived as well, constituting a major alternative theme in modern studies of the history of literacy and print. The clarion re-sounded in our century by Harold A. Innis – that writing and later print have always sapped the creative energies of culture, that throughout history, 'the dead hand of the written tradition threatened to destroy the spirit of Western man'[7] – has been echoed with various additional flourishes by a now long line of scholars. The *homo typographicus* of Marshall McLuhan, or the Ramus portrayed by Walter J. Ong, is a cold and abstracted fish, stranded from the 'warm' seas of oral traditions and oral community.[8] One recalls here Lévi-Strauss's fascinated and guilt-ridden observation of a Brazilian tribesman displaying the first symptoms of corruption and tyranny when introduced to writing. 'The primary function of writing', concluded Lévi-Strauss, '... is to facilitate the enslavement of other human beings.'[9] Jacques Derrida has done much to expose knots of illogic and contradiction in this and other condemnations of the written word.[10] Yet his own work is closely related to the tradition of modern scholarship that presents writing as a force of deception and corruption. Against Derrida's vision of Western thought, it needs to be emphasised that the evil reputation of writing represents only half the story. The 'logocentrism' that he describes belongs to a distinct tradition in European thought stemming less from Plato than from philosophers and rhetoricians of the mid and late eighteenth century.

During this era, European scholars became far more keenly attuned to the special powers of the speaking voice and oral communication. There was, indeed, something of a revolution in the study of intonation. Gesture also became a more central issue in linguistic and rhetorical literature. It cannot be said that people in previous centuries were either deaf to the emotive nuances of intonation, or blind to the contribution of the body to effective expression. Never before, however, had scholars studied these forms of communication not as mere rhetorical *additions* to the 'primary' meaning of language, but rather as central, indispensable features of any speech-act. It was, in part, this new sensitivity to the special capacities of oral communication that led to the diminished reputation of written language as a means of human expression. But scholars in the same age also began to recognise that writing had made its imprint even on their own ways of speaking. Was this influence good or bad? What Sheridan or Rousseau decried as the deadening spell of literate culture over expression, the Romantics more often applauded as a force moulding a sharper and more self-reflective language honed to the highest efforts of the human spirit.

We might even say that the late eighteenth century 'invented' our modern ideas of both writing and speech. This kind of sweeping generalisation is perhaps too often and too easily made. Yet an important legacy of eighteenth-century thought is the perception that writing and speech are distinct and dissimilar forms of communication, with quite different powers and functions. 'Writing' and 'speech' gained unprecedented sharpness and definition as linguistic concepts as they became separated in the minds of European scholars. Perhaps Thomas Sheridan can be given the last word on this issue:

These two kinds of language [writing and speech] are so early in life associated, that it is difficult ever after to separate them; or not to suppose that there is some kind of natural connection between them. And yet it is a matter of importance to us, always to bear in mind, that there is no sort of affinity between them, but what arises from a habitual association of ideas. Tho' we cannot so easily separate them in our own minds, yet when we come to separate them in relation to others, we see clearly enough their utter independence of each other.[11]

Even authors who did not share this elocutionist's hostility to writing were arriving at basically the same conclusion that writing and speech should not be confused. In England, evaporating interest in orthographic reform is one important indication of the consensus that writing could never fully duplicate the range and complexity of spoken language. In France, Rousseau's *Essai sur l'origine des langues* offered a similar challenge to the Aristotelian paradigm that presents writing as merely a 'copy' of speech. It is unfortunate that, early in our century, there was some reversion to the old attitude that writing fails as a medium precisely to the degree that it lacks a connection with speech sounds. Reacting against a perceived bias towards written language in nineteenth-century linguistics, Saussure and Jakobson insisted in their influential work on the exclusively 'phonetic' function of writing. Especially in the last forty years, however, linguists such as Joseph Vachek and William Haas have revived and greatly elaborated the conviction that alphabetical writing is an autonomous form of discourse that should not be confused with phonetic transcription.

In the eighteenth century, when this distinction was first formulated, there was a corresponding appreciation of the disparities between 'oral' and 'literate' cultures. Travellers to the New World began to recognise that their ways of life differed, for better or worse, from those of indigenous peoples in large part due to the impact of alphabetical writing. Scholars of language and *belles-lettres* began to differentiate between characteristically 'oral' and 'literate' modes of expression. Here again, the legacy of eighteenth-century thought continues in our time. But our own strong awareness of how writing and print influence culture needs also to be adjusted in the light of what we find in the seventeenth and eighteenth centuries. The general assumption of recent studies seems, initially, absolutely logical and straightforward: cultures dominated by visual media become more 'visual' in all their ways of considering language and the world, and more prone to think about language as it exists on the page rather than in oral exchange. Yet, on the contrary, scholars of the Renaissance and seventeenth century were far more inclined to think about language in specifically visual or written terms than were scholars of the mid eighteenth century. And eighteenth-century grammarians, rhetoricians and philosophers became sensitised to the special powers of speech, as well as to the unique advantages of 'orality', at precisely the time when their society was becoming dominated by books and other printed materials.

The history of European thought, in short, seems to cast doubt on the supposed correspondence between 'print culture' and the deadening of aural sensitivity – what McLuhan, echoing Yeats, called the 'Lockean swoon...induced by stepping up the visual component in experience until it filled the field of attention'.[12] It is true, as recent scholars have stressed, that even the elocutionists in fact 'textualised' the voice, making it the subject of philosophical analysis and certain written rules. But we should not forget that the primary aim of this movement was to recover the power and expressiveness that spoken language had lost, allegedly through the dominance of written texts. During the age of print, the direction of European scholarship on speech and sound is far better described as an 'awakening' than as a 'swoon'.

This pattern of change is, however, not so paradoxical as might at first appear. Predominately oral cultures are less aware of speech and orality because they do not generally reflect on language in literate and deliberate ways. In worlds where writing and books are rare – as was still the case even in the early seventeenth century – visual communication seems wondrously charged with as yet unrealised powers. But the mystique of writing is dispelled by the growth of literacy and reduction of books to mundane, domestic objects. In the eighteenth century, a greatly enlarged community of scholars achieved an ever more detailed and refined consciousness of language and culture. The effects of literacy were evident at every street corner. The differences between writing and speech, 'literate' and 'oral' worlds, became increasingly difficult to ignore.

And with the decline of the old oral ways of life came, inevitably, the pangs of nostalgia, loss and self-doubt. Condemnations of writing common in the late eighteenth century, the 'counter-Enlightenment', form part of a far broader disenchantment with European institutions, science, values and 'progress'. They reflect a backlash against the lofty status of alphabetical writing as the very emblem of civilisation, inventive genius and the wonders of the West. Beneath our ongoing debate concerning the benefits or dangers of writing, in short, lies a much deeper conflict – a conflict rooted in the extremely divided and ambivalent feelings of post-Enlightenment Westerners about their own civilisation. Pride and revulsion at the technological power of the West are the alternative moods of our consciousness, often displayed in the statements of a single author. Now, of course, our technologies infinitely exceed the first scratching of symbols in ancient Sumeria and Egypt: not only writing, but all kinds of activities and products from industry to television, automobiles to pesticides, are *pharmakon* – both remedy and poison. Yet writing has retained its traditional reputation as 'the primary Art', as Coleridge put it, the source of all the arts and sciences, all of 'civilisation'. Introduction to Western values and ideals still begins with a wobbly letter inscribed on a piece of paper, the slight but powerful fulcrum of modern culture with all its hopes and dangers.

In conclusion, the years 1600 to 1830 were the scene of dramatic changes in the ways European scholars understood written language – changes that still determine our outlook today. The nature and status of written language were re-evaluated in part as the result of significant advancements in linguistic scholarship: scholars simply learned more about both writing and language, and particularly about the limitations of writing in comparison with speech. But the transition of attitudes to writing was also caused by the emergence of new values and more critical appraisals of European life. The bright optimism of seventeenth-century science in technology and progress continued to shine throughout the Enlightenment, but became increasingly shadowed by doubts. Writing, invention of Hermes, father of arts and sciences, became the battleground for a wider debate concerning the very nature of Western civilisation, good or evil, bringer of light or corrupter of innocence.

Notes

INTRODUCTION

1 Quoted in William Massey, *The origin and progress of letters* (London, 1763), p. 4, n.

2 See Harvey J. Graff, *The literacy myth: literacy and social structure in the nineteenth-century city* (New York: Academic Press, 1976), preface, pp. xii–xvii, and *The legacies of literacy* (Bloomington: Indiana University Press, 1987), pp. 3ff. Of the vast range of works that have generally stressed the enlightening and progressive influence of literacy, writing and print, the following may be mentioned as representative: James Henry Breasted, *The conquest of civilisation*, (3rd edn, New York and London: Harper and Brothers, 1954), pp. 57–61; A. C. Moorhouse, *The triumph of the alphabet* (New York: Henry Schuman, 1953), pp. 178–215; David Diringer, *Writing* (London: Thames and Hudson, 1962), pp. 13–19; Lawrence Stone, 'Literacy and education in England 1640–1900', *Past and Present* 42 (1969), 69–139; Jack Goody, *The domestication of the savage mind* (Cambridge: University Press, 1977); Elizabeth L. Eisenstein, *The printing press as an agent of change*, 2 vols. (Cambridge: University Press, 1979), *Print culture and Enlightenment thought* (Chapel Hill: University of North Carolina Press, 1986).

3 Derrida's historical thesis concerning the 'logocentric' nature of Western thought is laid out most fully in the opening section, 'Writing before the letter', in *Of grammatology*, tr. Gayatri Chakravorty Spivak (Baltimore and London: Johns Hopkins University Press, 1974), pp. 3–93. For detailed discussion of the theme of writing in Derrida's philosophy, see Christopher Norris, *Derrida* (Cambridge, MA: Harvard University Press, 1987), pp. 28–141; Christopher Johnson, *System and writing in the philosophy of Jacques Derrida* (Cambridge: University Press, 1993). Many modern scholars of literacy – including Innis, MacLuhan, Ong and Havelock – have pointed to the alienating effects of literacy on culture. This debate will be discussed more fully in the final chapter.

4 Josef Vachek's major papers are collected in *Written language revisited*, ed. Philip A. Luelsdorff (Amsterdam and Philadelphia: John Benjamins, 1989). See also Dwight L. Bolinger, 'Visual morphemes', *Language* 22

(1946), 333–40; William Haas, *Phono-graphic transcription* (Manchester: University Press, 1970); Naomi S. Baron, *Speech, writing, and sign* (Bloomington: Indiana University Press, 1981), pp. 149–200.

5 On the growth of literacy in England and France of the eighteenth century, see Stone, 'Literacy and education in England', pp. 69–139; Carlo M. Cipolla, *Literacy and development in the West* (Harmondsworth: Penguin Books, 1969); François Furet and Jacques Ozouf, *Lire et écrire: l'alphabétisation des français de Calvin à Jules Ferry* (Paris: Les Éditions de Minuit, 1977); David Cressy, *Literacy and social order: reading and writing in Tudor and Stuart England* (Cambridge: University Press, 1980); Harvey J. Graff (ed.), *Literacy and social development in the West: a reader* (Cambridge: University Press, 1981), and *Legacies of literacy*, pp. 108–257; David Vincent, *Literacy and popular culture* (Cambridge: University Press, 1989).

6 See Marshall MacLuhan, *The Gutenberg galaxy* (Toronto: University Press, 1962); Walter J. Ong, *Ramus, method, and the decay of dialogue* (Cambridge, MA: Harvard University Press, 1958), *Rhetoric, romance and technology* (Ithaca and London: Cornell University Press, 1971), *Orality and literacy* (London and New York: Methuen, 1982).

7 On Medieval attitudes to writing and books, and the gradual demystification of the written word, see Ernst Robert Curtius, *European literature and the Latin Middle-Ages*, tr. Willard R. Trask (New York: Pantheon Books, 1953), pp. 303–46; Michael T. Clanchy, *From memory to written record: England 1066–1307* (2nd edn, Oxford and Cambridge, MA: Blackwell, 1993).

8 On the use of ceremonial emblems and marks in cultures where literacy is rare, see Clanchy, *From memory to written record*, pp. 254–60; Jack Goody, 'Introduction', in *Literacy in traditional societies* (Cambridge: University Press, 1968), pp. 11–20.

9 Jean-Jacques Rousseau, *Émile*, tr. Allan Bloom (New York: Basic Books, 1979), bk. 4, p. 303.

CHAPTER 1 SACRED AND OCCULT SCRIPTS IN THE RENAISSANCE TRADITION

1 Giorgio de Santillana, review of Frances A. Yates, *Giordano Bruno and the hermetic tradition*, in *American Historical Review* 70 (1965), 455.

2 On writing and education in the Renaissance, as influenced by Humanism and other factors, see Kenneth Chandler, *Education in Renaissance England* (London: Routledge and Kegan Paul; Toronto: University Press, 1965); Joan Simon, *Education and society in Tudor England* (Cambridge: University Press, 1966); Rosemary O'Day, *Education and society 1500–1800: the social foundations of education in Early Modern Britain* (London and New York: Longman, 1982), pp. 9–42.

3 See Frances A. Yates, *The occult philosophy in the Elizabethan Age* (London, Boston and Henley: Routledge and Kegan Paul, 1979), p. 1. Yates

clarifies here that 'hermetic-cabalist' is more accurate than her former term, 'hermetic', to denote the range of interests in occult philosophy of the Renaissance.

4 Herodotus, *Works*, tr. Henry Cary (London: George Bell and Sons, 1917), bk. 2, ch. 36, p. 108.

5 Diodorus of Sicily, *Library of history*, tr. C. H. Oldfather and Francis R. Walton, 12 vols. (Loeb Classical Library, London: William Heinemann; Cambridge, MA: Harvard University Press, 1933–67), bk 3, ch. 3, 2:95.

6 'Trois sortes d'écriture: épistolographique, hiéroglyphique, symbolique'. Porphyry, *La vie de Pythagore*, tr. E. des Places (Paris: Société d'Édition Les belles lettres, 1982), p. 41.

7 Clement of Alexandria, *Stromata*, in *The Writings of Clement of Alexandria*, tr. William Wilson, 2 vols. (Edinburgh: T. and T. Clark, 1867–9), bk 4, ch. 4, 2:233.

8 *Ibid.*, bk 5, ch. 2, 2:233.

9 See *ibid.*, bk 5, ch. 7, 2:245.

10 See A. J. Festugière, *La révélation d'Hermès Trismégiste* (Paris: Libraire Lecoffre, 1950), pp. 74–5.

11 See Manetho, *Works*, tr. W. G. Wadell (Loeb Classical Library, London: William Heinemann; Cambridge, MA: Harvard University Press, 1940), p. 211; Eusebius of Cæserea, *Evangelicæ Præparationis*, tr. (from Greek) E. H. Giffort, S. T. P. (Oxford, 1903), 31d–36a. Eusebius was actually recounting the report of Philo Byblius, as described in Porphyry's lost work, *Against the Christians*. This account distinguished between 'Taautus', inventor of the alphabet, and Hermes Trismegistus, inventor of hieroglyphics.

12 Cited by G. H. Gombrich, '*Icones symbolicæ*: the visual image in neo-platonic thought', *Journal of the Warburg and Courtauld Institutes* 48 (1948), 172.

13 See Michel Foucault, *The order of things* (New York: Vintage, 1970), pp. 17–45.

14 Sir Thomas Browne, *The major works*, ed. C. A. Patrides (Harmondsworth: Penguin Books, 1977), p. 428. The composition of *Christian morals* is of uncertain date; it was first published posthumously in 1716.

15 See Gombrich, '*Icones symbolicæ*', 163–92.

16 For a clear statement of this distinction, see Athanasius Kircher, *China Monumentis* (Amsterdam, 1667), p. 234.

17 Gombrich, '*Icones symbolicæ*', 163.

18 George Boas's introduction to his edition of *Hieroglyphics* (New York: Pantheon Books, 1950) is the best source for information on the nature of this work, and its importance in Renaissance thought. See also Karl Giehlow, 'Die Hieroglyphenkunde des Humanismus', *Jahrbuch der Kunsthistorishen Sammlungen des Allerhöchsten Kaiserhauses* 32 (1915), 1–218; Erik Iversen, *The myth of Egypt and its hieroglyphs* (Copenhagen: Gec Gad, 1961), pp. 57–87; Charles Dempsey, 'Renaissance hieroglyphic studies

and *Saint Mark preaching in Alexandria*', in Allen G. Debus and Ingrid Merkel (eds.), *Hermeticism and the Renaissance* (Washington: Folger Shakespeare Library; London and Toronto: Associated University Presses, 1988), pp. 342–65.

19 Horapollo, *Hieroglyphics*, bk 2, ch. 67, p. 100.

20 *Ibid.*, bk 2, ch. 65, p. 99.

21 Francesco Colonna, *Hypnerotomachia, or the strife of love in a dreame*, tr. 'R. D.' (London, 1592; facs. repr. Delmar, NY: Scholars Facsimiles and Reprints, 1973), p. 42.

22 John Dee, *Monas hieroglyphica*, tr. C. H. Josten, in *Ambix: Journal of the Society of Alchemy and Early Chemistry* 12 (1964), p. 147. Dee's monad was extremely influential on later scholars, as noted by Frances A. Yates in *The Rosicrucian enlightenment* (London and Boston: Routledge and Kegan Paul, 1972), p. 39. See also Peter J. French, *John Dee: the world of an Elizabethan magus* (London: Routledge and Kegan Paul, 1972), pp. 76–81; Nicholas H. Clulee, *John Dee's natural philosophy: between science and philosophy* (London and New York: Routledge, 1988), pp. 77–142.

23 Dee, *Monas hieroglyphica*, p. 171.

24 See Josten's introduction to *Monas hieroglyphica*, p. 105.

25 Henry Cornelius Agrippa, *Three books of occult philosophy* (London, 1651), p. 437.

26 See *Ibid.*, pp. 161–3.

27 'Eux aussi, les signes, les caractères, et les lettres ont leur force et leur efficacité.' Paracelsus, *Les sept livres de l'archidoxe magique* (Paris: Librairie du Merveilleux P. Dujos & A. Thomas, 1909), p. 21.

28 'La nature et l'essence propre des métaux, l'influence et le pouvoir du Ciel et des Planètes, la signification et la disposition des caractères, signes et lettres.' Paracelsus, *Septs livres*, p. 21.

29 On Kircher's life and work, see P. Conor Reilly, S. J., *Athanasius Kircher, S. J.: master of a hundred arts, 1602–1680* (Wiesbaden and Rome: Edizioni del Mondo, 1974); Joscelyn Godwin, *Athanasius Kircher: a Renaissance man and the quest for lost knowledge* (London: Thames and Hudson, 1979), pp. 5–24. More specifically on Kircher's place in the history of decipherment, see Iversen, *The myth of Egypt*, 89–98; Madeleine V.-David, *Le débat sur les écritures et l'hiéroglyphe aux XVIIe et XVIIIe siècles* (Paris: S.E.V.P.E.N., 1965), pp. 43–56.

30 On Casaubon's importance, see Frances A. Yates, *Giordano Bruno and the hermetic tradition* (London: Routledge and Kegan Paul, 1964), pp. 398–403; Garth Fowden, *The Egyptian Hermes: a historical approach to the late pagan mind* (Cambridge: University Press, 1986), p. xiv. For an example of continuing belief in the historical existence of Hermes, see John Jackson, *Chronological antiquities*, 3 vols. (London, 1752), 3:91–5; Thomas Astle, *The origin and progress of writing* (1784), 2nd edn (London, 1803), pp. 31–5.

31 See Athanasius Kircher, *Obeliscus pamphilius* (Rome, 1650), pp. 398–422.

32 See Athanasius Kircher, *Prodromus coptus sive ægyptiacus* (Rome, 1636), p. 260.

33 See Athanasius Kircher, *Œdipus ægyptiacus*, 4 vols. (Rome, 1652–4), 4:42–55. This section is repeated in Kircher's later book on the history of language and writing, *Turris Babel, sive archontologia* (Amsterdam, 1679), pp. 177–83.

34 On the connection between the Jesuits and mystical philosophy in the seventeenth century, see Yates, *The Rosicrucian enlightenment*, p. 230.

35 Cited in Joseph Leon Blau, *The Christian interpretation of the cabala in the Renaissance* (Port Washington: Kennikat Press, 1944), p. 24. For detailed discussion of Pico's cabalism and its sources, see Chaim Wirszubski, *Pico della Mirandola's encounter with Jewish mysticism* (Cambridge, MA and London: Harvard University Press, 1989).

36 Blau, *The Christian interpretation of the cabala*, p. 114.

37 Cited in Gershom G. Scholem, *Major trends in Jewish mysticism* (New York: Schocken Books, 1961), p. 76.

38 This was the doctrine of the thirteenth-century Spanish cabalist Abraham ben Samuel Abulafia. See *Ibid.*, p. 145.

39 See Leo Schaya, *The universal meaning of the kabbalah*, tr. Nancy Pearson (London: George Allen and Unwin, 1971), p. 18.

40 Claude Duret, *Thrésor de l'histoire des langues de cest univers* (Cologne, 1613), pp. 21–2.

41 On the Oral and Written Torah, with relation to cabala, see Gershom G. Scholem, *On the kabbalah and its symbolism*, tr. Ralph Manheim (New York: Schocken Books, 1956), pp. 47–50.

42 Alexander Top, *The oliue leafe; or universall abce* (London, 1603), sig. B2^v.

43 *Ibid.*, sig. A4^v.

44 See *Ibid.*, sig. B3^v–B4^r.

45 See Kircher, *Œdipus ægyptiacus*, 2:43–122; *Turris Babel*, pp. 153–67.

46 On Fludd's life and work, see Yates, *Rosicrucian enlightenment*, pp. 70–90 and 111–13; Serge Hutin, *Robert Fludd* (1570–1637): *alchimiste et philosophe rosicrucien* (Paris: Les Éditions de l'Omnium Littéraire, 1971).

47 Robert Fludd, *De præternaturali utriusque mundi historia*, in vol. 2 of *Utriusque cosmi, maioris scilicet et minoris, metaphysica, physica*, 2 vols. (Frankfurt, 1617–21), p. 2.

48 See the very similar description of the creation of the Hebrew letters in the first section 'Bereshith' of the *Zohar*, the huge and eclectic compendium of cabalistic teaching, 16b.

49 Fludd, *De præternaturali*, p. 7.

50 For Fludd's whole discussion of the relationship between the universe and Hebrew letters, which I have only sketched out here, see *ibid.*, pp. 2–33.

51 Dee, *Monas hieroglyphica*, p. 123.

52 See Fludd, *De præternaturali*, p. 82.

53 See, for example, Marin Mersenne's disdainful criticisms of Fludd's

speculations about the significance of Hebrew letters in *Traité de l'harmonie universelle* (Paris, 1627), pp. 421–2.

54 See Scholem, *On the kabbalah*, p. 11.

55 Jacob Boehme, *Mysterium magnum* (London, 1654), p. 160.

56 *Ibid.*, p. 242.

57 *Ibid.*, p. 161. On God's 'playing' on the 'signatures' of nature and the human spirit, see *Signatura rerum, or the signature of all things* (London, 1651), p. 2 and *passim*.

58 Boehme, *Mysterium magnum*, p. 170.

59 *Ibid.*, p. 228.

60 See *ibid.*, pp. 227–8.

61 On the popular cabalism of English sectaries in the Civil War and Commonwealth years, much of it influenced by Boehme, see Nigel Smith, *Perfection proclaimed: language and literature in English radical religion, 1640–1660* (Oxford: Clarendon Press, 1989), pp. 268–307. Boehme's own hostility to 'the dead letter' of Scripture reflects the mystical calvinism of his native Silesia, as remarked by Alexandre Koyré, in *La philosophie de Jacob Boehme* (New York: Burt Franklin, 1968), p. 7.

62 See N. Smith, *Perfection proclaimed*, pp. 288–94; Richard L. Greaves, *The Puritan revolution and educational thought* (New Brunswick, NJ: Rutgers University Press, 1969), pp. 80–4; Allen G. Debus, *Science and education in the seventeenth century: the Webster-Ward debate* (London: Macdonald; New York: American Elsevier, 1970), pp. 33–64.

63 These are the nine languages used in one of the great works of Anglican theology in the seventeenth century, the *Biblia sacra polyglotta* by Brian Walton, *ex officio* Bishop of Chester during the Interregnum. Against the belief that all these translations of the Bible were necessary to determine its original meaning, Robert Owen, Puritan Chancellor of Oxford University, contended that *only* the Hebrew version was directly dictated by the Holy Spirit, and that it should therefore be relied on before all other versions. See *Of the divine original, authority, self-evidencing light, and power of the Scriptures* (Oxford, 1659). Owen, in turn, was answered by the Quaker Samuel Fisher, who argued that no literal interpretation of the Bible was reliable without the direct and constant inspiration of the Spirit in the soul of the reader. See *Rusticus ad academicos* (London, 1660).

64 John Webster, *Academiarum examen, or the examination of the academies* (London, 1654), p. 18.

65 *Ibid.*, p. 8.

66 *Ibid.*, p. 24.

67 Seth Ward, *Vindiciæ academiarum, containing some briefe animadversions on Mr. Websters book* (London, 1654), p. 5.

68 *Ibid.*, p. 18.

69 *Ibid.*

CHAPTER 2 THE DEMYSTIFICATION OF WRITING IN THE SEVENTEENTH CENTURY

1 Frances A. Yates, *The art of memory* (London: Routledge and Kegan Paul, 1966), p. 234. See also French, *John Dee*, p. 144.

2 William Eamon, 'From the secrets of nature to public knowledge', in David C. Lindberg and Robert S. Westman (eds.), *Reappraisals of the scientific revolution* (Cambridge: University Press, 1990), pp. 333–65. See also Paolo Rossi, *Francis Bacon: from magic to science*, tr. Sacha Rabinovitch (London: Routledge and Kegan Paul, 1968), 27–31, and Martin C. Elsky's discussion of 'the transformation of the hieroglyphical tradition', as evidenced particularly by Bacon's works, in *Authorising words: speech, writing, and print in the English Renaissance* (Ithaca and London: Cornell University Press, 1989), pp. 147–83.

3 Paul Cornelius has discussed the debate concerning the primacy of Hebrew or Samaritan in *Languages in seventeenth- and early eighteenth-century imaginary voyages* (Geneva: Libraire Droz, 1965), pp. 5–23.

4 John Wilkins, *An essay towards a real character and a philosophical language* (London, 1668), p. 11. Wilkins was reasserting the defence of the primacy of Hebrew made by the Dutch Protestant scholar Hugo Grotius in *De veritate religionis christianæ* (Paris, 1627), bk 1.

5 Hermannus Hugo, *De prima scriblendi origine* (Antwerp, 1617), p. 29.

6 *Ibid.*, p. 42.

7 See *Ibid.*, pp. 78–9.

8 Wilkins, *Real character*, p. 365.

9 See *Ibid.*, p. 11.

10 See Brian Walton, *Biblia sacra polyglotta*, 9 vols. (London, 1659), 'prolegomena', 1:8.

11 Richard Simon, *A critical history of the Old Testament* (1678; tr. London, 1732), p. 155. See also Spinoza's denunciation of 'Kabbalistic triflers' in *Tractatus theologico-politicus* (1670), in *The chief works of Benedict de Spinoza*, tr. R. H. M. Elwes (London: George Bell and Sons, 1891), p. 140.

12 Thomas Sprat, *The history of the Royal-Society of London* (London, 1667), p. 5.

13 *Ibid.*, p. 40.

14 *Ibid.*, p. 22.

15 Edward Stillingfleet, *Origines sacræ, or a rational account of the grounds of Christian faith* (London, 1662), p. 103.

16 Joannes Amos Comenius, *Linguarum methodus novissima* (1649), in *Opera didactica omnia*, 2 vols. (Amsterdam, 1657), 1:27.

17 Stillingfleet, *Origines sacræ*, p. 19.

18 Wilkins, *Real character*, p. 10. See Cicero, *Tusculan disputations*, tr. J. E. King (Loeb Classical Library, Cambridge, MA.: Harvard University Press; London: William Heinemann, 1927), bk 1, ch. 25, p. 73.

19 See Walton, *Biblia sacra polyglotta*, 'prolegomena', 1:6.

20 Galileo Galilei, *Dialogue concerning the two chief world systems*, tr. Stillman Drake, 2nd edn (Berkeley, Los Angeles and London: University of California Press, 1967), first day, p. 105. See also *Dialogo sopra i due massimi sistemi del mondo* (1632), in *Opere*, 20 vols. (Firenze: G. Barbera, 1929–39), 7:130–1.

21 Thomas Hobbes, *Leviathan* (Oxford: Clarendon Press, 1909), pt 1, ch. 4, p. 23. In books on writing, the printing press was usually discussed only briefly as an improvement on the advantages already created by the alphabet. See Hugo, *De prima scriblendi*, ch. 34, pp. 210–11; Daniel Defoe, *An essay upon literature; or, an enquiry into the antiquity and original of letters* (London, 1726), p. 2.

22 See Stillingfleet, *Origines sacræ*, p. 19; Walton, *Biblia sacra polyglotta*, 'prolegomena', 1:7.

23 On the rise of atomism in seventeenth-century science, see Robert Hugh Kargon, *Atomism in England from Harriot to Newton* (Oxford: Clarendon Press, 1966); Richard W. F. Kroll, *The material word: literate culture in the Restoration and early eighteenth century* (Baltimore and London: Johns Hopkins University Press, 1991).

24 See Lucretius, *De rerum natura*, ed. and tr. Cyril Bailey, 3 vols. (Oxford: Clarendon Press, 1948), bk 1, lines 823–9 (1:216–19).

25 See Francis Bacon, *The advancement of learning*, ed. Arthur Johnson (Oxford: Clarendon Press, 1974), bk 2, ch. 7, U5, pp. 91–2. The alphabet image is often used by Robert Boyle, as in *The origin of forms and qualities* (1666), in *Works*, ed. Thomas Birch, 6 vols. (London, 1772; Hildesheim: Georg Olms, 1965–6), 3:298.

26 See J. G. Leibniz, *Opscules et fragments inédits*, ed. Louis Couturat (Hildesheim: Georg Olms, 1961), p. 435; John Locke, *An essay concerning human understanding*, ed. Peter H. Nidditch (Oxford: Clarendon Press, 1975), bk 2, ch 7, p. 132; George Berkeley, *A treatise concerning the principles of human understanding*, in *Works*, 9 vols., ed. A. A. Luce and T. E. Jessop (London: Thomas Nelson and Sons, 1948–57), 2:69; David Hartley, *Observations on man* (London, 1749; facs. repr. Gainesville, FL: Scholars Facsimiles, 1966), p. 75.

27 Michael Harbsmeier, 'Writing and the other: travellers' literacy, or towards an archaeology of writing', in Karen Schousboe and Morgens Trolle Larsen *Literacy and society* (Copenhagen: Akademisk Forlag, 1989), pp. 201–2. See also Michel de Certeau, *The writing of history* (New York: Columbia University Press, 1988), pp. 209–43. Both Harbsmeier and Certeau point to Jean de Léry's *Histoire d'un voyage faict en la terre du Brésil* (1578) as the first European work to single out writing as the mark distinguishing civilised from 'savage' peoples.

28 Joseph de Acosta, *The natural and moral history of the Indies*, tr. Edward Grimston, 2 vols. (London, 1588–90; repr. London: Hakluyt Society, 1880), 2:407.

29 See Antonio de Solis y Ribadeneyra, *Histoire de la conqueste du Mexique* (1684), 2 vols. (Paris, 1730), 1:532 and 548–9.

30 Francisco Lopez de Gómara, *Histoire géneralle des Indes occidentales* & *terres neuues* (1554), tr. M. Fumée (Paris, 1569), ch. 28, sig. D5ᵛ.

31 'Il leur ont mõtré les lettres, qui est vne chose si necessaire aux hõmes que sans icelles il sont cõme vraies bestes.' *Ibid.*, ch. 114, sig. Kk2ᵛ.

32 Stephen Greenblatt, *Marvellous possessions: the wonder of the New World* (Chicago: University Press, 1991), p. 10.

33 Samuel Purchas, *Hakluytus posthumus, or Purchas his pilgrimes*, 4 vols. (London, 1625), 1:176.

34 *Ibid.*, 1:178–9.

35 See Thomas Hariot, *A brief and true report of the new found land of Virginia* (London, 1588; facs. repr. New York: The History Book Club, 1951), sigs. E1ᵛ–F2ᵛ. The same judgement was of course made of pre-literate peoples in Africa, although Arab traders and Islam had already introduced writing to many parts of this continent.

36 See Gómara, *Histoire géneralle*, ch. 34, sig. E2ʳ⁻ᵛ. Gómara's is the earliest version of this story that I have found. It was recounted with variations by numerous authors in later decades. See Hugo, *De prima scriblendi*, pp. 14–15; Geraldus Vossius, *Quatuor artibus popularibus* (Amsterdam, 1650), p. 7; John Wilkins, *Mercury: or the secret and swift messenger*, 3rd edn (London, 1707; facs. repr., with an introduction by Brigitte Asbach-Schnitker, Amsterdam and Philadelphia: John Benjamins, 1984), pp. 3–4.

37 Defoe, *Essay upon literature*, pp. 5–6.

38 On the use of writing for magical purposes in Africa, see John Ogilby, *Africa: being an accurate description of the regions of Ægypt, Barbary, Lybia, and Billedulgerid, the land of the Negroes, Guinee, Æthiopia, and the Abyssines* (London, 1670), pp. 667 and 670.

39 For detailed discussion of the short-hand, cryptology and scripts for the deaf, particularly as backgrounds to schemes for a universal language, see Vivian Salmon's excellent introduction to *The works of Francis Lodwick* (London: Longmans, 1972), pp. 60–71.

40 René Descartes, letter to Marin Mersenne, 20 November 1629, in *Œuvres*, ed C. Adam and P. Tanney, 11 vols. (Paris: Libraire Philosophique J. Vrin, 1964–86), 1:79–80. Descartes was responding to a plan by des Valées. See James Knowlson, *Universal language schemes in England and France 1600–1800* (Toronto and Buffalo: University of Toronto Press, 1975), pp. 48–51; M. M. Slaughter, *Universal languages and scientific taxonomy in the seventeenth century* (Cambridge: University Press, 1982), p. 109.

41 See Cave Beck, *The universal character* (London, 1657). Lodwick's various experiments with a new language, including *A common writing* (1647) and *The groundwork or foundation laid, for the forming of a new perfect language* (1652), are compiled in Vivian Salmon's edition of his *Works*. Wilkins's *Essay towards a real character* (1668) will be discussed further.

42 See Sir Thomas Urquhart, *Logopandecteifon, or an introduction to the universal language* (1653), in *Works* (Edinburgh: The Maitland Club, 1834);

George Dalgarno, *Ars signorum* (London, 1661; facs. repr. Menston: Scolar Press, 1968); Ralph W. V. Elliot, 'Isaac Newton's "Of an universall language"', *Modern Language Review* 52 (1957), 1–18. This article reproduces Newton's unpublished manuscript, dating from just before or after his matriculation at Trinity College, Cambridge, in 1661.

43 Murray Cohen, *Sensible words: linguistic practice in England 1640–1785* (Baltimore and London: Johns Hopkins University Press, 1977), p. 7. On the tendency of seventeenth-century authors to view language as an aggregate of signs, rather than as a system of syntactical relations, see also Stephen K. Land, *From signs to propositions: the concept of form in eighteenth-century semantic theory* (London: Longman, 1974), pp. 1–20.

44 See Kroll, *Material word*, pp. 183–238.

45 Dalgarno, *Ars signorum*, p. 15. Concerning Bacon's influence on the British language planners, see Vivian Salmon, 'Language-planning in seventeenth-century England', in *The study of language in 17th-century England* (Amsterdam: John Benjamins, 1979), pp. 129–56.

46 See David, *Le débat sur les écritures*, pp. 35–40.

47 Bacon, *The advancement of learning*, bk 2, ch. 16, §2, p. 131.

48 Francis Bacon, *Novum organum*, in *Works*, ed. J. Spedding, R. L. Ellis and D. D. Heath (London: Longman, 1870), bk 1, ¶101, 4:96.

49 *Ibid.*, bk 1, ¶71, 4:73.

50 *Ibid.*, bk 1, ¶43, 4:54–5.

51 See Matthew Ricci, *China in the sixteenth century: the journals of Matthew Ricci, 1583–1610*, tr. Louis J. Gallagher, S. J. (New York: Random House, 1942), pp. 27–30; Juan Gonzales de Mendoza, *The history of the great and mighty kingdom of China* (1585), tr. Robert Parke, ed. George T. Staunton (London: Hakluyt Society, 1853), pp. 120–2. On the importance of Chinese as an influence on the universal language schemes, see Cornelius, *Languages*, pp. 25–38.

52 These are the precedents for a 'universal character' mentioned by Wilkins in *Mercury*, pp. 56–7.

53 See A. R. Hall, *The scientific revolution 1500–1800* (Boston: Beacon Press, 1956), p. 228.

54 See Descartes, letter to Mersenne, 20 November 1629, in *Œuvres*, 1:80–2.

55 On Leibniz's use of Descartes' letter, see Jonathan Cohen, 'On the project of a universal character', *Mind*, n.s. 63 (1954), 49–63.

56 G. W. Leibniz, 'On the general characteristic' (written c. 1679), in *Philosophical papers and letters*, ed. Leroy E. Loemaker, 2 vols. (Chicago: University Press, 1956), 1:343. Leibniz wrote various papers on his 'general characteristic' during the 1660s and 1670s, the earliest of which is 'De arte combinatoria' (1666), reproduced in *Logical papers*, ed. G. H. R. Parkinson (Oxford: Clarendon Press, 1966). For discussion of Leibniz's 'combinatory art', see Louis Couturat, *La logique de Leibniz* (Hildesheim: Georg Olms, 1961), pp. 33–118; Knowlson, *Universal language schemes*, pp. 107–11.

57 See G. W. Leibniz, *Discourse on the natural theology of the Chinese*, tr. Henry Rosemont, jr., and Daniel J. Cook (Honolulu: University of Hawaii Press, 1977).

58 See Dalgarno, *Ars signorum*, p. 13.

59 See Robert Fitzgibbon Young, *Comenius in England* (Oxford: University Press; London: Humphrey Milford, 1937), p. 65.

60 On the importance of shorthand, see Salmon's introduction to *The Works of Lodwick*, pp. 60–4 and 144; Knowlson, *Universal language schemes*, pp. 15–27.

61 George Dalgarno, *Didascalocophus; or the deaf and dumb mans tutor* (London, 1680), p. 118.

62 Wilkins, *Real character*, p. 385.

63 *Ibid.*

64 Michel de Montaigne, *Essays*, tr. Jacob Zeitlin, 3 vols. (New York: Alfred A. Knopf, 1934), 2:288.

65 See Cicero, *De oratore*, tr. E. W. Sutton and H. Rackham, 2 vols. (Loeb Classical Library, Cambridge, MA: Harvard University Press; London: William Heinemann, 1942), bk 3, ch. 53, vol 2, pp. 173–77; Quintilian, *Institutio oratoria*, tr. H. E. Butler, 4 vols. (Loeb Classical Library, London: William Heinemann; New York: G. P. Putnam, 1920), bk. 1, ch. 10, 1:24.

66 An arguable exception here is Marin Mersenne, who speculated on the possibility of a 'natural' language based on onomatopoeic sounds. But Mersenne thought that such a language would be too narrow, and abandoned this plan in favour of a written language. See Salmon, *Works of Lodwick*, introduction, pp. 25, 90, 154–5; Knowlson, *Universal language*, pp. 68–9.

67 There are exceptions. Alexander Gil briefly touches on 'prosodia' in *Logonomia anglica* (London, 1619; Menston: Scolar Press, 1968), p. 128. But there are no sections on prosody in, to cite only a few examples, Paul Greaves's *Grammatica anglicana* (1594), John Wallis's *Grammatica linguæ anglicæ* (1655), Owen Price's *The vocal organ* (1665), Guy Miege's *The English grammar* (1688), or James Greenwood's *An essay towards a practical English grammar* (1711).

68 See Antoine Arnauld and Pierre Nicole, *La logique, ou l'art de penser*, ed. Pierre Clair and François Girbal (Paris: Presses Universitaires de France, 1965), pt I, ch. 14, pp. 94–5.

69 Locke, *Essay*, bk 3, ch. 2, pp. 405 and 408.

70 See *ibid.*, bk 3, ch. 10, p. 508. See also Lord Shaftesbury's warnings against the deceptive powers of spoken rhetoric in 'Soliloquy, or advice to an author', in *Characteristics of men, manners, opinions, times etc.*, 2 vols., ed. J. M. Robertson (London: Grant Richards, 1900), 1:111.

71 See Yates, *Art of memory*, p. 378; Knowlson, *Universal language schemes*, p. 87; Hugh Ormsby-Lennon, 'Rosicrucian linguistics: twilight of a Renaissance tradition', in Allen G. Debus and Ingrid Merkel (eds.),

Hermeticism and the Renaissance, pp. 311–41; Thomas S. Singer, 'Hieroglyphs, real characters, and the idea of natural language in English seventeenth-century thought', *Journal of the History of Ideas* 50 (1989), 49–70.

72 Kircher's plans for a new written language were presented in *Polygraphia nova et universalis ex combinatoria arte delecta* (Rome, 1663) and *Ars magna sciendi* (Amsterdam, 1669). He was strongly influenced by Ramon Llull, as well as by Egyptian hieroglyphics. Another advocate of occult science, John Webster, endorsed the idea of a universal language as an 'almost *Catholic Cure* for the confusion of tongues' (*Academiarum examen*, p. 25).

73 On Llull's influence on Leibniz, see J. Cohen, 'Universal character', pp. 60–1. In *The advancement of learning* (bk 2, ch. 17, pp. 138–9), Bacon was dismissive of Llull's method as 'nothing of worth'. Yet Llull evidently had some influence on Bacon's own plan for a scientific notation, set out in a fragment entitled 'Abecedarium naturæ'.

74 Wilkins, *Real character*, p. 21.

75 See Slaughter, *Universal languages*, pp. 157–219. The influence of ancient grammatical theory on Wilkins and other language-planners is examined by G. A. Padley in *Grammatical theory in western Europe, 1500–1700*, 2 vols. (Cambridge: University Press, 1985), 1:325–81.

76 Wilkins, *Real character*, p. 289. According to M. M. Slaughter, Wilkins meant only to say that humans are *temporarily* ignorant of the 'essences' of nature. But I do not see that this inference is justified by Wilkins's statements in *An essay towards a real character* or elsewhere. See Slaughter, *Universal languages*, pp. 162–3.

77 See Dalgarno, *Ars signorum*, p. 52. For discussion of Dalgarno's scepticism about the knowledge of 'essences' or 'forms', see Wayne Shumaker, 'George Dalgarno's universal language', in *Renaissance curiosa* (Binghamton, NY: Medieval and Renaissance Texts and Studies, 1982), pp. 147–8.

78 Locke, *Essay*, bk 3, ch. 4, p. 457. For discussion of how Locke's philosophy undermined projects for a universal language, see Slaughter, *Universal languages*, pp. 194–212; Lia Formigari, *Language and experience in 17th-century British philosophy* (Amsterdam and Philadelphia: John Benjamins, 1988), pp. 99–131.

79 See Brigitte Asbach-Schnitker's introduction to Wilkins's *Mercury*, pp. xlvii–lvi.

80 Wallis acted as a cryptographer for the parliamentary armies in the Civil Wars. For discussion of seventeenth-century cryptology and its legacy, see Paul J. Korshin, 'Deciphering Swift's codes', in *Proceedings of the first Münster symposium on Jonathan Swift*, ed. Hermann J. Real and Heinz J. Vienken (München: Wilhelm Fink Verlag, 1985), pp. 123–34.

81 Wilkins, *Essay*, p. 13.

82 *Ibid.*, p. 12.

83 See Ovid, *Metamorphoses*, tr. Horace Gregory (New York and Scar-

borough, Ont.: New American Library, 1958), bk 3, pp. 85–9; Desiderius Erasmus, *De recta latini græcique sermonis pronuntiatione*, ed. M. Cytowska (Amsterdam: North-Holland, 1973), p. 38. On Cadmus' bringing letters to Greece, see Herodotus, *Works*, bk 5, ch. 58, pp. 327–8; Diodorus Sicilus, *Library of history*, bk 5, ch. 57, 3:253.

84 Plato, *Phædrus*, tr. R. Hackforth, 275a–b, in *Collected dialogues*, ed. Edith Hamilton and Huntington Cairns (Bollingen Series LXXI, Princeton: University Press, 1961), p. 520.

85 See *ibid.*, pp. 520–2.

86 Jacques Derrida, 'Plato's Pharmacy', in *Dissemination*, tr. Barbara Johnson (Chicago: University Press, 1981), pp. 63–171. Derrida's interpretation of the *Phædrus* has been challenged by a number of classical historians. According to one scholar, the *Phædrus* should be read not as a condemnation but as an ironic *defence* of the art of writing. See Ronna Burger, *Plato's 'Phædrus': a defence of the philosophical art of writing* (University, AL: University of Alabama Press, 1980). A less extreme interpretation suggests that Socrates was not rejecting writing outright, but was merely warning against abuses possible in both writing and speech. See G. R. F. Ferrari, *Listening to the cicadas: a study of Plato's 'Phædrus'* (Cambridge: University Press, 1987), pp. 204–22; and George A. Kennedy's discussion of the *Phædrus* in *The Cambridge history of literary criticism*, vol. 1, ed. George A. Kennedy (Cambridge: University Press, 1989), p. 147. In his well-known *Preface to Plato* (Cambridge, MA: Belknap Press, 1963), p. 57, n. 17, Eric A. Havelock described the disparagement of writing in the *Phædrus* as 'illogical' given Plato's general hostility to oral culture.

87 John Milton, *Areopagitica*, in *Works*, ed. Frank Allen Patterson (gen. ed.), 18 vols. (New York: Columbia University Press, 1931–40), 4:297–8.

88 Wilkins, *Mercury*, p. 90. For similar vindications of writing from attacks by Plato and others, see Duret, *Thrésor de l'histoire des langues*, pp. 5–6; Hugo, *De prima scriblendi*, pp. 24–5.

89 Wilkins, *Mercury*, p. 89.

90 Stillingfleet, *Origines sacræ*, pp. 34–5. Stillingfleet had in mind the remark by the third-century author Iamblichus that the ancient Egyptians inscribed 'all their own writings with the name of Hermes'. See *On the Mysteries of the Egyptians*, tr. Thomas Taylor (London: G. Dobell, 1968), pp. 17–18. The same passage later inspired Giambattista Vico's similar portrayal of Hermes as the 'poetic character' of useful inventions. See *The new science of Giambattista Vico*, tr. Thomas Goddard Bergin and Max Harold Fisch (Ithaca and London: Cornell University Press, 1948), p. 132.

91 See Stillingfleet, *Origines sacræ*, p. 594.

92 Sir Isaac Newton, *The chronology of ancient kingdoms amended* (London, 1728), p. 212.

93 *Ibid.*, pp. 193–234. Euhemeristic doctrines, which seek a basis for myth

in real historical figures and events, became increasingly fashionable in the late seventeenth and early eighteenth century. See Frank E. Manuel, *The eighteenth century confronts the gods* (New York: Atheneum, 1967), pp. 85–125.

94 See Plato, *Philebus*, tr. R. Hackforth, 18b, in *Collected dialogues*, p. 1094.

95 Jean-Jacques Rousseau, *The first and second discourses together with replies to critics, and Essay on the origin of languages*, tr. Victor Gourevitch (New York: Perennial Library, 1968), p. 14.

96 James Burnet, Lord Monboddo, *Of the origin and progress of language*, 5 vols. (Edinburgh, 1774–93), 2:25.

CHAPTER 3 'THE UNIFORM VOICE OF NATURE':
CONJECTURAL HISTORIES OF WRITING IN THE
EARLY EIGHTEENTH CENTURY

1 William Warburton, *The divine legation of Moses*, 4 vols. (London, 1738–41; facs. repr. New York and London: Garland Publishing, 1978), 3:105.

2 See Étienne Bonnot, Abbé de Condillac, *Essay on the origin of human knowledge* (1746), tr. Thomas Nugent (London, 1756; repr. Gainesville, FL: Scholars Facsimiles, 1971); Pierre Louis Moreau de Maupertuis, *Réflexions philosophiques sur l'origine des langues* (1748) in Ronald Grimsby (ed.), *Sur l'origine du langage* (Genève: Libraire Droz, 1971); Adam Smith, *Considerations concerning the first formation of languages* (1761) in *Lectures on rhetoric and belles lettres*, ed. J. C. Bryce (Oxford: Clarendon Press, 1983); Monboddo, *Of the origin and progress of language*. On the conjectural history of language, particularly as developed by Condillac and his admirers, see Hans Aarsleff, 'The tradition of Condillac: the problem of the origin of language in the eighteenth century and the debate in the Berlin academy before Herder', in *From Locke to Saussure: essays on the study of language and intellectual history* (Minneapolis: University of Minnesota Press, 1982), pp. 146–209. The impact of Condillac's tradition on British linguistic thought in the nineteenth century is examined in Aarsleff's *The study of language in England, 1780–1860* (2nd edn, Minneapolis: University of Minnesota Press, 1983).

3 See Dugald Stewart, *Account of the life and writings of Adam Smith, LLD*, in Adam Smith, *Essays on philosophical subjects*, ed. W. P. D. Wightman, J. C. Bryce and I. S. Ross (Oxford: Clarendon, 1980), p. 293.

4 See Manuel, *The eighteenth century confronts the gods*, pp. 107–11.

5 Fréret's history of writing is discussed by Madeleine V.-David, particularly in connection with this scholar's more accurate understanding of Chinese writing. See *Le débat sur les écritures*, pp. 83–92.

6 Nicolas Fréret, *De la langue des Chinois; réflexions sur les principes généraux de l'art d'écrire*, in *Œuvres complètes*, 20 vols. (Paris, 1796), 6:229.

7 See *ibid.*, 6:229–30.

8 *Ibid.*, 6:231.

9 *Ibid.*, 6:231–2.

10 See *ibid.*, 6:237–46.

11 Warburton's dissertation on writing comprises bk 4, §4 of the second volume of *The divine legation of Moses* (London, 1738–41). The second (1765) edition of *The divine legation* is reprinted together with the first edition in a four-volume facsimile reprint by Garland.

12 Maurice Pope, *The story of decipherment from Egyptian hieroglyphics to Linear B* (London: Thames and Hudson, 1975), pp. 52–3. On Warburton's importance in the history of decipherment, see also Iversen, *The myth of Egypt*, pp. 103–5; David, *Le débat sur les écritures*, pp. 95–104. On Warburton's life and works, see A. W. Evans, *Warburton and the Warburtonians: a study in some eighteenth-century controversies* (London: Oxford University Press, 1932); Robert M. Ryley, *William Warburton* (Boston: Twayne Publishers, 1984).

13 James Boswell, *Life of Johnson*, ed. G. B. Hill, rev. L. F. Powell, 6 vols. (Oxford: Clarendon Press, 1934–50), 4:48–9. On the nature of Warburton's arguments, see Roland N. Stromberg, *Religious liberalism in eighteenth-century England* (Oxford: University Press, 1954), pp. 79–81; Ryley, *Warburton*, pp. 23–31.

14 See Warburton, *Divine legation*, bk. 4, §4., 2:140.

15 See the 'Advertisement by the bookseller', *ibid.*, 2: sig. b^{r-v}.

16 *Essai sur les hieroglyphes des Egyptiens*, tr. Marc-Antoine Léonard des Malpeines, 2 vols. (Paris, 1744). On Léonard's revisions to Warburton's original work, see David, *Le débat sur les écritures*, pp. 95–6.

17 See Condillac, *Essay*, pt 2, §1, ch. 13, pp. 173–83.

18 Warburton cites Fréret's discussions of Chinese writing in the second edition of *Divine legation*, 3:93.

19 See Warburton, *Divine legation*, bk 4, §4., 2:67–70.

20 See *ibid.*, 2:70.

21 *Ibid.*, 3:88–9.

22 On the collections of Egyptian artifacts by Bernard de Montfaucon and Jean-Pierre Rigord, including some of the first transciptions of Egyptian cursive writing, see Pope, *The story of decipherment*, pp. 43–6. The jewellery trader Jean Chardin is especially important for his detailed reproductions of Persian cuneiform inscriptions at the ruins of Persepolis. See *Voyages de Monsieur le Chevalier Chardin en Perse* (1686), 3 vols. (Amsterdam, 1711), 3:118–19.

23 Warburton, *Divine legation*, bk 4, §4, 2:71.

24 *Ibid.*, 2:71.

25 *Ibid.*, 2:72.

26 *Ibid.*, 2:110. See also Bernard de Montfaucon, *Antiquity explained* (1719), tr. David Humphreys, 3 vols. (London, 1721), 2:221.

27 Warburton, *Divine legation*, bk 4, §4, 2:109.

28 *Ibid.*, 2:105.

29 *Ibid.*, 2:110–11. By isolating a class of 'symbolical' marks, Warburton intended to explicate Porphyry's report that the Egyptians used 'three sorts of writing: epistolographic, hieroglyphic, symbolic'. See Porphyry, *La vie de Pythagore*, p. 41.

30 Warburton, *Divine legation*, bk 4, §4, 2:73.

31 Warburton was essentially correct in his conjecture, not yet confirmed by archaeological evidence, that the Egyptians developed a 'running-hand' or cursive form of hieroglyphics. See *ibid.*, 2:115.

32 *Ibid.*, 2:114.

33 *Ibid.*, 2:78.

34 Francis Wise, *Some enquiries concerning the first inhabitants, language, religion, learning and letters of Europe* (Oxford, 1758), p. 93. See also Jean-Jacques Barthélemy's important remarks on Warburton's theories in Anne-Claude-Philippe de Tubières, Comte de Caylus, *Recueil d'antiquités Égyptiennes, Étrusques, Grecques et Romaines*, 7 vols. (Paris, 1752–67), 1:70, n.(a).

35 Warburton, *Divine legation*, 2nd edn, bk 4, §4, 3:153.

36 *Ibid.*, 1st edn, 2:124–31; 2nd edn, 3:148–51.

37 *Ibid.*, 1st edn, 2:132.

38 Jacques Derrida, 'Scribble (writing-power)', tr. Cary Plotkin, in *Yale French Studies* 58 (1979), 118.

39 Derrida, 'Scribble', 124.

40 On Warburton's arguments and their importance in eighteenth-century debate on religious rights, see Norman Sykes, *Church and state in England in the XVIIIth century* (Cambridge: University Press, 1939), pp. 316–26; Nicholas Hudson, *Samuel Johnson and eighteenth-century thought* (Oxford: Clarendon Press, 1988), pp. 223–8.

41 Derrida, 'Scribble', 132 and 142.

42 Warburton, *Divine legation*, bk. 4, §4, 2:105.

43 *Ibid.*, 2nd edn, 3:91.

44 *Ibid.*, 3:151.

45 See *Ibid.*, 2:132; 2nd edn, 3:154–5; Clement of Alexandria, *Stromata*, in *Writings*, bk 5, ch. 4, 2:233.

46 John Turberville Needham, *De inscriptione quadam Ægyptiaca Taurini inventa, et characteribus Ægyptiis, olim Sinis communibus, exarata, idolo cuidam antiquo in regia universitate servato* (Rome, 1761).

47 Joseph de Guignes, *Memoire dans lequel on prouve que les Chinois sont une colonie Égyptienne* (Paris, 1759). This tract is actually an abbreviated version of a lecture delivered to the Académie des Inscriptions et Belles-Lettres on 14 November, 1758. It includes a transcription of Barthélemy's lecture on Phoenician which inspired Guignes' speculations.

48 See Michel-Ange-André Leroux Deshautesrayes, *Doutes sur la dissertation de M. de Guignes* (Paris, 1759).

49 See Barthélemy's discussion of the evolution of letters in the Comte de Caylus' *Receuil*, 1:70–5. Barthélemy's analysis was inspired in part by

Warburton's conjectures about the development of a 'running-hand' hieroglyphic. But Barthélemy took the crucial step of actually showing the similarity between Egyptian cursive writing and hieroglyphic characters. Warburton, highly gratified by this attention from the prestigious Barthélemy, reproduced this comparison in the second edition of *Divine legation*, plate 7, 3:102 ff.

50 Warburton, *Divine legation*, 2nd edn, bk 4, §4, 3:96, n. (u).

51 *Ibid.*, 3:99, n. (u).

52 *Ibid.*, 3:91–2.

53 See Wilhelm von Humboldt, *On language*, tr. Peter Heath, with an introduction by Hans Aarsleff (Cambridge: University Press, 1988), pp. 231–2. On the development of the theory that linguistic difference stemmed from differences of innate ability or racial character, see Aarsleff's introduction to this volume, pp. xvii–xxxii, and *passim*; Nicholas Hudson, 'The individual and the collective in eighteenth-century language theory', in *Man and nature; the proceedings of the Canadian society for eighteenth-century studies*, vol. 10, ed. Josiane Boulad-Ayoub, Michael Cartwright, Michel Grenon and William Kinsley (Edmonton: Academic Publishers, 1991), pp. 157–66.

54 Antoine Court de Gébelin, *Monde primitif, analysé et comparé avec le monde moderne* (1771–82), 9 vols., (2nd edn, Paris, 1777–93), 1:61.

55 Little attention has been paid to Vico's theories about writing, or even to his linguistic ideas, despite their great originality and richness. For an examination of Vico's discussion of writing in the light of modern linguistic theories, see Naomi S. Baron, 'Writing and Vico's functional approach to language change', in Giorgio Tagliacozzo (ed.), *Vico: past and present* (Atlantic Highlands, NJ: Humanities Press, 1981), pp. 115–31. On the related issues of literacy and orality, see Patrick H. Hutton, 'The problem of oral tradition in Vico's historical scholarship', *Journal of the History of Ideas* 53 (1992), 3–23.

56 Vico, *New science*, ¶209, p. 74.

57 See *Ibid.*, ¶¶428–29, pp. 138–9; but compare ¶447, p. 150.

58 See *Ibid.*, ¶377, pp. 117–18.

59 *Ibid.*, ¶¶486–7, pp. 162–3.

60 *Ibid.*, ¶378, p. 118.

61 See, eg., how Aesop was invented as 'a poetic character' to inculcate the virtue of veiling thoughts in fables, and to represent the *famuli* as enslaved and ugly. *Ibid.*, ¶¶424–6, pp. 136–7.

62 *Ibid.*, ¶439, p. 145.

63 *Ibid.*

64 See Derrida, 'Plato's pharmacy', pp. 144–5.

65 Vico, *New science*, ¶460, p. 154.

66 *Ibid.*, ¶501, p. 169.

67 See Vico's description of the dissolution of the popular commonwealths, and the rise of philosophical scepticism and impiety that inevitably

follows from the refinement of abstract thought. *Ibid.*, ¶¶1102–6, pp. 423–4.

CHAPTER 4 CONSERVATIVE REACTION: THE STUDY OF WRITING AFTER WARBURTON

1 Defoe, *Essay upon literature*, pp. 15–16.
2 *Ibid.*, p. 16.
3 Wise, *Some enquiries*, pp. 96–7.
4 Hartley, *Observations on man*, p. 299.
5 *Ibid.*, p. 290.
6 *Ibid.*, p. 308.
7 *Ibid.*, p. 289.
8 James Beattie, *The theory of language* (London, 1788), pp. 109–10.
9 On Süssmilch's argument, first delivered in lectures to the Berlin Academy in 1756, see Aarsleff, *From Locke to Saussure*, pp. 187–8.
10 Wise, *Some enquiries*, p. 93.
11 Charles Davy, *Conjectural observations on the origin and progress of alphabetical writing* (London, 1772), pp. 1–2.
12 *Ibid.*, p. 4.
13 'Écriture', in *Encyclopédie; ou dictionnaire raisonné des sciences, des arts et des métiers*, ed. Jean le Rond d'Alembert and Denis Diderot, 35 vols. (Paris, 1951–80), 5:360.
14 See Franciscus Mercurius van Helmont, *Alphabeti vere naturalis Hebraici* (Sulzbaci, 1657). Some of Helmont's contemporaries were interested in the possibility of designing a new 'natural' alphabet wherein the shape of the characters would resemble the corresponding movement of the vocal organs. See Wilkins, *Real character*, p. 17.
15 Rowland Jones, *Hieroglyfic: or, a grammatical introduction to an universal hieroglyfic language* (London, 1768; facs. repr. Menston: Scolar Press, 1972), pp. 15–16.
16 See Johann Wachter, *Naturæ et scripturæ concordia* (Lipsiæ et Hafniæ, 1752), pp. 54–7.
17 L. D. Nelme, *An essay towards an investigation of the origin and elements of language and letters* (London, 1772), p. 25.
18 *Ibid.*, p. 8.
19 *Ibid.*, p. 26.
20 *Ibid.*, p. 2.
21 Wachter, *Naturæ et scripturæ concordia*, p. 57.
22 Charles de Brosses, *Traité de la formation méchanique des langues et des principes physiques de l'étymologie*, 2 vols. (Paris, 1801), 1:4–5.
23 Nelme, *Essay*, p. 14.
24 Court de Gébelin, *Monde primitif*, 3:xii. For discusssion of Court de Gébelin's linguistic theories, particularly in connection with the natural basis of all language, see André Robinet, *Le langage à l'âge classique* (Paris: Éditions Klincksieck, 1978), pp. 234–9.

25 See Court de Gébelin, *Monde primitif.*, 3:xi.
26 *Ibid.*, 3:i.
27 *Ibid.*, 3:412.
28 *Ibid.*, 3:410.
29 Quotations from Blake's poetry are taken from *Complete writings*, ed. Geoffrey Keynes (London: Oxford University Press, 1966).
30 On Boehme's influence on Blake, see Nelson Hilton, *Literal imagination: Blake's vision of words* (Berkeley, Los Angeles and London: University of California Press, 1983), pp. 13–14; Robert N. Essick, *William Blake and the language of Adam* (Oxford: Clarendon Press, 1989), pp. 48–54.
31 On Blake's use of images modelled on letters, or as 'hieroglyphical' symbols contributing to the meaning of his poetry, see W. J. T. Mitchell, *Blake's illuminated art: a study of the illuminated poetry* (Princeton: University Press, 1978), pp. 58–69; Grant Holly, 'William Blake and the dialogue of discourse and figure', in Kevin L. Cope (ed.), *Compendious conversations: the methods of dialogue in the early Enlightenment* (Frankfurt am Main: Peter Lang, 1992), pp. 15–33. See also Blake's experiments with positioning human forms in alphabetical shapes in his *Notebook*, ed. David V. Erdman and Donald K. Moore (Oxford: Clarendon Press, 1973), p. 46, and plate 74.
32 This sentence is written on the first end paper of this copy, call no. Douce N. 297.
33 See Massey, *The origin and progress of letters*, p. 80; Thomas Astle, *The origin and progress of writing* (1784), (2nd edn, London, 1803), pp. 62–3.
34 Jean-Jacques Barthélemy, *Les ruines de Balbec*, in *Œuvres diverses*, 2 vols. (Paris, 1798), 1:252.
35 Warburton, *Divine legation*, 2nd edn, bk 4, §4, 3:80 n.(i).
36 For discussion of the decipherment of hieroglyphics and other Middle Eastern scripts in the late eighteenth and early nineteenth centuries, see Ernst Doblhofer, *Voices in stone: the decipherment of ancient scripts and writings*, tr. Mervyn Savill (New York: Viking, 1961), pp. 44–74; Iversen, *The myth of Egypt*, pp. 124–45; David, *Le débat sur les écritures*, pp. 105–39; Pope, *The story of decipherment*, pp. 43–110.
37 Young's ground-breaking exegesis of the Rosetta Stone was first published anonymously as the article 'Egypt' in the 1819 supplement to the *Encyclopedia Britannica*. For Young's description of the phonographic values of some hieroglyphics, see *Supplement to the fourth, fifth and sixth editions of the Encyclopedia Britannica*, 6 vols. (Edinburgh and London, 1824), 4:62–3, and plates 74–8. Champollion presented his far more accurate analysis of Egyptian writing in *Lettre à M. Dacier* (Paris, 1822). On the 'semi-alphabetic' procedures of the Egyptians, see p. 34.
38 See Champollion, *Lettre à M. Dacier*, pp. 42–3.
39 Stewart, *Account of the life and writings of Adam Smith*, p. 296.
40 *Ibid.*, p. 310.
41 See Doblhofer, *Voices in stone*, pp. 121–48; Pope, *The story of decipherment*, pp. 85–110.

CHAPTER 5 WRITING AND SPEECH: THE DEBATE IN BRITAIN

1 The evidence of marriage registers suggests that more than half of the male population in England was literate by the middle of the eighteenth century. Female literacy lagged behind, but seems to have reached the level of about thirty-five to forty per cent in the same period. See Roger S. Schofield, 'Dimensions of illiteracy in England 1750–1850', in Graff (ed.), *Literacy and social development in the West*, pp. 201–13; Graff, *The legacies of literacy*, pp. 230–3. The growth of 'print culture' is not revealed by the number of new titles produced each year: that number remained fairly steady during the first half of the century. Nonetheless, the influence of printed materials increased with the rise of circulating libraries and newspapers, and with the more efficient retailing and distribution of books. See Marjorie Plant, *The English book trade: an economic history of the making and sale of books* (London: George Allen and Unwin, 1939), pp. 53–8 and 462; Terry Belanger, 'Publishers and writers in eighteenth-century England', in Isabel Rivers (ed.), *Books and their readers in eighteenth-century England* (London: St Martin's Press, 1982), pp. 5–25; Alvin Kernan, *Printing technology, letters and Samuel Johnson* (Princeton: University Press, 1987), pp. 48–9.

2 Galileo, *Dialogue concerning the two chief world systems*, p. 105. See ch. 2 above.

3 Sir Thomas Smith, *De recta et emendata linguæ anglicæ scriptione* (London, 1568; facs. repr. Menston: Scolar Press, 1968), sig. b2^v. See John Hart's similarly dismissive comments on hieroglyphical writing in *An orthographie* (1569), in *Works on English orthography and pronunciation*, ed. Bror Danielsson, 2 parts (Stockholm and Almquist: Wiksell, 1955), 1:170.

4 On the rise of the vernacular as a background to linguistic reform, see Charlton, *Education in Renaissance England*, pp. 102–4.

5 See Alexander Gil, *Logonomia anglica* (London, 1619; facs. repr. Menston: Scolar Press, 1968); Charles Butler, *The English grammar, or the institution of letters* (Oxford, 1633).

6 See Robert Robinson, *The art of pronunciation*, in *Phonetic writings*, ed. E. J. Dobson (London, New York and Toronto: Oxford University Press, 1957), pp. 22–3 and *passim*.

7 See Wilkins, *Real character*, p. 376; Lodwick, *An essay towards an universal alphabet* (1686), in *Works*.

8 See Richard Mulcaster, *The first part of the elementarie* (London, 1582; facs. repr. Menston: Scolar Press, 1970), pp. 61ff.

9 See Robinson, *The art of pronunciation*, in *Phonetic writings*, p. 7; Lodwick, *Essay towards an universal alphabet*, in *Works*, pp. 126–7.

10 William Holder, *Elements of speech* (London, 1669; Menston: Scolar Press, 1967), pp. 47 and 56–7.

11 *Ibid.*, p. 18.

12 David Abercrombie, 'Parameters and phonemes', in *Studies in phonetics and linguistics* (London: Oxford University Press, 1965), pp. 120–4.

13 See J. A. Kemp's excellent introduction to John Wallis, *Grammar of the English tongue* (1653), tr. J. A. Kemp (London: Longman, 1972), pp. 62–3.

14 See Priscian, *Institutionum grammaticarum*, bk 1, ch. 2, §4; Abercrombie, 'What is a "letter"?', in *Studies in phonetics*, pp. 76–85.

15 See Wallis, *Grammar*, pp. 205, 220 and 250

16 All quotations are from Samuel Johnson, *A dictionary of the English language* (London, 1755; facs. repr. New York: AMS, 1967).

17 Roy Harris, *The origin of writing* (London: Duckworth, 1986), p. 114.

18 Edward Sapir, 'The psychological reality of phonemes', in *Selected writings*, ed. David G. Mandelbaum (Berkeley and Los Angeles: University of California Press, 1949), pp. 46–60. See also Daniel Jones, *The history and meaning of the term 'phoneme'* (London: International Phonetic Association, 1957), pp. 1–2.

19 Robinson, *The art of pronunciation*, in *Phonetic writings*, pp. 19–20.

20 D. G. Scragg, *A history of English spelling* (Manchester: University Press; New York: Barnes and Noble, 1974), p. 80. See also F. H. Brengelman, 'Orthoepists, printers, and the rationalization of English spelling', *Journal of English and Germanic Philology* 79 (1980), 332–54. Debate has surrounded the question of who was responsible for the regularisation of orthography. Brengelman takes issue with the conventional view that the printers led this reform, arguing instead that it was promoted by 'theoretical linguists and schoolmasters'. Yet Brengelman's own evidence that spelling became more regularised comes from 'printed texts'. It seems that printers must at least have understood and co-operated with the theoretical reforms.

21 Wilkins, *Real character*, p. 18.

22 Guy Miege, *The English grammar* (London, 1688), p. 108.

23 Vico, *New science*, ¶440, p. 145.

24 Beattie, *Theory of language*, pp. 44–5.

25 Abercrombie, 'Isaac Pitman', in *Studies in phonetics*, p. 94.

26 Mulcaster, *The first part of the elementarie*, p. 104.

27 Wilkins, *Real character*, p. 365. For discussion of Wilkins's phonetic analysis, see Joseph L. Subbiondo, 'John Wilkins's theory of articulatory phonetics', in Hans Aarsleff, Louis G. Kelly and Josef Niederehe (eds.), *Papers in the history of linguistics: proceedings of the third international conference on the history of language sciences* (Amsterdam and Philadelphia: John Benjamin, 1987), pp. 263–70.

28 Abraham Tucker, *Vocal sounds* (London, 1773; facs. repr. Menston: Scolar Press, 1969), p. 40.

29 *Ibid.*, pp. 4–5.

30 *Ibid.*, p. 1. See Harris, *The origin of writing*, pp. 29–56.

31 See Johnson, *Grammar of the English tongue*, in *Dictionary*, sig. a2ᵛ.

32 *Ibid.*

33 *Ibid.*, preface, sig. a2ʳ. Johnson's conservative approach to orthographic reform is evident from his initial 1746 'Scheme' for the *Dictionary*. Allen Reddick suggests that his views on this question may have been influenced by that great arbiter of linguistic taste, Lord Chesterfield. See *The making of Johnson's Dictionary 1746–1773* (Cambridge: University Press, 1990), pp. 19–20.

34 Johnson, *Grammar of the English tongue*, in *Dictionary*, sig. a2ᵛ.

35 *Ibid.*

36 Interestingly, Johnson's own spellings often differed from those in his *Dictionary*. See N. E. Osselton, 'Informal spelling systems in Early Modern English', in *English historical linguistics: studies in development*, ed. N. F. Blake and Charles Jones (Sheffield: Centre for English Cultural Tradition and Language, 1984), pp. 127–37. Particularly in the Early Modern Period, as Osselton points out, authors felt at liberty to adopt some personal spellings that differed from the 'official' spellings found in dictionaries and used by printers.

37 Robert Nares, *Elements of orthoepy* (London, 1784; Menston: Scolar Press, 1968), pp. 268–323.

38 See James Macpherson, 'A dissertation concerning the antiquity, &c. of the poems of Ossian the son of Fingal', in *Fingal, an ancient epic poem in six books* (London, 1762), pp. x–xv. On Macpherson's use of the oral traditions of the Highlands, see also Fiona J. Stafford, *The sublime savage: a study of James Macpherson and the poems of Ossian* (Edinburgh: University Press, 1988), pp. 81–2.

39 See Robert Wood, *An essay on the original genius and writings of Homer* (London: John Richardson, 1824), pp. 151–75. The term 'oral tradition' was originally used in the counter-Reformation to describe 'unwritten' traditions of belief and worship in the Catholic church. See George H. Tavard, *Holy Writ or Holy Church? The crisis of the Protestant Reformation* (New York: Harper and Brothers, 1959). Not until the eighteenth century was the term 'oral tradition' normally used to describe the beliefs and practices of pre-literate cultures rather than the extra-Scriptural doctrines of the church. See, eg., Jean François Lafitau in *Customs of the American Indians (Moeurs des sauvages amériquains, comparées aux moeurs des premiers temps)* (1723), tr. William N. Fenton and Elizabeth L. Moore, 2 vols. (Toronto: Champlain Society, 1974–7), 1:308.

40 Samuel Johnson, *A journey to the western isles of Scotland*, ed. Mary Lascelles (New Haven and London: Yale University Press, 1971), vol. 9 of *The Yale Works of Samuel Johnson*, p. 114. Johnson's claim that Earse did not have a written form until the eighteenth century was later supported by the Highland lexicographer William Shaw. See Shaw, *An enquiry into the authenticity of the poems ascribed to Ossian* (1781), (2nd edn, London, 1782), p. 8. According to the Scottish literati who defended Macpherson, however, the Highlanders possessed an indigenous written language

even in the time of Ossian, whose poems were disseminated by both oral and written means. See Donald M'Nicol, *Remarks on Dr. Samuel Johnson's journey to the Hebrides* (London, 1779), pp. 257–76; John Clark, *An answer to Dr. Shaw's Inquiry* (Edinburgh, 1781), pp. 26–7.

41 Johnson, *Journey to the western isles*, p. 115.

42 *Ibid.*, pp. 115–16.

43 Goody, *The domestication of the savage mind*, p. 44.

44 Joseph Priestley, *Course of lectures on the theory of language and universal grammar* (Warrington, 1763), p. 156.

45 *Ibid.*, p. 159.

46 Hugh Blair, *A critical dissertation on the poems of Ossian* (London, 1763), p. 18.

47 For background on the life and career of Thomas Sheridan, see W. Benzie, *The Dublin orator: Thomas Sheridan's influence on eighteenth-century rhetoric and belles-lettres* (Leeds: University School of English, 1972). On the 'elocutionary movement' that Sheridan did much to launch, see Wilbur Samuel Howell, *Eighteenth-century British logic and rhetoric* (Princeton: University Press, 1971), pp. 143–256. See also Michael Shortland, 'Moving speeches: language and elocution in eighteenth-century Britain', *History of European Ideas* 8 (1987), 639–53; Peter de Bolla, *The discourse of the sublime: readings in history, aesthetics and the subject* (Oxford and New York: Basil Blackwell, 1989), pp. 163–82.

48 Boswell, *Life of Johnson*, 1:386.

49 Thomas Sheridan, *A course of lectures on elocution, together with two dissertations on language* (London, 1762), p. 43.

50 *Ibid.*, p. 245.

51 Thomas Sheridan, *Elements of English* (London, 1786; Menston: Scolar Press, 1968), p. vi.

52 Sheridan, *Course of lectures*, p. 235.

53 *Ibid.*, p. 8.

54 Sheridan was not the first to provide a written guide to pronunciation, this method having been used previously by Nathaniel Bailey in the third edition of his *Universal etymological dictionary* (1731) and by a few later lexicographers and grammarians. The *General dictionary* (London, 1780) nonetheless offered the most regular and comprehensive standard of pronunciation to date. See Benzie, *The Dublin orator*, pp. 97–113.

55 Sheridan, *Course of lectures*, p. 71.

56 On seventeenth-century attitudes to intonation, see chapter 2, pp. 46–7, above.

57 For brief discussion of early studies of intonation, see David Crystal, *Prosodic systems and intonation in English* (Cambridge: University Press, 1967), pp. 20–5.

58 See Johnson, *Dictionary*, sigs. c2^{r-v}.

59 Daniel Fenning, *A new grammar of the English tongue* (London, 1771), p. 181. See also Ann Fisher, *A new grammar* (Newcastle upon Tyne, 1750;

repr. Menston: Scolar Press, 1968), pp. 141–3; James Buchanan, *The British grammar* (London, 1762), pp. 67–8.

60 The terminology in Sheridan's discussions of prosody is admirably clear. He reserved 'accent' to describe stress in single words and 'emphasis' to describe patterns of stress in whole sentences or phrases. He believed that 'accent' or regular patterns of syllable stress were created by changes of 'quantity' (duration) not 'tone' (pitch). Changes of 'tone', affecting only 'emphasis', were prompted by the emotional states of the speaker. See *Course of lectures*, pp. 39–49.

61 James Burgh, *The art of speaking* (London, 1761), p. 21.

62 See Kroll, *Material word*, pp. 183–238, and my discussion in chapter 2 above, pp. 42–3.

63 Conjectural historians frequently traced the origin of language to gestures and 'cries of passion'. See Condillac, *Essay on the origin of human knowledge*, pt 2, §1, ch. 1, pp. 171–9; Bernard Mandeville, *Fable of the bees* (1724–9), ed. F. B. Kaye, 2 vols. (Oxford: Clarendon Press, 1924), pt 2, 2:286–90.

64 Sheridan, *Course of lectures*, p. 97.

65 *Ibid.* p. 100.

66 Murray Cohen has commented on the increased importance of sound in late eighteenth-century grammatical literature in *Sensible words*, pp. 105–22. He has ascribed this trend to a greater emphasis on the 'communication of intention' in a social context, in contrast with the preoccupying concern of language planners of the seventeenth century with the philosophical truth of language. While this argument has merit, it is inaccurate to suggest that seventeenth-century scholars of language were indifferent to the general needs of communication. Clearer and wider communication (to 'remedy...the Curse of Babel') was, arguably, their primary aim in contriving new 'universal' languages. Nor did the philosophical study of language disappear in the mid eighteenth century, as demonstrated by the popular works of James Harris, Lord Monboddo and William Ward. A more consistent difference between the seventeenth- and eighteenth-century authors, as I am arguing, is that later grammarians stressed the importance of oral delivery, with all its special resources, in order fully to achieve 'the communication of intention'. The inventors of the 'real character' tended to assume that there was no essential difference between writing and speech in fulfilling this end, for all language consisted of 'arbitrary signs' for things or ideas.

67 Sheridan, *Course of lectures*, p. xv.

68 Hugh Blair, *Lectures on rhetoric and belles lettres*, 3 vols., 2nd edn (London, 1785; facs. repr. New York: Garland Publishing, 1970), 1:172.

69 See Thomas Sheridan, *British education: or, the source of disorders in Great Britain* (Dublin, 1756; facs. repr. New York: Garland Publishing, 1970), pp. 185–6.

70 Sheridan, *Course of lectures*, p. x.

71 See Sheridan, *British education*, pp. 53–6.

72 *Ibid.*, pp. 63–8. Ironically, the co-founder and leader of the Methodist movement, John Wesley, seems to have benefited from the lessons of elocutionism. He went on to write his own tract on this subject, *Directions concerning pronunciation and gesture* (Bristol, 1770).

73 Oliver Goldsmith, 'Of eloquence', in *The bee*, in *Collected works*, ed. Arthur Friedman, 5 vols. (Oxford: Clarendon Press, 1966), 1:481.

74 Sheridan, *Course of lectures*, p. 139.

75 *Ibid.*, p. 148.

76 *Ibid.*, p. 181.

77 Thomas Reid, *Inquiry into the human mind on the principles of common-sense*, in *Works*, ed. Sir William Hamilton (Edinburgh: Maclachlan and Stewart, 1863), ch. 4, §2, pp. 118–19.

78 John Rice, *An introduction to the art of reading* (London, 1765; facs. repr. Menston: Scolar Press, 1969), p. 195.

79 *Ibid.*, p. 219.

80 See Olivia Smith, *The politics of language* 1791–1819 (Oxford: Clarendon Press, 1984), pp. 13–29. I obviously disagree with Smith that Sheridan was 'most unusual' (p. 99) in advocating the superiority of speech to writing.

81 See Boswell, *Life of Johnson*, 2:188. The best known statement of the view that it was socially dangerous to educate the poor, who would be made more cunning and less satisfied with their lowly status, was Bernard Mandeville's *Essay on charity and charity-schools*, added in 1723 to the full *Fable of the bees*. By Johnson's time, Mandeville's opinion had a wide popular currency.

82 Monboddo, *Of the origin and progress of language*, 2:25.

83 See De Bolla, *Discourse of the sublime*, pp. 175–7.

84 Rice, *Introduction to the art of reading*, pp. 388–9.

85 Henry Home, Lord Kames, *Elements of criticism*, 3 vols. (Edinburgh, 1762; facs. repr. New York: Johnson Reprint Corp., 1967), 2:119–20.

86 Joseph Priestley, *A course of lectures on oratory and criticism* (London, 1778; facs. repr. New York: Garland Publishing, 1971), p. 297.

87 Sheridan, *British education*, pp. 144–5.

88 Rice, *Introduction to the art of reading*, p. 235.

89 *Ibid.*, p. 208.

90 William Cockin, *The art of delivering written language* (London, 1775), p. 9.

91 *Ibid.*, p. 86.

92 See Boswell, *Life of Johnson*, 4:323.

93 There remained some interest in a universal written language, especially very late in the century in France and continental Europe. See Knowlson, *Universal language schemes*, pp. 150–60; Robin E. Rider, 'Measure of ideas, rule of language: mathematics and language in the 18th century', in Tore Frängsmyr, J. L. Heilbron and Robin E. Rider (eds.), *The quantifying spirit of the eighteenth century* (Berkeley, Los Angeles

and Oxford: University of California Press, 1990), pp. 113–40. I will look briefly at this movement in the next chapter.

94 Sheridan, *Course of lectures*, p. 14.

95 Cockin, *Art of delivering written language*, p. 125.

96 John Walker, *The melody of speaking* (London, 1787; facs. repr. Menston: Scolar Press, 1970), p. ii.

97 On the differences between the 'mechanical' and 'natural' schools of elocution, see Benzie, *Dublin orator*, pp. 35–54.

98 See John Walker, *Elements of elocution*, 2 vols. (London, 1781; facs. repr. Menston: Scolar Press, 1969), 1:113.

99 Laurence Sterne, *The life and opinions of Tristram Shandy*, ed. Ian Campbell Ross (Oxford: Clarendon Press, 1983), vol. 2, ch. 11, p. 87.

100 *Ibid.*, vol. 1, ch. 20, p. 47. Grammarians in Sterne's time had become more aware that *length* of pause was an important factor in the meaning of speech and that variations of length could be marked in an ideal system of punctuation. See, for example, Robert Lowth, *A short introduction to English grammar* (London, 1762), pp. 154–8.

101 Sterne, *Tristram Shandy*, vol. 4, ch. 27, p. 254.

102 Crystal, *Prosodic systems*, p. 23.

103 Monboddo, *Origin and progress of language*, 2:300.

104 See Sheridan, *Course of lectures*, p. 41. Grammarians of this period widely agreed with Monboddo that the regular stress patterns of English were created by changes of quantity or loudness, not pitch, as was the case in Greek. See also Anselm Bayly, *An introduction to languages*, 3 parts (London, 1758; facs. repr. Menston: Scolar Press, 1968), 3:181–3; Buchanan, *British grammar*, p. 63.

105 See Dwight Bolinger, *Intonation and its parts* (Stanford: University Press, 1986), pp. 3–23; Alan Crittenden, *Intonation* (Cambridge: University Press, 1986), pp. 16–17.

106 See Joshua Steele in *An essay towards establishing the melody and measure of speech* (London, 1775; facs. repr. Menston: Scolar Press, 1969), pp. 18–55.

107 Boswell, *Life of Johnson*, 2:326–7.

108 *Ibid.*, 2:326.

109 See Cohen, *Sensible words*, p. 109.

CHAPTER 6 ROUSSEAU'S *ESSAI SUR L'ORIGINE DES LANGUES* AND ITS CONTEXT

1 See Derrida's 'Introduction to the "Age of Rousseau"', in *Of grammatology*, pp. 97–100, as well as the whole section on Rousseau, pp. 141–316. For discussion of Derrida's reading of Rousseau, see Paul de Man, 'The rhetoric of blindness: Jacques Derrida's reading of Rousseau', in *Blindness and insight*, (2nd edn Minneapolis: University of Minnesota Press, 1983), pp. 102–41; Christie V. McDonald, 'Jacques

Derrida's reading of Rousseau', *The Eighteenth Century: Theory and Interpretation* 20 (1979), 82–95; Gregory L. Ulmer, 'Jacques Derrida and Paul de Man on/in Rousseau's faults', *The Eighteenth Century: Theory and Interpretation* 20 (1979), 164–81; Norris, *Derrida*, pp. 97–141; Johnson, *System and Writing*, pp. 112–20.

2 For brief discussion of Leibniz's general characteristic, see chapter 2, pp. 44–5, above. Like Derrida, André Robinet has presented Rousseau as reacting against the elevation of written language by Leibniz and language planners of the seventeenth century. But Robinet also portrays Rousseau as opposing Vico's theory that visual signs played an essential role in the birth of language. Writing, Rousseau insisted, was only of late invention, and had the effect of retarding, not advancing, the progress of language. Unfortunately, there is no evidence that Rousseau knew of Vico's thesis about the primordial status of the written mark, or about its essential contribution to linguistic development, positions that were not shared by Warburton or Condillac. See *Le langage à l'âge classique*, pp. 243–61.

3 For a detailed account of the progress of orthographic reform in France from the Renaissance to the nineteenth century, see Ambroise Firmin Didot, *Observations sur orthographe ou orthografie française* (Paris: Typographie d'Ambroise Firmin Didot, 1868), pp. 99ff.

4 Louis de Lesclache, *Les véritables régles de l'orthografe francèze* (Paris, 1668; facs. repr. Genève: Slatkine Reprints, 1972), p. 5. See also Étienne de Blegny, *L'ortografe françoise* (Paris, 1667; facs. repr. Genève: Slatkine Reprints, 1972); Antoine Lartigaut, *Les progrès de la véritable ortografe* (Paris, 1669; facs. repr. Genève: Slatkine Reprints, 1972).

5 Antoine Arnauld and Claude Lancelot, *General and rational grammar* (London, 1753; facs. repr. Menston: Scolar Press, 1968), p. 15.

6 See *Le grand dictionnaire de l'Académie Françoise*, 2nd impression (Paris, 1695; facs. repr. Genève: Slatkine Reprints, 1968), preface, sig. *4^{r–v}.

7 François-Séraphin Régnier-Desmarais, *Traité de la grammaire françoise* (Paris, 1706; facs. repr. Genève: Slatkine Reprints, 1973), p. 89.

8 See Nicolas Beauzée, 'Orthographe', in *Encyclopédie*, 11:669.

9 Voltaire, 'Orthographe', in *Questions sur l'Encyclopédie*, in *Œuvres complètes*, ed. L. Moland, 52 vols. (Paris: Garnier Frères, 1877–85), 20:157.

10 Charles Pinot Duclos, *Remarques sur La grammaire générale et raisonnée*, in *Œuvres complètes*, 9 vols. (Paris, 1820–1), 8:35.

11 *Ibid.*, 8:42.

12 See *ibid.*, 8:41.

13 See Pierre Delattre, 'Comparing the prosodic features of English, German, Spanish and French', *International Review of Applied Linguistics in Language Teaching* 1 (1963), 193–210; Mario Rossi, 'Le cadre accentuel et le mot en italien et en français', in Pierre Léon and Mario Rossi (eds.), *Problèmes de prosodie*, 2 vols. (Ottawa: Didier, 1979–80), 1:9–22; Philippe Martin, 'Sur les principes d'une théorie syntaxique de l'intonation',

in Léon and Rossi (eds.), *Problèmes de prosodie*, 1:91–101; Jacqueline Vaissière, 'Language-independent prosodic features', in A. Culter and D. R. Ladd (eds.), *Prosody: models and measurements* (Berlin, Heidelberg, New York and Tokyo: Springer-Verlag, 1983), pp. 53–66.

14 Pierre Joseph Thoulier d'Olivet, *Traité de la prosodie françoise*, 2nd edn (Genève, 1750), pp. 29–30.

15 *Ibid.*, p. 27.

16 *Ibid.*, p. 19.

17 Duclos, *Remarques*, in *Œuvres complètes*, 8:30.

18 *Ibid.*, 8:28.

19 Du Marsais, 'Accent', in *Encyclopédie*, 1:64.

20 See *ibid.*, 1:67.

21 Pierre Restaut, *Principes généraux et raisonnés de la grammaire françoise*, 6th edn (Paris, 1750), pp. 525–33.

22 Duclos, *Remarques*, in *Œuvres complètes*, 8:9.

23 *Ibid.*

24 See Rice, *Introduction to the art of reading*, p. 88.

25 Jean-Jacques Rousseau, 'Prononciation', in *Œuvres complètes*, ed. Bernard Gagnebin and Marcel Raymond, 4 vols. (in progress, Paris: Pléiade, 1959–), 2:1249.

26 See the English translation of this essay, *A dissertation on the influence of opinions on language and of language on opinions* (London, 1769), pp. 77–92. It was originally published as *Beantwortung der Frage von dem Einfluss der Meinungen in die Sprache und der Sprache in die Meinungen* (Berlin, 1760). For discussion of Michaëlis's linguistic doctrines, see Aarsleff, *From Locke to Saussure*, pp. 189–91.

27 'Écriture', in *Encyclopédie*, 5:360. See chapter 4, p. 81, above.

28 See Joseph de Maimieux, *Pasigraphie* (Paris, 1797), p. 65. On these universal language projects, see Knowlson, *Universal language schemes*, pp. 150–60; Rider, 'Measure of ideas, rule of language', in Frängsmyr et al. (eds.), *The quantifying spirit of the eighteenth century*, pp. 113–40.

29 Rousseau, 'Prononciation', in *Œuvres complètes* (Pléiade), 2:1252.

30 See *ibid.*, 2:1251.

31 *Ibid.*, 2:1249.

32 The dating of Rousseau's *Essai sur l'origine des langues* has been the subject of a long and inconclusive controversy. The debate has concerned whether Rousseau's description of the origin of civilisation in chapter 9 of the *Essai* represents an earlier, concurrent or later version of the presentation of the same subject in the 1754 *Discours sur l'inégalité*. For a detailed account of this debate, see Charles Porset, 'L'*inquiétante étrangeté* de l'*Essai sur l'origine des langues*: Rousseau et ses exégètes', *Studies on Voltaire and the Eighteenth Century* 154 (1976), 4715–58; Robert Wokler, 'l'*Essai sur l'origine des langues* en tant que fragment du *Discours sur l'inégalité*: Rousseau et ses "mauvais" interprètes', in *Rousseau et Voltaire en 1978: actes du colloque international de Nice* (Genève: Éditions Slatkine,

1981), pp. 145–61. In my view, the centrality of Duclos's ideas to chapters 5 and 7, along with the long note on Du Marsais's 1751 article on 'Accent', are strong indications that these parts of the *Essai* were written soon after the 1754 *Remarques*. It is possible that other sections of the *Essai* were composed long afterwards. Nevertheless, scholars need to reconsider the assumption that the remarks on writing in the *Essai* are entirely consistent with those in the fragment on 'Prononciation', which can be placed with some certainty in the early 1760s.

33 See the commentary on the *Essai* by Victor Gourevitch, in his translation of *The first and second discourses, together with replies to critics, and Essay on the origin of languages* (New York: Perennial Library, 1986), p. 362.

34 Rousseau, *ibid.*, *Essay on the origin of languages*, p. 249. I will use the Gourevitch translation in preference to the translation by John H. Moran (Chicago and London: University of Chicago, 1966). The Moran translation contains some significant inaccuracies in chapter 7 on prosody, which is central to my discussion.

35 See I. C. Gelb, *A study of writing*, 2nd edn (Chicago and London: University of Chicago Press, 1963), pp. 13–18 and 106–7.

36 Rousseau, *Essay on the origin of languages*, tr. Gourevitch, pp. 249–50. All citations of the original French version of the *Essai* are from Charles Porset's standard edition (Bordeaux: Guy Ducros, 1970).

37 *Ibid.*, p. 251.

38 See Newton, *The chronology of ancient kingdoms amended*, p. 212, and discussion in chapter 2, pp. 53–4, above.

39 See Voltaire, 'ABC, ou Alphabet', in *Questions sur l'Encyclopédie* (1770), in *Œuvres complètes*, 17:42–3.

40 Rousseau, *Essay on the origin of languages*, tr. Gourevitch, pp. 252–3.

41 Bernard Lamy, *La rhétorique, ou l'art de parler*, 4th edn (Amsterdam, 1699), pp. 165–6.

42 *Ibid.*, p. 166.

43 Rousseau, *Essay on the origin of languages*, tr. Gourevitch, p. 253.

44 Aristotle, *De interpretatione*, tr. E. M. Edghill, 16a, in vol. 1 of *Works*, 12 vols., ed. W. D. Ross (Oxford: Clarendon Press, 1908–52).

45 J. G. Herder, *Essay on the origin of language*, tr. Alexander Gode, in Jean-Jacques-Rousseau and J. G. Herder, *On the origin of language*, ed. John H. Moran and Alexander Gode (Chicago and London: University of Chicago Press,) pp. 90–1.

46 Derrida, *Of grammatology*, p. 228.

47 Rousseau, *Dictionnaire de musique*, in *Œuvres complètes*, 4 vols. (Paris: Chez Alexandre Houssiaux, 1852–3), 3:591–2.

48 Rousseau, *Essay on the origin of languages*, tr. Gourevitch, p. 256.

49 *Ibid.*, pp. 257–8.

50 *Ibid.*, p. 257.

51 See Duclos's commentary on chapter 4 of the Port-Royal *Grammaire* in *Remarques*, in *Œuvres complètes*, 8:26–7.

52 *Ibid.*, 8:28.
53 Rousseau, *Essay on the origin of languages*, tr. Gourevitch, p. 255.
54 See *ibid.*, pp. 255–6 and note.
55 See *ibid.*, p. 258.
56 *Ibid.*, p. 258.
57 *Ibid.*, ch. 12, p. 277.
58 See *ibid.*, ch. 19, pp. 290–1.
59 See *ibid.*, ch. 5, pp. 253–4.
60 See Condillac, *Essay on the origin of human knowledge*, pt 2, §1, ch. 8, p. 229.
61 See Rousseau, *Essay on the origin of languages*, tr. Gourevitch, ch. 20, pp. 293–4.
62 Duclos, *Remarques*, in *Œuvres complètes*, 8:9.
63 Rousseau, *Essay on the origin of languages*, tr. Gourevitch, ch. 20, p. 294.
64 *Essai sur l'origine des langues*, ed. Jean Starobinski (Paris: Éditions Gallimard, 1990), p. 53.
65 On the controversy generated by the first *Discourse*, see Robert Wokler, 'The *Discours sur les sciences et les arts* and its offspring: Rousseau in reply to his critics', in Simon Harvey, Mariam Hobson, David Kelley and Samuel S. B. Taylor (eds.), *Reappraisals of Rousseau: studies in honour of R. A. Leigh* (Totowa, NJ: Barnes and Noble Books, 1980), pp. 250–78.
66 Rousseau, 'Letter to Grimm', in *The first and second discourses, together with replies to the critics*, tr. Gourevitch, p. 55.
67 See Jean Starobinski, *Jean-Jacques Rousseau: transparency and obstruction*, tr. Arthur Goldhammer (Chicago and London: University of Chicago Press, 1988), pp. 141–2. Starobinski's book was first published in 1958.
68 See Jean-Jacques Rousseau, *Les confessions*, in *Œuvres complètes* (Pléiade), bk 3, 1:113–17; Starobinski, *Jean-Jacques Rousseau*, p. 125; Roland Mortier, 'Rousseau et la dissemblance', in Harvey et al. (eds.), *Reappraisals of Rousseau*, pp. 24–36.
69 Starobinski, *Jean-Jacques Rousseau*, p. 148.
70 Rousseau, *Discourse on the sciences and arts*, tr. Gourevitch, p. 27.
71 Rousseau, *Émile*, bk 3, p. 184.
72 See *ibid.*, bk 2, p. 160.
73 *Ibid.*, p. 204.
74 Louis Armand de Lom d'Acre, Baron de Lahontan, *Voyages*, ed. Stephen Leacock (Ottawa: Graphic Publishers, 1932), pp. 218–19.
75 *Ibid.*, p. 317.
76 *Ibid.*, pp. 318–19.
77 *Ibid.*, p. 319.
78 See *ibid.*, p. 27.
79 Lafitau, *Customs of the American Indians*, 1:298.
80 Guillaume-Thomas-François Raynal, *A philosophical and political history of the settlements and trade of the Europeans in the East and West Indies*, 3 vols. (Glasgow, 1811), 3:79.
81 See ch. 6 of the *Essai sur l'origine des langues*, 'S'il est probable qu'Homére

ait su écrire'. Rousseau has a good claim to being the first author of the eighteenth century to propose explicitly that Homer was illiterate. In doing so, however, he was reviving a claim made by the first-century AD Jewish scholar Flavius Josephus, in his critique of Greek civilisation, *Against Apion*, bk 1. ch. 2.

82 See Wood, *An essay on the original genius and writings of Homer*, 151–75; F. A. Wolf, *Prolegomena to Homer* (1798), tr. James E. G. Zetzel (Princeton: University Press, 1985), pp. 71–116 and *passim*. Some readers may think of Thomas Blackwell's *An enquiry into the life and writings of Homer* (1735) as a possible precursor to the view that Homer was a bard in an oral tradition, for Blackwell portrays the Homeric epic as the product of a society still dominated by primitive manners and language. But Blackwell never touches on the question of whether Homer knew letters. On Wood, Wolf and eighteenth-century discussions of Homer's literacy, see J. A. Davison, 'Homeric criticism: the transmission of the text', in Frank H. Stubbings and Alan J. B. Wace (eds.), *A companion to Homer* (London: Macmillan, 1962), pp. 215–33; Kristi Simonsuuri, *Homer's original genius: eighteenth-century notions of the early Greek epic* (Cambridge: University Press, 1979), pp. 107 and 139–40.

83 Yves Goguet, *The origin of laws, arts, and sciences, and their progress among the most ancient nations*, 3 vols. (Edinburgh, 1761), 1:190.

CHAPTER 7 THE NEW MEDIATION: PERCEPTIONS OF WRITING IN THE ROMANTIC ERA

1 William Wordsworth, Preface to *Lyrical ballads*, in *Prose Works*, ed. W.J.B. Owen and Jane Worthington Smyser, 3 vols. (Oxford: Clarendon Press, 1974), 1:138.

2 William Wordsworth, *The Prelude* (1850), ed. W. J. B. Owen (Ithaca and London: Cornell University Press, 1985), bk 13, 263–4.

3 *Ibid.*, bk 6, 111–12.

4 William Wordsworth, *The Excursion*, bk 6, 612–13, in *Poetical works*, ed. E. de Selincourt and Helen Darbishire, 5 vols. (Oxford: Clarendon Press, 1940–49), volume 5.

5 James K. Chandler, *Wordsworth's second nature: a study of the poetry and politics* (Chicago and London: University of Chicago Press, 1984), pp. 140–1.

6 M. H. Abrahms, *The mirror and the lamp: Romantic theory and the critical tradition* (New York: Oxford University Press, 1953), p. 112.

7 Chandler, *Wordsworth's second nature*, p. 140.

8 On Wordsworth's scrupulous revision of his work, see E. de Selincourt's introduction to his edition of the *Poetic Works*, 1:v–vii. See also Wordsworth's second 'Essay upon epitaphs', in *Prose works*, 2:77.

9 Wordsworth, Preface to *Lyrical ballads*, in *Prose works*, 1:123.

10 *Ibid.*, 1:149.

11 *Ibid.*, 1:138.
12 Wordsworth, 'Preface to the edition of 1815', in *Prose Works*, 3:29.
13 *Ibid.*, 3:27.
14 Wordsworth, *The Prelude*, bk 8, 421.
15 *Ibid.*, 507–8.
16 *Ibid.*, bk 5, 171.
17 See *ibid.*, bk 8, 617–664. J. Douglas Kneale has described 'the alternating priority' of images of speech and writing throughout *The Prelude*. See 'Wordsworth's images of language: voice and letter in *The Prelude*', *PMLA* 101 (1986), 351–61.
18 Wordsworth, *The Prelude*, bk 3, 368–9.
19 Wordsworth, 'Lines left upon a seat in a yew-tree', 1–3, in *Poetical works*, vol. 1.
20 See Geoffery H. Hartman, 'Inscriptions and romantic nature poetry', in *The unremarkable Wordsworth* (Minneapolis: University of Minnesota Press, 1987), pp. 31–46. See also Cynthia Chase, '*Monument and inscription*: Wordsworth's "rude embryo" and the remaining of history', in Gilbert Chaitlin, Kenneth R. Johnson, Karen Hanson and Herbert Marks (eds.), *Romantic revolutions: criticism and theory* (Bloomington and Indianapolis: Indiana University Press, 1990), pp. 50–77.
21 Wordsworth, 'Essay upon epitaphs, I', in *Prose works*, 2:49.
22 *Ibid.*, 2:60.
23 Wordsworth, 'Essay upon epitaphs, III', in *Prose works*, 2:88. Walter J. Ong has argued that Wordsworth set out to remove all commonplaces from poetry, an indication of his antipathy to the last vestiges of oral tradition, which relies on commonplace formulae. See *Rhetoric, romance, and technology*, pp. 281–3. But it is inaccurate to suggest that Wordsworth was uniformly hostile to the repetitive locutions typical of speech. Indeed, he set out to imitate such repetitions in a number of poems, and strongly defended 'tautologies' in a long note to his poem 'The Thorn' in *Lyrical ballads* (*Poetical works*, 2:513). See Hugh Sykes Davies' analysis of 'The Thorn' and of Wordsworth's use of oral formulae in *Wordsworth and the worth of words* (Cambridge: University Press, 1986), pp. 38–48 and 102.
24 Wordsworth, 'Essay upon epitaphs, II', in *Prose works*, 2:78.
25 Wordsworth, 'Essay upon epitaphs, III', in *Prose works*, 2:84.
26 *Ibid.*, 2:83.
27 *Ibid.*, 2:78.
28 See Susan Eilenberg, 'Mortal pages: Wordsworth and the reform of copyright', *ELH* 56 (1989), 351–74.
29 Samuel Taylor Coleridge, *Logic*, ed. J. R. de J. Jackson (London: Routledge and Kegan Paul; Princeton: University Press, 1981), p. 17. This is volume 13 of *The collected works of Samuel Taylor Coleridge*, ed. Kathleen Coburn, Bollingen Series LXXV.
30 Samuel Taylor Coleridge, *Notebooks*, ed. Kathleen Coburn and Merton

Christensen, 4 vols. (London: Routledge and Kegan Paul, 1957–89), 3:4396–7.

31 *Ibid.*, 3:4397.

32 Samuel Taylor Coleridge, *Biographia literaria*, ed. W. Jackson Bate and James Engell, 2 vols. (London: Routledge and Kegan Paul; Princeton: University Press, 1983), ch. 13, 1:304–5. These are volumes 7:1 and 7:2 of *The collected works of Samuel Taylor Coleridge*. For detailed discussion of the distinction between primary and secondary Imagination, see Owen Barfield, *What Coleridge thought* (Middletown: Wesleyan University Press, 1971), pp. 76–91.

33 Coleridge, *Notebooks*, 3:4396.

34 Coleridge, *Logic*, p. 16. For discussion of language and self-reflection in the *Logic*, see James C. McKusick, 'Coleridge's *Logic*: a systematic theory of language', in Aarsleff et al. (eds.), *Papers in the history of linguistics*, pp. 479–89.

35 Wordsworth, Preface to *Lyrical ballads*, in *Prose works*, 1:52.

36 Coleridge, *Biographia literaria*, ch. 17, 2:52.

37 *Ibid.*, 2:54.

38 *Ibid.*, ch. 18., 2:60, n.

39 *Ibid.*, ch. 17, 2:57. For related discussion of the disagreement between Coleridge and Wordsworth on the nature of language, particularly as revealed in *Biographia literaria*, see James C. McKusick, *Coleridge's philosophy of language* (New Haven and London: Yale University Press, 1986), pp. 110–18.

40 For a provocative case that Coleridge misrepresented Wordsworth in *Biographia literaria*, see Don H. Bialostosky, 'Coleridge's interpretation of Wordsworth's Preface to *Lyrical ballads*', *PMLA* 93 (1978), 912–24.

41 Joseph Marie Degérando, *Des signes et de l'art de penser considérés dans leurs rapports mutuels*, 4 vols. (Paris, 1800) 2:408–9.

42 *Ibid.*, 2:404.

43 *Ibid.*, 2:400.

44 Mary Wollstonecraft, *Thoughts on the education of daughters* (London, 1787), p. 46.

45 For a comparable analysis of literacy as the foundation of philosophical thought, see, eg., Jack Goody and Ian Watt, 'The consequences of literacy', in Goody (ed.), *Literacy in traditional societies*, pp. 27–68.

46 See Degérando, *Des signes*, 2:392–400.

47 William Hazlitt, *Lectures on the English poets*, in *Complete works*, ed. P. P. Howe, 21 vols. (London and Toronto: J. M. Dent, 1930–4), lecture 1, 5:6; see also G. W. F. Hegel, *The philosophy of fine art* (1835), tr. F. P. B. Osmaston, 4 vols. (London: G. Bell and Sons, 1920), introduction.

48 William Lamb, Viscount Melbourne, *Essay on the progressive improvement of mankind* (London, 1860), p. 7. See also William Godwin, *Enquiry concerning political justice* (London, 1798; Harmondworth: Penguin Books, 1978), bk 4, ch. 2, p. 277.

49 Hazlitt, *Life of Napoleon*, in *Complete works*, 13:38.
50 See Robert Darnton's excellent delineation of the clandestine book trade in eighteenth-century France, fuelled by entrepreneurial printers in neighbouring countries, in *The literary underground of the old regime* (Cambridge, MA and London: Harvard University Press, 1982).
51 See Hazlitt, *Complete works*, vol. 17; see Chandler, *Wordsworth's second nature*, pp. 144–7.
52 Hazlitt, 'On the difference between writing and speaking', in *Complete works*, 12:276.
53 *Ibid.*, 12:266.
54 *Ibid.*, 12:279.
55 Hazlitt, *Lectures on the English poets*, in *Complete works*, lecture 1, 5:1.
56 *Ibid.*, 5:12.
57 *Ibid.*
58 Hazlitt, 'On the conversation of authors', in *Complete works*, 12:40.
59 Coleridge, *Biographia literaria*, ch. 1, 1:22.
60 Degérando, *Des signes*, 2:409.
61 Antoine Destutt de Tracy, *Élémens d'idéologie*, 5 vols. (Bruxelles, 1826), 2:197.
62 *Ibid.*, 2:196–7.
63 *Ibid.*, 2:201.
64 *Ibid.*, 1:274–5.
65 See, eg., Hegel, *Philosophy of fine art*, pt 2, §1, ch. 1, 2:75–84.
66 G. W. F. Hegel, *Philosophy of subjective spirit* (Part 3 of *The encyclopedia of philosophical sciences*), tr. M. J. Petry, 3 vols. (Dordrecht and Boston: D. Reidel, 1978), §459, 3:185.
67 See *ibid.*, §459 (addition), 3:197.
68 G. W. F. Hegel, *The philosophy of history*, tr. J. Sibree (New York: Colonial Press, pt 1, §2), p. 200. This work was first delivered in lectures in the winter of 1830–1. See also *Philosophy of fine art*, pt 2, §1, ch. 1, 2:79.
69 Hegel, *Philosophy of subjective spirit*, §459, 3:183–5.
70 See Coleridge, *Biographia literaria*, ch. 4, 1:82–3 n. On Coleridge's neologisms and 'desynonymisation' of words, see Timothy Corrigan, *Coleridge, language, and criticism* (Athens: University of Georgia Press, 1982), pp. 19–32.
71 Humboldt, *On language*, p. 49.
72 Hegel, *Philosophy of subjective spirit*, §459, 3:185.
73 *Ibid.*, 3:199.
74 Hegel, *Philosophy of history*, pt 1, §1, p. 135.
75 Jacques Derrida, 'Le puits et la pyramide: introduction à la sémiologie de Hegel', in *Marges de la philosophie* (Paris: Éditions de Minuit, 1972), p. 121. 'Nefarious' is the translation by Alan Bass in 'The pit and the pyramid: introduction to Hegel's semiology', in *Margins of philosophy*, (Chicago: University Press, 1982), p. 103.
76 See Hegel, *Philosophy of fine art*, introduction, 1:120, and pt 3, §3. ch. 3,

4:10. On Hegel's depreciation of music and his emphasis on poetical content, see Stephen Bungay, *Beauty and truth: a study of Hegel's aesthetics* (Oxford: University Press, 1984), pp. 133–46.

77 Hegel, *Philosophy of subjective spirit*, §459, 3:189–91.
78 *Ibid.*, §459 (addition), 3:197.
79 *Ibid.*, §459, 3:191.

CONCLUSIONS: A CONTINUING LEGACY OF DEBATE

1 See chapter 6, p. 127, above.
2 See, eg., Ong, *Rhetoric, romance and technology*, p. 256; Terry Eagleton, *Literary theory: an introduction* (Oxford: Basil Blackwell, 1983), pp. 18–22.
3 Gelb, *A study of writing*, p. 221. This statement might be compared to the opening sentences of Thomas Astle's 1784 *The origin and progress of writing*: 'The noblest acquisition of mankind is SPEECH, and the most useful art is WRITING. The first, eminently distinguishes MAN, from the brute creation; the second, from uncivilised savages' (p. i).
4 Gelb, *A study of writing*, p. 222. See also Harvey J. Graff's summary of the eminent place given to writing and literacy in the post-Enlightenment tradition, *Literacy and social development in the West*, p. 3.
5 See, eg., Jack Goody's introduction to *Literacy and traditional societies*, pp. 20–6.
6 See Eisenstein, *The printing-press as an agent of change* and *Print culture and Enlightenment thought*.
7 Harold J. Innis, *Empire and communication*, rev. Mary Q. Innis (Toronto and Buffalo: University of Toronto Press, 1972), p. 57. Innis's book was first published in 1950.
8 See McLuhan, *The Gutenberg galaxy*; Ong, *Ramus, method, and the decay of dialogue*.
9 Claude Lévi-Strauss, *A world on the wane [Tristes tropiques]*, tr. John Russell (London: Hutchinson, 1961), p. 292.
10 Lévi-Strauss's attack on writing in *Tristes tropiques* is deconstructed by Derrida in *Of grammatology*, pp. 118–40.
11 Sheridan, *Course of lectures*, p. 7.
12 McLuhan, *Gutenberg galaxy*, p. 17.

Bibliography

PRIMARY SOURCES

Académie Française, *Le grand dictionnaire de l'Académie Française* (1694), 2nd impression, Paris, 1695; facs. repr. Genève: Slatkine Reprints, 1968

Acosta, Joseph de, *The natural and moral history of the Indies* (1590), tr. Edward Grimston, 2 vols., London, 1588–90; repr. London: Hakluyt Society, 1880

Agrippa, Henry Cornelius, *Three books of occult philosophy* (1530), London, 1651

Alembert, Jean le Rond d', and Denis Diderot, *Encyclopédie; ou dictionnaire raisonné des sciences, des arts et des métiers*, 35 vols., Paris, 1751–80

Aristotle, *Works*, 12 vols., ed. W. D. Ross, Oxford: Clarendon Press, 1908–52

Arnauld, Antoine, and Claude Lancelot, *General and rational grammar* (1660), London, 1753; facs. repr. Menston: Scolar Press, 1968

Arnauld, Antoine, and Pierre Nicole, *La logique, ou l'art de penser* (1662) ed. Pierre Clair and François Girbal, Paris: Presses Universitaires de France, 1965

Astle, Thomas, *The origin and progress of writing* (1784), 2nd edn, London, 1803

Bacon, Francis, *The advancement of learning* (1605), ed. Arthur Johnson, Oxford: Clarendon Press, 1974

Works, ed. J. Spedding, R. L. Ellis and D. D. Heath, London: Longman, 1870

Bailey, Nathaniel, *Universal etymological dictionary* (1721), 3rd edn, London, 1731

Barthélemy, Jean-Jacques, *Œuvres diverses*, 2 vols., Paris, 1798

Bayly, Anselm, *An introduction to languages*, 3 parts, London, 1758; facs. repr. Menston: Scolar Press, 1968

Beattie, James, *The theory of language*, London, 1788

Beck, Cave, *The universal character*, London, 1657

Berkeley, George, *Works*, 9 vols., ed. A. A. Luce and T. E. Jessop, London: Thomas Nelson and Sons, 1948–57

Blackwell, Thomas, *An enquiry into the life and writings of Homer*, London, 1735

Blair, Hugh, *A critical dissertation on the poems of Ossian*, London, 1763
    Lectures on rhetoric and belles lettres (1783), 3 vols., 2nd edn, London, 1785;
    facs. repr. New York: Garland Publishing, 1970
Blake, William, *Complete writings*, ed. Geoffrey Keynes, London: Oxford
    University Press, 1966
    Notebook, ed. David V. Erdman and Donald K. Moore, Oxford:
    Clarendon Press, 1973
Blegny, Étienne de, *L'ortografe françoise*, Paris, 1667; facs. repr. Genève:
    Slatkine Reprints, 1972
Boehme, Jacob, *Mysterium magnum* (1622), London, 1654
    Signatura rerum, or the signature of all things (1621), London, 1651
Boswell, James, *Life of Johnson* (1791), ed. G. B. Hill, rev. L. F. Powell,
    6 vols., Oxford: Clarendon Press, 1934–50
Boyle, Robert, *Works*, ed. Thomas Birch, 6 vols., London, 1772; Hildesheim:
    Georg Olms, 1965–6
Brosses, Charles de, *Traité de la formation méchanique des langues et des principes*
    physiques de l'étymologie (1765), 2 vols., Paris, 1801
Browne, Sir Thomas, *The major works*, ed. C. A. Patrides, Harmondsworth:
    Penguin Books, 1977
Buchanan, James, *The British grammar*, London, 1762
Burgh, James, *The art of speaking*, London, 1761
Butler, Charles, *The English grammar, or the institution of letters*, Oxford,
    1633
Caylus, Anne-Claude-Philippe de Tubières, Comte de, *Recueil d'antiquités*
    Égyptiennes, Étrusques, Grecques et Romaines, 7 vols., Paris, 1752–67
Champollion, Jean François, *Lettre à M. Dacier*, Paris, 1822
Chardin, Jean, *Voyages de Monsieur le Chevalier Chardin en Perse* (1686), 3 vols.,
    Amsterdam, 1711
Cicero, *De oratore*, tr. E. W. Sutton and H. Rackham, 2 vols., Loeb Classical
    Library, Cambridge, MA: Harvard University Press; London: Wil-
    liam Heinemann, 1942
    Tusculan disputations, tr. J. E. King, Loeb Classical Library, Cambridge,
    MA: Harvard University Press; London: William Heinemann, 1927
Clark, John, *An answer to Dr. Shaw's inquiry*, Edinburgh, 1781
Clement of Alexandria, *Writings*, tr. William Wilson, 2 vols., Edinburgh:
    T. and T. Clark, 1867–9
Cockin, William, *The art of delivering written language*, London, 1775
Coleridge, Samuel Taylor, *Biographia literaria* (1817), ed. W. Jackson Bate
    and James Engell, 2 vols., London: Routledge and Kegan Paul;
    Princeton: University Press, 1983
    Logic, ed. J. R. de J. Jackson, London: Routledge and Kegan Paul;
    Princeton: University Press, 1981
    Notebooks, ed. Kathleen Coburn and Merton Christensen, 4 vols., London:
    Routledge and Kegan Paul, 1957–89
Colonna, Francesco, *Hypnerotomachia, or the strife of love in a dreame* (1499),

tr. 'R. D.', London, 1592; facs. repr. Delmar, NY: Scholars Facsimiles and Reprints, 1973

Comenius, Joannes Amos, *Opera didactica omnia*, 2 vols., Amsterdam, 1657

Condillac, Étienne Bonnot, Abbé de, *Essay on the origin of human knowledge* (1746), tr. Thomas Nugent, London, 1756; repr. Gainesville, FL: Scholars Facsimiles, 1971

Court de Gébelin, Antoine, *Monde primitif, analysé et comparé avec le monde moderne* (1771–82), 9 vols., 2nd edn, Paris, 1777–93

Dalgarno, George, *Ars signorum*, London, 1661; facs. repr. Menston: Scolar Press, 1968

Didascalocophus; or the deaf and dumb mans tutor, London, 1680

Davy, Charles, *Conjectural observations on the origin and progress of alphabetical writing*, London, 1772

Dee, John, *Monas hieroglyphica* (1564), tr. C. H. Josten, in *Ambix: Journal of the Society of Alchemy and Early Chemistry* 12 (1964)

Defoe, Daniel, *Essay upon literature; or, an enquiry into the antiquity and original of letters*, London, 1726

Degérando, Joseph Marie, *Des signes et de l'art de penser considérés dans leurs rapports mutuels*, 2 vols., Paris, 1800

Descartes, René, *Œuvres*, ed. C. Adam and P. Tanney, 11 vols., Paris: Libraire Philosophique J. Vrin, 1964–86

Destutt de Tracy, Antoine, *Élémens d'idéologie* (1804–15), 5 vols., Bruxelles, 1826

Diordorus of Sicily, *Library of history*, tr. C. H. Oldfather and Francis R. Walton, 12 vols., Loeb Classical Library, London: William Heinemann; Cambridge, MA: Harvard University Press, 1933–67

Duclos, Charles Pinot, *Œuvres complètes*, 9 vols., Paris, 1820–1

Duret, Claude, *Thrésor de l'histoire des langues de cest univers*, Cologne, 1613

Erasmus, Desiderius, *De recta latini græcique sermonis pronuntiatione*, ed. M. Cytowska, Amsterdam: North-Holland, 1973

Eusebius of Cæserea, *Evangelicæ præparationis*, tr. E. H. Giffort, S. T. P., Oxford, 1903

Fenning, Daniel, *A new grammar of the English tongue*, London, 1771

Fisher, Ann, *A new grammar*, Newcastle upon Tyne, 1750; facs. repr. Menston: Scolar Press, 1968

Fisher, Samuel, *Rusticus ad academicos*, London, 1660

Fludd, Robert, *Utriusque cosmi, maioris scilicet et minoris, metaphysica, physica*, 2 vols., Frankfurt, 1617–21

Fréret, Nicolas, *Œuvres complètes*, 20 vols., Paris, 1796

Galilei, Galileo, *Dialogue concerning the two chief world systems* (1632), tr. Stillman Drake, 2nd edn, Berkeley, Los Angeles and London: University of California Press, 1967

Opere, 20 vols., Firenze: G. Barbera, 1929–39

Gill, Alexander, *Logonomia anglica*, London, 1619; facs. repr. Menston: Scolar Press, 1968

Godwin, William, *Enquiry concerning political justice*, London, 1798; Harmondsworth: Penguin Books, 1978

Goguet, Yves, *The origin of laws, arts, and sciences, and their progress among the most ancient nations* (1758), 3 vols., Edinburgh, 1761

Goldsmith, Oliver, *Collected works*, ed. Arthur Friedman, 5 vols., Oxford: Clarendon Press, 1966

Gómara, Francisco Lopez de, *Histoire généralle des Indes occidentales & terres neuues* (1554), tr. M. Fumée, Paris, 1569

Grotius, Hugo, *De veritate religionis christianæ*, Paris, 1627

Guignes, Joseph de, *Memoire dans lequel on prouve que les Chinois sont une colonie Égyptienne*, Paris, 1759

Hariot, Thomas, *A brief and true report of the new found lands of Virginia*, London, 1588; facs. repr. New York: The History Club, 1951

Harris, James, *Hermes: or, a philosophical inquiry concerning language and universal grammar*, London, 1751

Hart, John, *Works on English orthography and pronunciation*, ed. Bror Danielsson, 2 parts, Stockholm and Almquist: Wiksell, 1955

Hartley, David, *Observations on man*, London, 1749; Gainesville, FL: Scholars Facsimiles, 1966

Hazlitt, William, *Complete works*, ed. P. P. Howe, 21 vols., London and Toronto: J. M. Dent, 1930–4

Hegel, G. W. F., *The philosophy of fine art* (1835), tr. F. P. B. Osmaston, 4 vols., London: G. Bell and Sons, 1920

The philosophy of history (1833), tr. J. Sibree, New York: Colonial Press, 1900

Philosophy of subjective spirit (1817), tr. M. J. Petry, 3 vols., Dordrecht and Boston: D. Reidel, 1978

Helmont, Franciscus Mercurius van, *Alphabeti vere naturalis Hebraici*, Sulzbaci, 1657

Herder, J. G., and Jean-Jacques Rousseau, *On the origin of language*, tr. John H. Moran and Alexander Gode, Chicago and London: University of Chicago Press, 1966

Herodotus, *Works*, tr. Henry Cary, London: George Bell and Sons, 1917

Hobbes, Thomas, *Leviathan* (1651), Oxford: Clarendon Press, 1909

Holder, William, *Elements of speech*, London, 1669; facs. repr. Menston: Scolar Press, 1967

Horapollo, *Hieroglyphics*, ed. George Boas, New York: Pantheon Books, 1950

Hugo, Hermannus, *De prima scriblendi origine*, Antwerp, 1617

Humboldt, Wilhelm von, *On language*, tr. Peter Heath, with an introduction by Hans Aarsleff, Cambridge: University Press, 1988

Iamblichus, *On the mysteries of the Egyptians*, tr. Thomas Taylor, London: G. Dobell, 1968

Jackson, John, *Chronological antiquities*, 3 vols., London, 1752

Johnson, Samuel, *A dictionary of the English language*, London, 1755; facs. repr. New York: AMS, 1967

A journey to the western isles of Scotland (1775), ed. Mary Lascelles, New Haven and London: Yale University Press, 1971, vol. 9 of *The Yale works of Samuel Johnson*

Jones, Rowland, *Hieroglyfic: or, a grammatical introduction to an universal hieroglyfic language*, London, 1768; facs. repr. Menston: Scolar Press, 1972

Kames, Henry Home, Lord, *Elements of criticism*, 3 vols., Edinburgh, 1762; facs. repr. New York: Johnson Reprint Corp., 1967

Kircher, Athanasius, *Ars magna sciendi*, Amsterdam, 1669
China Monumentis, Amsterdam, 1667
Obeliscus pamphilius, Rome, 1650
Œdipus ægyptiacus, 4 vols., Rome, 1652–4
Polygraphia nova et universalis ex combinatoria arte delecta, Rome, 1663
Prodromus coptus sive ægyptiacus, Rome, 1636
Turris Babel, sive archontologia, Amsterdam, 1679

Lafitau, Joseph François, *Customs of the American Indians* (1723), tr. William N. Fenton and Elizabeth L. Moore, 2 vols., Toronto: Champlain Society, 1974–7

Lahontan, Louis Armand de Lom d'Acre, Baron de, *Voyages* (1704–5), ed. Stephen Leacock, Ottawa: Graphic Publishers, 1932

Lamy, Bernard, *La rhétorique, ou l'art de parler* (1670), 4th edn, Amsterdam, 1699

Lartigaut, Antoine, *Les progrès de la véritable ortografe*, Paris, 1669; facs. repr. Genève: Slatkine Reprints, 1972

Leibniz, G. W., *Discourse on the natural theology of the Chinese*, tr. Henry Rosemont, jr., and Daniel J. Cook, Honolulu: University of Hawaii Press, 1977
New essays on the human understanding, tr. Peter Remnant and Jonathan Bennett, Cambridge: University Press, 1981
Logical papers, ed. G. H. R. Parkinson, Oxford: Clarendon Press, 1966
Opscules et fragments inédits, ed. Louis Couturat, Hildesheim: Georg Olms, 1961
Philosophical papers and letters, ed. Leroy E. Loemaker, 2 vols., Chicago: University Press, 1956

Leroux Deshautesrayes, Michel-Ange-André, *Doutes sur la dissertation de M. de Guignes*, Paris, 1759

Lesclache, Louis de, *Les véritables régles de l'orthografe francèze*, Paris, 1668; facs. repr. Genève: Slatkine Reprints, 1972

Locke, John, *An essay concerning human understanding* (1690), ed. Peter H. Nidditch, Oxford: Clarendon Press, 1975

Lodwick, Francis, *Works*, ed. Vivian Salmon, London: Longmans, 1972

Lowth, Robert, *A short introduction to English grammar*, London, 1762

Lucretius, *De rerum natura*, ed. and tr. Cyril Bailey, 3 vols., Oxford: Clarendon Press, 1948

M'Nicol, Donald, *Remarks on Dr. Samuel Johnson's journey to the Hebrides*, London, 1779

Macpherson, James, *Fingal, an ancient epic poem in six books*, London, 1762

Maimieux, Joseph de, *Pasigraphie*, Paris, 1797

Mandeville, Bernard, *Fable of the bees* (1724–9), ed. F. B. Kaye, 2 vols., Oxford: Clarendon Press, 1924

Manetho, *Works*, tr. W. G. Wadell, Loeb Classical Library, London: William Heinemann; Cambridge, MA: Harvard University Press, 1940

Massey, William, *The origin and progress of letters*, London, 1763

Maupertuis, Pierre Louis Moreau de, *Réflexions philosophiques sur l'origine des langues* (1748), in Ronald Grimsby (ed.), *Sur l'origine du langage*, Genève: Libraire Droz, 1971

Melbourne, William Lamb, Viscount, *Essay on the progressive improvement of mankind* (1798), London, 1860

Mendoza, Juan Gonzales de, *The history of the great and mighty kingdom of China* (1585), tr. Robert Parke, ed. George T. Staunton, London: Hakluyt Society, 1853

Mersenne, Marin, *Traité de l'harmonie universelle*, Paris, 1627

Michaëlis, Johann David, *A dissertation on the influence of opinions on language and of language on opinions* (1760), London, 1769

Miege, Guy, *The English grammar*, London, 1688

Milton, John, *Works*, ed. Frank Allen Patterson (gen. ed.), 18 vols., New York: Columbia University Press, 1931–40

Monboddo, James Burnet, Lord, *Of the origin and progress of language*, 5 vols., Edinburgh, 1774–93

Montaigne, Michel de, *Essays* (1580–8), tr. Jacob Zeitlin, 3 vols., New York: Alfred A. Knopf, 1934

Montfaucon, Bernard de, *Antiquity explained* (1719), tr. David Humphreys, 3 vols., London, 1721

Mulcaster, Richard, *The first part of the elementarie*, London, 1582; facs. repr. Menston: Scolar Press, 1970

Nares, Robert, *Elements of orthoepy*, London, 1784; facs. repr. Menston: Scolar Press, 1968

Needham, John Turberville, *De inscriptione quadam Ægyptiaca Taurini inventa, et characteribus Ægyptiis, olim Sinis communibus, exarata, idolo cuidam antiquo in regia universitate servato*, Rome, 1761

Nelme, L. D., *An essay towards an investigation of the origin and elements of language and letters*, London, 1772

Newton, Sir Isaac, *The chronology of ancient kingdoms amended*, London, 1728

Ogilby, John, *Africa: being an accurate description of the regions of Ægypt, Barbary, Lybia, and Billedulgerid, the land of the Negroes, Guinee, Æthiopia, and the Abyssines*, London, 1670

Olivet, Pierre Joseph Thoulier d', *Traité de la prosodie françoise* (1736), 2nd edn, Genève, 1750

Ovid, *Metamorphoses*, tr. Horace Gregory, New York and Scarborough, Ont.: New American Library, 1958

Owen, Robert, *Of the divine original, authority, self-evidencing light, and power of the Scriptures*, Oxford, 1659

Paracelsus, *Les sept livres de l'archidoxe magique*, Paris: Libraire du Merveilleux P. Dujos & A. Thomas, 1909

Plato, *Collected dialogues*, ed. Edith Hamilton and Huntington Cairns, Bollingen Series LXXI, Princeton: University Press, 1961

Porphyry, *La vie de Pythagore*, tr. E. des Places, Paris: Société d'Édition Les belles lettres, 1982

Priestley, Joseph, *A course of lectures on oratory and criticism*, London, 1778; facs. repr. New York: Garland Publishing, 1971

    Course of lectures on the theory of language and universal grammar, Warrington, 1763

Priscian, *Institutionum grammaticarum*, in Heinrich Keil (ed.), *Grammatici Latini*, 8 vols., Hildeshiem, Georg Olms, 1961

Purchas, Samuel, *Hakluytus posthumus, or Purchas his pilgrimes*, 4 vols., London, 1625

Quintilian, *Institutio oratoria*, tr. H. E. Butler, 4 vols., Loeb Classical Library, London: William Heinemann; New York: G. P. Putnam, 1920

Raynal, Guillaume-Thomas-François, *A philosophical and political history of the settlements and trade of the Europeans in the East and West Indies* (1770), 3 vols., Glasgow, 1811

Régnier-Desmarais, François-Séraphin, *Traité de la grammaire françoise*, Paris, 1706; facs. repr. Genève: Slatkine Reprints, 1973

Reid, Thomas, *Works*, ed. Sir William Hamilton, Edinburgh: Maclachlan and Stewart, 1863

Restaut, Pierre, *Principes généraux et raisonnés de la grammaire françoise* (1732), 6th edn, Paris, 1750

Ricci, Matthew, *China in the sixteenth century: the journals of Matthew Ricci, 1583–1610*, tr. Louis J. Gallagher, S. J., New York: Random House, 1942

Rice, John, *An introduction to the art of reading*, London, 1765; facs. repr. Menston: Scolar Press, 1969

Robinson, Robert, *Phonetic writings*, ed. E. J. Dobson, London, New York and Toronto: Oxford University Press, 1957

Rousseau, Jean-Jacques, *Émile* (1762), tr. Allan Bloom, New York: Basic Books, 1979

    Essai sur l'origine des langues (1781), ed. Charles Porset, Bordeaux: Guy Ducros, 1970

    Essai sur l'origine des langues, ed. Jean Starobinski, Paris: Éditions Gallimard, 1990

    The first and second discourses together with replies to critics, and Essay on the origin of languages, tr. Victor Gourevitch, New York: Perennial Library, 1968

    Œuvres complètes, 4 vols., Paris: Chez Alexandre Houssiaux, 1852–3

    Œuvres complètes, ed. Bernard Gagnebin and Marcel Raymond, 4 vols. (in progress), Paris: Pléiade, 1959–

Shaftesbury, Anthony Ashley Cooper, Lord, *Characteristics of men, manners, opinions, times etc.* (1711), 2 vols., ed. J. M. Robertson, London: Grant Richards, 1900

Shaw, William, *An enquiry into the authenticity of the poems ascribed to Ossian* (1781), 2nd edn, London, 1782

Sheridan, Thomas, *British education: or, the source of disorders in Great Britain*, Dublin, 1756; facs. repr. New York: Garland Publishing, 1970

A course of lectures on elocution, together with two dissertations on language, London, 1762

A general dictionary of the English language, 2 vols., London, 1780

Simon, Richard, *A critical history of the Old Testament* (1678), London, 1732

Smith, Adam, *Considerations concerning the first formation of languages* (1761), in *Lectures on rhetoric and belles lettres*, ed. J. C. Bryce, Oxford: Clarendon Press, 1983

Smith, Sir Thomas, *De recta et emendata linguæ anglicæ scriptione*, London, 1568; facs. repr. Menston: Scolar Press, 1968

Solis y Ribadeneyra, Antonio de, *Histoire de la conqueste du Mexique* (1684), 2 vols., Paris, 1730

Spinoza, Benedict de, *The chief works*, tr. R. H. M. Elwes, London: George Bell and Sons, 1891

Sprat, Thomas, *The history of the Royal-Society of London*, London, 1667

Steele, Joshua, *An essay towards establishing the melody and measure of speech*, London, 1775; facs. repr. Menston: Scolar Press, 1969

Sterne, Laurence, *The life and opinions of Tristram Shandy* (1760–7), ed. Ian Campbell Ross, Oxford: Clarendon Press, 1983

Stewart, Dugald, *Account of the life and writings of Adam Smith, LLD* (1794), in Adam Smith, *Essays on philosophical subjects*, ed. W. P. D. Wightman, J. C. Bryce and I. S. Ross, Oxford: Clarendon, 1980

Stillingfleet, Edward, *Origines sacræ, or a rational account of the grounds of Christian faith*, London, 1662

Top, Alexander, *The oliue leafe; or universall abce*, London, 1603

Tucker, Abraham (alias 'Edward Search'), *Vocal sounds*, London, 1773; facs. repr. Menston: Scolar Press, 1969

Urquhart, Sir Thomas, *Works*, Edinburgh: The Maitland Club, 1834

Valieriano Bolzani, Giovani Pierio, *Hieroglyphica* (1556), Lyon, 1602; facs. repr. New York: Garland Publishing, 1976

Vico, Giambattista, *The new science* (1725–44), tr. Thomas Goddard Bergin and Max Harold Fisch, Ithaca and London: Cornell University Press, 1948

Voltaire, *Œuvres complètes*, ed. L. Moland, 52 vols., Paris: Garnier Frères, 1877–85

Vossius, Geraldus, *Quatuor artibus popularibus*, Amsterdam, 1650

Wachter, Johann, *Naturæ et scripturæ concordia*, Lipsiæ et Hafniæ, 1752

Walker, John, *Elements of elocution*, 2 vols., London, 1781; facs. repr. Menston: Scolar Press, 1969

The melody of speaking, London, 1787; facs. repr. Menston: Scolar Press, 1970

Wallis, John, *Grammar of the English tongue* (1653), tr. J. A. Kemp, London: Longman, 1972

Walton, Brian, *Biblia sacra polyglotta*, 9 vols., London, 1659

Warburton, William, *The alliance of church and state*, London, 1736
   The divine legation of Moses, 4 vols., London, 1738–41; facs. repr. New York and London: Garland Publishing, 1978
   Essai sur les hiéroglyphes des Égyptiens, tr. Marc-Antoine Léonard des Malpeines, 2 vols., Paris, 1744

Ward, Seth, *Vindiciæ academiarum, containing some briefe animadversions on Mr. Websters book*, London, 1654

Ward, William, *An essay on grammar*, London, 1765

Webster, John, *Academiarum examen, or the examination of the academies*, London, 1654

Wesley, John, *Directions concerning pronunciation and gesture*, Bristol, 1770

Wilkins, John, *An essay towards a real character and a philosophical language*, London, 1668
   Mercury: or the secret and swift messenger (1641), 3rd edn, London, 1707; facs. repr., with an introduction by Brigitte Asbach-Schnitker, Amsterdam and Philadelphia: John Benjamins, 1984

Wise, Francis, *Some enquiries concerning the first inhabitants, language, religion, learning and letters of Europe*, Oxford, 1758

Wolf, F. A., *Prolegomena to Homer* (1798), tr. James E. G. Zetzel, Princeton: University Press, 1985

Wollstonecraft, Mary, *Thoughts on the education of daughters*, London, 1787

Wood, Robert, *An essay on the original genius and writings of Homer* (1769), London: John Richardson, 1824

Wordsworth, William, *Poetical works*, ed. E. de Selincourt and Helen Darbishire, 5 vols., Oxford: Clarendon Press, 1940–9
   The Prelude (1850), ed. W. J. B. Owen, Ithaca and London: Cornell University Press, 1985
   Prose Works, ed. W. J. B. Owen and Jane Worthington Smyser, 3 vols., Oxford: Clarendon Press, 1974

Young, Thomas, 'Egypt,' in *Supplement to the fourth, fifth and sixth editions of the Encyclopedia Britannica*, 6 vols., Edinburgh and London, 1824

SECONDARY SOURCES

Aarsleff, Hans, *From Locke to Saussure: essays on the study of language and intellectual history*, Minneapolis: University of Minnesota Press, 1982
   The study of language in England, 1780–1860, 2nd edn, Minneapolis: University of Minnesota Press, 1983

Aarsleff, Hans, Louis G. Kelly and Josef Niederehe (eds.), *Papers in the history of linguistics: proceedings of the third international conference on the history of language sciences*, Amsterdam and Philadelphia: John Benjamin, 1987

Abercrombie, David, *Studies in phonetics and linguistics*, London: Oxford University Press, 1965
Abrahms, M. H., *The mirror and the lamp: Romantic theory and the critical tradition*, New York: Oxford University Press, 1953
Barfield, Owen, *What Coleridge thought*, Middletown: Wesleyan University Press, 1971
Baron, Naomi S., *Speech, writing, and sign*, Bloomington: Indiana University Press, 1981
Benzie, W., *The Dublin orator: Thomas Sheridan's influence on eighteenth-century rhetoric and belles-lettres*, Leeds: University School of English, 1972
Bialostosky, Don H., 'Coleridge's interpretation of Wordsworth's Preface to *Lyrical ballads*', *PMLA* 93 (1978), 912–24
Blake, N. F., and Charles Jones, *English historical linguistics: studies in development*, Sheffield: Centre for English Cultural Tradition and Language, 1984
Blau, Joseph Leon, *The Christian interpretation of the cabala in the Renaissance*, Port Washington: Kennikat Press, 1944
Bolinger, Dwight, *Intonation and its parts*, Stanford: University Press, 1986
'Visual morphemes', *Language* 22 (1946), 333–40
Breasted, James Henry, *The conquest of civilization*, 3rd edn, New York and London: Harper and Brothers, 1954
Brengelman, F. H., 'Orthoepists, printers, and the rationalization of English spelling', *Journal of English and Germanic Philology* 79 (1980), 332–54
Bungay, Stephen, *Beauty and truth: a study of Hegel's aesthetics*, Oxford: University Press, 1984
Burger, Ronna, *Plato's 'Phædrus': a defence of the philosophical art of writing*, University, AL: University of Alabama Press, 1980
Certeau, Michel de, *The writing of history*, New York: Columbia University Press, 1988
Chaitlin, Gilbert, Kenneth R. Johnson, Karen Hanson and Herbert Marks (eds.), *Romantic revolutions: criticism and theory*, Bloomington and Indianapolis: Indiana University Press, 1990.
Chandler, James K., *Wordsworth's second nature: a study of the poetry and politics*, Chicago and London: University of Chicago Press, 1984
Chandler, Kenneth, *Education in Renaissance England*, London: Routledge and Kegan Paul; Toronto: University Press, 1965
Cipolla, Carlo M., *Literacy and development in the West*, Harmondsworth: Penguin Books, 1969
Clanchy, Michael T., *From memory to written record: England 1066–1307*, 2nd edn, Oxford and Cambridge, MA: Blackwell, 1993
Clulee, Nicholas H., *John Dee's natural philosophy: between science and philosophy*, London and New York: Routledge, 1988
Cohen, Jonathan, 'On the project of a universal character', *Mind*, n.s. 63 (1954), 49–63
Cohen, Murray, *Sensible words: linguistic practice in England 1640–1785*, Baltimore and London: Johns Hopkins University Press, 1977

Cornelius, Paul, _Languages in seventeenth- and early eighteenth-century imaginary voyages_, Geneva: Libraire Droz, 1965

Corrigan, Timothy, _Coleridge, language, and criticism_, Athens, GA: University of Georgia Press, 1982

Couturat, Louis, _La logique de Leibniz_, Hildesheim: Georg Olms, 1961

Cressy, David, _Literacy and social order: reading and writing in Tudor and Stuart England_, Cambridge: University Press, 1980

Crittenden, Alan, _Intonation_, Cambridge: University Press, 1986

Crystal, David, _Prosodic systems and intonation in English_, Cambridge: University Press, 1967

Culter, A., and D. R. Ladd (eds.), _Prosody: models and measurements_, Berlin, Heidelberg, New York and Tokyo: Springer-Verlag, 1983

Curtius, Ernst Robert, _European literature and the Latin Middle-Ages_, tr. Willard R. Trask, New York: Pantheon Books, 1953

Darnton, Robert, _The literary underground of the old regime_, Cambridge, MA, and London: Harvard University Press, 1982

David, Madeleine V.-, _Le débat sur les écritures et l'hiéroglyphe aux XVIIe et XVIIIe siècles_, Paris: S.E.V.P.E.N., 1965

Davies, Hugh Sykes, _Wordsworth and the worth of words_, Cambridge: University Press, 1986

De Bolla, Peter, _The discourse of the sublime: readings in history, aesthetics and the subject_, Oxford and New York: Basil Blackwell, 1989

Debus, Allen G., _Science and education in the seventeenth century: the Webster-Ward debate_, London: Macdonald; New York: American Elsevier, 1970

Debus, Allen G., and Ingrid Merkel (eds.), _Hermeticism and the Renaissance_, Washington: Folger Shakespeare Library; Toronto and London: Associated University Presses, 1988

Delattre, Pierre, 'Comparing the prosodic features of English, German, Spanish and French', _International Review of Applied Linguistics in Language Teaching_ 1 (1963), 193–210

De Man, Paul, _Blindness and insight_, 2nd edn, Minneapolis: University of Minnesota Press, 1983

Derrida, Jacques, _Of grammatology_, tr. Gayatri Chakravorty Spivak, Baltimore and London: Johns Hopkins University Press, 1974

'Plato's pharmacy', in _Dissemination_, tr. Barbara Johnson, Chicago: University Press, 1981

'Le puits et la pyramide: introduction à la sémiologie de Hegel', in _Marges de la philosophie_, Paris: Éditions de Minuit, 1972. Tr. by Alan Bass as 'The pit and the pyramid: introduction to Hegel's semiology', in _Margins of philosophy_, Chicago: University Press, 1982

'Scribble (writing-power)', tr. Cary Plotkin, _Yale French Studies_ 58 (1979), 117–47

De Santillana, Giorgio, review of Frances A. Yates, _Giordano Bruno and the hermetic tradition_, in _American Historical Review_ 70 (1965), 455–7.

Didot, Ambroise Firmin, _Observations sur orthographe ou orthografie française_, Paris: Typographie d'Ambroise Firmin Didot, 1868

Diringer, David, *Writing*, London: Thames and Hudson, 1962
Doblhofer, Ernst, *Voices in stone: the decipherment of ancient scripts and writings*, tr. Mervyn Savill, New York: Viking, 1961
Eagleton, Terry, *Literary theory: an introduction*, Oxford: Basil Blackwell, 1983
Eilenberg, Susan, 'Mortal pages: Wordsworth and the reform of copyright', *ELH* 56 (1989), 351–74
Eisenstein, Elizabeth L., *Print culture and Enlightenment thought*, Chapel Hill: University of North Carolina Press, 1986
   The printing press as an agent of change, 2 vols., Cambridge: University Press, 1979
Elliot, Ralph W. V., 'Isaac Newton's "Of an universall language"', *Modern Language Review* 52 (1957), 1–18
Elsky, Martin C., *Authorising words: speech, writing, and print in the English Renaissance*, Ithaca and London: Cornell University Press, 1989
Essick, Robert N., *William Blake and the language of Adam*, Oxford: Clarendon, 1989
Evans, A. W., *Warburton and the Warburtonians: a study in some eighteenth-century controversies*, London: Oxford University Press, 1932
Ferrari, G. R. F., *Listening to the cicadas: a study of Plato's 'Phædrus'*, Cambridge: University Press, 1987
Festugière, A. J., *La révélation d'Hermès Trismégiste*, Paris: Libraire Lecoffre, 1950
Formigari, Lia, *Language and experience in 17th-Century British philosophy*, Amsterdam and Philadelphia: John Benjamins, 1988
Foucault, Michel, *The order of things*, New York: Vintage, 1970.
Fowden, Garth, *The Egyptian Hermes: a historical approach to the late pagan mind*, Cambridge: University Press, 1986
Frängsmyr, Tore, J. L. Heilbron and Robin E. Rider (eds.), *The quantifying spirit of the eighteenth century*, Berkeley, Los Angeles and Oxford: University of California Press, 1990
French, Peter J., *John Dee: the world of an Elizabethan magus*, London: Routledge and Kegan Paul, 1972
Furet, François, and Jacques Ozouf, *Lire et écrire: l'alphabétisation des français de Calvin à Jules Ferry*, Paris: Les Éditions de Minuit, 1977
Gelb, I. C., *A study of writing*, 2nd edn, Chicago and London: University of Chicago Press, 1963
Giehlow, Karl, 'Die Hieroglyphenkunde des Humanismus', *Jahrbuch der Kunsthistorishen Sammlungen des Allerhöchsten Kaiserhauses* 32 (1915), 1–218
Godwin, Joscelyn, *Athanasius Kircher: a Renaissance man and the quest for lost knowledge*, London: Thames and Hudson, 1979
Gombrich, G. H., '*Icones symbolicæ*: the visual image in neo-platonic thought', *Journal of the Warburg and Courtauld Institutes* 48 (1948), 163–92
Goody, Jack, *The domestication of the savage mind*, Cambridge: University Press, 1977
   (ed.), *Literacy in traditional societies*, Cambridge: University Press, 1968

Graff, Harvey, *The legacies of literacy*, Bloomington and Indianapolis: University of Indiana Press, 1987
The literacy myth: literacy and social structure in the nineteenth-century city, New York: Academic Press, 1976
(ed.), *Literacy and social development in the West: a reader*, Cambridge: University Press, 1981
Greaves, Richard L., *The Puritan revolution and educational thought*, New Brunswick, NJ: Rutgers University Press, 1969
Greenblatt, Stephen, *Marvellous possessions: the wonder of the New World*, Chicago: University Press, 1991
Haas, William, *Phono-graphic transcription*, Manchester: University Press, 1970
Hall, A. R., *The scientific revolution 1500–1800*, Boston: Beacon Press, 1956
Harris, Roy, *The origin of writing*, London: Duckworth, 1986
Hartman, Geoffery H., *The unremarkable Wordsworth*, Minneapolis: University of Minnesota Press, 1987
Harvey, Simon, Mariam Hobson, David Kelley and Samuel S. B. Taylor (eds.), *Reappraisals of Rousseau: studies in honour of R. A. Leigh*, Totowa, NJ: Barnes and Noble Books, 1980
Havelock, Eric A., *Preface to Plato*, Cambridge, MA: Belknap Press, 1963
Hilton, Nelson, *Literal imagination: Blake's vision of words*, Berkeley, Los Angeles and London: University of California Press, 1983
Holly, Grant, 'William Blake and the dialogue of discourse and figure', in Kevin L. Cope (ed.), *Compendious conversations: the methods of dialogue in the early enlightenment*, Frankfurt am Main: Peter Lang, 1992, 15–33
Howell, Wilbur Samuel, *Eighteenth-century British logic and rhetoric*, Princeton: University Press, 1971
Hudson, Nicholas, *Samuel Johnson and eighteenth-century thought*, Oxford: Clarendon Press, 1988
'The individual and the collective in eighteenth-century language theory', *Man and nature*; *the proceedings of the Canadian society for eighteenth-century studies*, vol. 10, ed. Josiane Boulad-Ayoub, Michael Cartwright, Michel Grenon and William Kinsley, Edmonton: Academic Publishers, 1991, 157–66
Hutin, Serge, *Robert Fludd (1570–1637): alchimiste et philosophe rosicrucien*, Paris: Les Éditions de l'Omnium Littéraire, 1971
Hutton, Patrick H., 'The problem of oral tradition in Vico's historical scholarship', *Journal of the History of Ideas* 53 (1992), 3–23
Innis, Harold J., *Empire and communication*, rev. Mary Q. Innis, Toronto and Buffalo: University of Toronto Press, 1972
Iversen, Erik, *The myth of Egypt and its hieroglyphs*, Copenhagen: Gec Gad, 1961
Johnson, Christopher, *System and writing in the philosophy of Jacques Derrida*, Cambridge: University Press, 1993
Jones, Daniel, *The history and meaning of the term 'phoneme'*, London: International Phonetic Association, 1957

Kargon, Robert Hugh, *Atomism in England from Harriot to Newton*, Oxford: Clarendon Press, 1966

Kennedy, George A. (ed.), *The Cambridge history of literary criticism*, vol. 1, Cambridge: University Press, 1989

Kernan, Alvin, *Printing technology, letters and Samuel Johnson*, Princeton: University Press, 1987

Kneale, J. Douglas, 'Wordsworth's images of language: voice and letter in *The Prelude*', *PMLA* 101 (1986), 351–61

Knowlson, James, *Universal language schemes in England and France 1600–1800*, Toronto and Buffalo: University of Toronto Press, 1975

Korshin, Paul J., 'Deciphering Swift's codes', in *Proceedings of the first Münster symposium on Jonathan Swift*, ed. Hermann J. Real and Heinz J. Vienken, München: Wilhelm Fink Verlag, 1985, 123–34

Koyré, Alexandre, *La philosophie de Jacob Boehme*, New York: Burt Franklin, 1968

Kroll, Richard W. F., *The material word: literate culture in the Restoration and early eighteenth century*, Baltimore and London: Johns Hopkins University Press, 1991

Land, Stephen K., *From signs to propositions: the concept of form in eighteenth-century semantic theory*, London: Longman, 1974

Léon, Pierre, and Mario Rossi (eds.), *Problèmes de prosodie*, 2 vols., Ottawa: Didier, 1979–80

Lévi-Strauss, Claude, *A world on the wane [Tristes tropiques]*, tr. John Russell, London: Hutchinson Press, 1961

Lindberg, David C., and Robert S. Westman (eds.), *Reappraisals of the scientific revolution*, Cambridge: University Press, 1990

McDonald, Christie V., 'Jacques Derrida's reading of Rousseau', *The Eighteenth Century: Theory and Interpretation* 20 (1979), 2–95

McKusick, James C., *Coleridge's philosophy of language*, New Haven and London: Yale University Press, 1986

MacLuhan, Marshall, *The Gutenberg galaxy*, Toronto: University Press, 1962

Manuel, Frank E., *The eighteenth century confronts the gods*, New York: Atheneum, 1967

Mitchell, W. J. T., *Blake's illuminated art: a study of the illuminated poetry*, Princeton: University Press, 1978

Moorhouse, A. C., *The triumph of the alphabet*, New York: Henry Schuman, 1953

Norris, Christopher, *Derrida*, Cambridge, MA: Harvard University Press, 1987

O'Day, Rosemary, *Education and society 1500–1800: the social foundations of education in Early Modern Britain*, London and New York: Longman, 1982

Ong, Walter J., *Orality and literacy*, London and New York: Methuen, 1982
Ramus, method, and the decay of dialogue, Cambridge, MA: Harvard University Press, 1958

Rhetoric, romance and technology, Ithaca and London: Cornell University Press, 1971

Padley, G. A., *Grammatical theory in western Europe, 1500–1700*, 2 vols., Cambridge: University Press, 1985

Plant, Marjorie, *The English book trade: an economic history of the making and sale of books*, London: George Allen and Unwin, 1939

Pope, Maurice, *The story of decipherment from Egyptian hieroglyphics to Linear B*, London: Thames and Hudson, 1975

Porset, Charles, '*L'inquiétante étrangeté* de l'*Essai sur l'origine des langues*: Rousseau et ses exégètes', *Studies on Voltaire and the Eighteenth Century* 154 (1976), 4715–58

Reddick, Allen, *The making of Johnson's Dictionary 1746–1773*, Cambridge: University Press, 1990

Reilly, P. Conor, S. J., *Athanasius Kircher, S. J.: master of a hundred arts, 1602–1680*, Wiesbaden and Rome: Edizioni del Mondo, 1974

Rivers, Isabel (ed.), *Books and their readers in eighteenth-century England*, London: St Martin's Press, 1982

Robinet, André, *Le langage à l'âge classique*, Paris: Éditions Klincksieck, 1978

Rossi, Paolo, *Francis Bacon: from magic to science*, tr. Sacha Rabinovitch, London: Routledge and Kegan Paul, 1968

Ryley, Robert M., *William Warburton*, Boston: Twayne Publishers, 1984

Salmon, Vivian, *The study of language in 17th-century England*, Amsterdam: John Benjamins, 1979

Sapir, Edward, *Selected writings*, ed. David G. Mandelbaum, Berkeley and Los Angeles: University of California Press, 1949

Schaya, Leo, *The universal meaning of the kabbalah*, tr. Nancy Pearson, London: George Allen and Unwin, 1971

Scholem, Gershom G., *Major trends in Jewish mysticism*, New York: Schocken Books, 1961

   On the kabbalah and its symbolism, tr. Ralph Manheim, New York: Schocken Books, 1956

Schousboe, Karen, and Morgens Trolle Larsen (eds.), *Literacy and society*, Copenhagen: Akademisk Forlag, 1989

Scragg, D. G., *A history of English spelling*, Manchester: University Press; New York: Barnes and Noble, 1974

Shortland, Michael, 'Moving speeches: language and elocution in eighteenth-century Britain', *History of European Ideas* 8 (1987), 639–53

Shumaker, Wayne, *Renaissance curiosa*, Binghamton, NY: Medieval and Renaissance Texts and Studies, 1982

Simon, Joan, *Education and society in Tudor England*, Cambridge: University Press, 1966

Simonsuuri, Kristi, *Homer's original genius: eighteenth-century notions of the early Greek epic*, Cambridge: University Press, 1979

Singer, Thomas S., 'Hieroglyphs, real characters, and the idea of natural language in English seventeenth-century thought', *Journal of the History of Ideas* 50 (1989), 49–70

Slaughter, M. M., *Universal languages and scientific taxonomy in the seventeenth century*, Cambridge: University Press, 1982

Smith, Nigel, *Perfection proclaimed: language and literature in English radical religion, 1640–1660*, Oxford: Clarendon Press, 1989

Smith, Olivia, *The politics of language 1791–1819*, Oxford: Clarendon Press, 1984

Stafford, Fiona J., *The sublime savage: a study of James Macpherson and the poems of Ossian*, Edinburgh: University Press, 1988

Starobinski, Jean, *Jean-Jacques Rousseau: transparency and obstruction*, tr. Arthur Goldhammer, Chicago and London: University of Chicago Press, 1988

Stone, Lawrence, 'Literacy and education in England 1640–1900', *Past and Present* 42 (1969), 69–139

Stromberg, Roland N., *Religious liberalism in eighteenth-century England*, Oxford: University Press, 1954

Stubbings, Frank H. and Alan J. B. Wace (eds.), *A companion to Homer*, London: Macmillan, 1962

Sykes, Norman, *Church and state in England in the XVIIIth century*, Cambridge: University Press, 1939

Tagliacozzo, Giorgio (ed.), *Vico: past and present*, Atlantic Highlands, NJ: Humanities Press, 1981

Tavard, George H., *Holy Writ or Holy Church? The crisis of the Protestant Reformation*, New York: Harper and Brothers, 1959

Ulmer, Gregory L., 'Jacques Derrida and Paul de Man on/in Rousseau's faults', *The Eighteenth Century: Theory and Interpretation* 20 (1979), 164–81

Vachek, Josef, *Written language revisited*, ed. Philip A. Luelsdorff, Amsterdam and Philadelphia: John Benjamins, 1989

Vincent, David, *Literacy and popular culture*, Cambridge: University Press, 1989

Wirszubski, Chaim, *Pico della Mirandola's encounter with Jewish mysticism*, Cambridge, MA, and London: Harvard University Press, 1989

Wolkler, Robert, '*l'Essai sur l'origine des langues* en tant que fragment du *Discours sur l'inégalité*: Rousseau et ses "mauvais" interprètes', in *Rousseau et Voltaire en 1978: actes du colloque international de Nice*, Genève: Éditions Slatkine, 1981, 145–61

Yates, Frances A., *The art of memory*, London: Routledge and Kegan Paul, 1966

   Giordano Bruno and the hermetic tradition, London: Routledge and Kegan Paul, 1964

   The occult philosophy in the Elizabethan Age, London, Boston and Henley: Routledge and Kegan Paul, 1979

   The Rosicrucian enlightenment, London and Boston: Routledge and Kegan Paul, 1972

Young, Robert Fitzgibbon, *Comenius in England*, Oxford: University Press; London: Humphrey Milford, 1937

Index

Simple references to modern scholarship are not listed.

218